JAMES LUCAS

PANZER
ARMY AFRICA

This book is dedicated, generally, to all who fought in Africa, irrespective of national allegiance and, specifically, to all who died or were killed in action there. But particularly this book commemorates two men: one German and one Englishman, whose lives were an example to the men they led and whose deaths brought a loss which is still felt by their comrades.

The British officer is Lieutenant Sidney Keyes, my platoon commander in 'C' Company, 1st Battalion The Queen's Own Royal West Kent Regiment. The German is Oberleutnant Schuster of 1st Battalion Fallschirmjäger Regiment Hermann Goering.

JAMES LUCAS

PANZER
ARMY AFRICA

PRESIDIO PRESS
San Rafael, California & London, England

Copyright © 1977 by James Lucas

Published by Presidio Press of San Rafael, California,
and London, England, with editorial offices at
1114 Irwin Street, San Rafael, California 94901

First American edition 1978

First published in Great Britain in 1977 by
Macdonald and Jane's Publishers Limited
ISBN 0-354-01056-5

Library of Congress Cataloging in Publication Data
Lucas, James Sidney.
  Panzer Army Africa.

  Bibliography: p.
  Includes index.
  1. World War, 1939-1945—Campaigns—Africa, North.
2. World War, 1939-1945—Regimental histories—Germany—
Panzerarmeekorps Afrika.   3. Germany. Heer.
Panzerarmeekorps Afrika.   I. Title.
D766.82.L83 1978   940.54'23   78-18175
ISBN 0-89141-064-3

Printed in the United States of America

Contents

List of Illustrations   vii

Acknowledgments   x

Foreword by Rudolf Witzig   xi

Introduction   xii

Prologue   1

1. Background to war   7

2. Conditions in the desert: 17
Food, hygiene, and other regulations
Uniform
Terrain
Tactics
The Commander-in-Chief – Erwin Rommel
The Italian Ally
The British and their Allies

3. The Germans come to Africa, February 1941   35

4. The advance upon Tobruk and the first siege, April–May 1941   45

5. The tank battle of Sollum, June 1941   57

6. Rommel deflects Operation Crusader, November 1941   63

7. The pre-emptive blow at Gazala, June 1942   93

8. The Axis tide ebbs, November 1942   111

9. The Tunisian bridgehead, November–December 1942;   127

Tunisian prelude
The preliminary encounters
The Allied drive for Tunis
The German riposte
Quiet on the north-western front

10. The attempts to expand the bridgehead, February 1943   161

**11. Army Group Africa fights in the north, west, and south,
     March–April 1943:**   171
The Mareth line
The Schott position

12. Towards the end in Africa, May 1943   181

Epilogue   187

Appendixes: 189
1. Chronology of the war in Africa
2. Order of battle of the German divisions which served in Africa
3. The major groupings of the German Army in Africa
4. Establishment tables:
Panzer Division
Panzer Battalion of a Panzer Division
Panzerjager Battalion
Panzer Division Reconnaissance Battalion
Panzer Division Lorried Infantry Battalion
Infantry Battalion of Infantry Division

Select Bibliography   201

Index   205

LIST OF ILLUSTRATIONS

Photographs
Between pages 36 and 37

General Field Marshal Erwin Rommel

Field Marshal Albert Kesselring, Supreme Commander South

German armoured fighting vehicles drawn up in a street in Tripoli

The first units of the German Army in Africa parade through Tripoli

Reinforcements were sometimes flown into the African theatre of operations in JU 52 aircraft

Reinforcements on a desert airfield

A half-tracked prime mover towing an 8.8cm anti-aircraft tank gun

A Panzer I Ausf. B, mounting a 4.7cm Pak L/43 tank destroyer

The face of the German infantry soldier in the desert

German tanks enter an Italian fort in Libya

Rommel's command vehicle

Panzer IIs on a desert battlefield

A young tank commander of the German armoured force

A tank destroyer and infantry move forward

A Panzer III passing a burning Honey tank

During one of the pauses in the fighting there is time to write home

The crew of an MG 34 on outpost duty

Between pages 68 and 69

A light field howitzer with its half-track prime mover

German soldiers wearing nets to keep the flies away

The Arco Fileni on the Via Balbia marked the border of Cyrenaica and Tripolitania

The German view of the desert fighting

Rommel in an armoured wireless command vehicle (SPW)

Bersaglieri motorcycle reconnaissance troops of the Italian Army on patrol

Rommel watches Italian troops move up to the front during the Gazala battles

Desert soldiers enjoying the unusual luxury of an all-over wash

German infantry move through Bir Hachim

Dusk in the desert and the Panzer Army is formed in battle position

Rommel in his armoured command half-track

A Luftwaffe Volkswagen throwing up clouds of dust

Grenadier Halm, winner of the Knight's Cross of the Iron Cross

Infantry assaulting under cover of a smoke screen during the battle of Alam Halfa

The 8.8cm anti-tank/anti-aircraft gun in action

An infantry assault moving across the soft going of sand dunes at Mersa Brega

Between pages 100 and 101

The infantryman's view of battle

Gunners manhandling an 8.8cm gun into position in Tunisia

Armour to reinforce the Africa Corps being unloaded at Tripoli

General Bismarck of 21st Panzer Division

An Axis airfield after an Allied bombing raid

A gun line of 8.8cm guns in defensive positions

A French 15.5cm GPF gun used by the Germans in Libya

A Panzer IV speeds past a knocked out Bren carrier

Junkers aircraft fly in supplies and petrol to Tobruk aerodrome

Rounding up British prisoners of war during the Gazala battle

Gunners examining the damage caused to the turret of a Matilda tank

Italian infantry towing the 47/28 anti-tank gun during a march past

Panzer IIs moving up the line for the Gazala battle

Between pages 132 and 133

The crew of an Italian 11/40 Ansaldo tank

The artillery forward observation officer watching the fall of shot from his sangar

A Panzer III in action against British armour in the Gazala battle

An aerial view of Halfaya Pass under bombardment by Axis aircraft

Men of a 17cm gun crew holding a funeral service

An SdKfz 251 armoured personnel carrier

A heavy field howitzer 15cm sFH 18 taking up position

Rommel and his staff visiting the battle area

Field artillery in action

A 15cm heavy howitzer sFH 13 mounted on a French Lorraine chassis, moving forward at Alamein

An Italian gun crew manning a German 15cm field howitzer

An 8.8cm gun in a well constructed defensive position

Light field artillery supporting an infantry attack

The grave of a German corporal

Maps   *Page*

Operation Crusader, November–December 1941   64

Operation Crusader, 7th Armoured Division is trapped, November–December 1941   65

Operation Crusader, Rommel's dash to the wire, November–December 1941   66

Operation Crusader and its consequences, November–December 1941   78

Rommels second drive towards Egypt, January–July 1942   80
The battle at Gazala, May–June 1942   94
Battle of Alam Halfa, 1st Alamein, August–September 1942   112
Battle of El Alamein, October–November 1942   121
The withdrawal from El Alamein to Tunisia, November 1942–February 1943 124
The Tunisian battle area   128

Acknowledgments

A book is not the individual effort of the author but the result of collaboration with his family and his friends both personal and professional. To all of these I am indebted but particularly to Traude, my wife, to Barbara Shaw, and to Mary Harris who typed and retyped my manuscript; to Matthew Cooper who collaborates with me in the writing of our books; and, finally, on the British side, to Isobel Smythe-Wood and to Michael Stevens of Macdonald and Jane's, upon whose expert advice I have depended.

On the German side my thanks are due, particularly, to Oberst Witzig who very kindly wrote the foreword to this book; to Heinz Teske, Franz Josef Kugel, Paul Beck, and Rudi Hambuch, all formerly members of Fallschirm-jager Sturmregiment Koch; and to other comrades of the German Paratroop Association and former members of Panzer Army Africa.

Foreword by Rudolf Witzig

In this book an Englishman who fought against us in Tunisia has undertaken the task of recounting the campaign in Africa from the German point of view and to do this objectively, carefully, and fairly has used all available German sources.

In Tunisia I commanded a Paratroop Engineer Battalion posted to a division which was made up in the early days of units which had been hastily thrown together. Ours were not major battles like those of the Africa Corps but limited advances carried out by understrength formations, hard defensive struggles often fought to the bitter end without heavy weapons support and with only the minimum of supplies and equipment. The actions in which my battalion fought, in so many ways different to those of other units, typify the unconventional course of the Tunisian campaign.

The battalion was air transported from Greece and southern Italy to Bizerta and except for personal weapons was issued only with a few motor-cycles and field kitchens. The westward thrust, during which we came up against the British at Djebel Abiod, was made on lorries which we had had to requisition in Bizerta. The few heavy weapons and tanks under command were all that were available at that time. During the campaign we fought, principally, as infantry and only during breaks in the fighting were we able to return to being engineers, to mine-laying, or to acting as divisional reserve.

Improvisation, the exploitation of all resources and opportunities with minimal support; the forming into battle groups whose varied compositions depended upon the job in hand: these were our daily lot. Although it lacked numbers my battalion was made up of officers, non-commissioned officers, and men who could act upon their own initiative. Each man was an individual warrior, brave, self-reliant, and intelligent. The esprit de corps shown by all ranks was incomparable.

When I was reading this book I thought of my comrades who fell in Africa, offering their lives for Germany, serving bravely and loyally unto death. I thought, also, of our Italian comrades in arms who down to the smallest units were our equals in battle. And I thought, too, of our brave opponents who, like us, fought and suffered.

I see the author's intention as not merely to present a factual and correct account but also to strive for better understanding between both sides; to build bridges. Let us hope that that friendship which has grown out of the battles of thirty-five years ago will continue and be of benefit to our peoples.

Oberschleizsheim,   *Rudolf Witzig*
Germany   *31 January 1977*

Introduction

War is, by definition, an armed struggle engaged in by two or more nations. During a war it is understandable that the accounts of the conflict and the records of its battles reflect a national bias. Even years after a major war histories tend to be subjective and decades need to elapse before authors are able to present, in anything but an unfavourable light, the policies, opinions, and actions of former enemy nations and armies.

Objective accounts can only be written when the historians or the war diaries of the nations involved become generally available for comparison and analysis. The time has now come when authors can write historically objective accounts of the fighting which occurred during the Second World War and restore the balance which propaganda and partisanship had upset.

This book sets out to trace the history of the whole German Army in Africa and to recount the course of the campaign as seen by the men of that Army who fought in that theatre of operations. Most of the information upon which the narrative was written was gained from German sources and reflects the attitudes and opinions of the men of that Army. It follows, necessarily, that those men had their own priorities as to what battles were important and those considered to be of far-reaching significance by our historians, are not considered to be such by the authors of the contemporary war diaries written on the other side of 'no man's land'. The reader will, therefore, seek through this book in vain for a detailed account of the battle of El Alamein in October 1942 for, to the commanders of the German and the Italian forces the climax had been reached much earlier, during the fighting which we have named as the battle of Alam Halfa and which the German military historians call First Alamein.

The politics of command form no part of the narrative for there was no space to describe in detail the conflicts between commanders and their subordinates. Nor has it been possible to give more than basic details of the arms, equipment, or clothing used by the German armies in the desert.

The book falls logically into two parts: the fighting in the desert and that in Tunisia. In the former campaign the German forces are fighting for victory; in the second part they are battling for their very existence. The description of the fighting in these two campaigns requires different treatment. In the western desert the swift tank thrust, the sweep of massed armour across the tactician's paradise and, in the second, the clawing struggle for every important mountain crest with the bitter realisation that the loss of a platoon of panzers in 1943 had a more sombre significance than the loss of a whole regiment would have had in the earlier and headier days of victory.

Prologue

*'The loss of the Libyan area must be
prevented under all circumstances ...'*
Hitler, January 1941

For a period of some twenty-eight months of the Second World War, from February 1941 to May 1943, the battlefield fought upon by one German army extended across twenty degrees of longitude and through a sickle of Arab countries from Egypt to Tunisia. That German formation was conceived as a small contingent in approximately divisional strength whose task it would be to support the Italians and to act as a block against a British advance. It was to be subordinate to the Italians, on whose colonial territories it would serve and who had been fighting the British for nearly a year. This small unit rapidly developed to become the spearhead of Axis advances, commanded by a man whose plans and strategies were carried through often against the orders of his superiors in Libya, Rome, and Berlin. The German Africa Corps, as it was first known and under which title it has become a legend, rose in status to become Panzer Group Africa, Panzer Army Africa, and, finally in the closing months of the war, Army Group Africa.

But by whatever name it was known and under whatever conditions it fought this contingent, almost invariably inferior in numbers and supplies to its principal enemy Britain, was further burdened by being shackled to the less military potent Italian Army.

In order to understand what was so important about North Africa that years of fighting had to be conducted across its hot and desert wastes we must first consider the major combatant nations in relation to the area of the southern Mediterranean. The Germans, with whom this book principally deals, were drawn into that region because the demands of alliance compelled her to aid the weaker partner, Italy, who was there because of her geographical position. The presence of the other main protagonist, Great Britain, whom both Axis partners were seeking to drive from the Mediterranean, was due to Imperial policy. Britain's position needs to be explained in detail for the relationship of the Mediterranean with British foreign policies cannot be too highly stressed. To the Italians it was *Mare Nostrum*, but to the British it was the short sea route to the Imperial possessions in the Far East. The great inland sea and the land area surrounding it bound the continents of Europe, Africa, and Asia; there was no other region of the world which held this special strategic position of being at the epicentre of a world-wide war.

For more than two hundred years British Imperial strategy had been a maritime policy based upon British control of the seas. Through this control any land-based enemy could, in time of war, be blockaded into submission. Alternatively, being vulnerable to sea-borne attack at many points of his domain he could be financially ruined by being forced to the expense of maintaining a very large army to defend his territory against such attacks. British sea control would, at some time during that war, allow the Imperial strategists to establish a base convenient to some point at which the enemy was weakest and there, by rapid build-up, convert this into a springboard from which an assault on the mainland could be made. Then would be fought the decisive battle in conjunction with Britain's allies; a pre-requisite this for her own man-power resources were too small to allow her to dispose both a large navy and army.

Beginning in the eighteenth century Britain established her presence in the Mediterranean by the capture of Gibraltar and Minorca. A century later Malta was occupied and during the decades of the nineteenth century, as more bases were acquired at Alexandria and in Cyprus, the Royal Navy controlled the Mediterranean and thus the land and sea routes to the East. The British position was expressed in a single sentence by that great member of the Imperial Defence Committee, Lord Esher. 'Great Britain', he wrote, 'either is or is not one of the great powers of the world. Her position in this respect depends solely upon sea command – and upon sea command in the Mediterranean.'

In 1940 the Mediterranean and specifically North Africa was the only military theatre in which the British forces were fighting the enemy on land and the operations which were being carried out there, from the time of Italy's entry into the war until the surrender of the Axis armies in Tunisia, can be seen as a continuation of the traditional British policy. A proper acknowledgment must be made to each of the British bases there – Gibraltar, Malta, and Egypt – for these were the vital links in the Imperial chain which Britain strove to keep intact and which the Axis partners sought to break; but Egypt was the key to the whole southern Mediterranean. German grand strategy considered the possibility of a military pincer advancing along the northern and southern shores of the Mediterranean and aimed at the capture of the Middle East. The northern arm had a choice of three different routes along which it could thrust: through Turkey, from Crete into Syria, or else through the Caucasus; but on the southern shore the pincer arm had, of necessity, to go via Egypt for there was no other route. Barring the path of the Axis thrusts stood the forces of Great Britain and her Empire and the failure of Germany and Italy to capture and hold Egypt was a strategic defeat of immense importance.

The course and the outcome of the campaign in the desert was influenced, decided is perhaps the better word, by conclusions reached and orders given by the chief political leaders of Germany, Italy, and Great Britain, each of whom was thousands of miles removed from the battlefields and not one of whom comprehended the peculiar characteristics of desert warfare nor sympathised with the difficulties of their respective commanders in the field.

Mussolini grasped the political need to hold the Italian African empire but in his Army he had a tool which was too weak to carry out his grandiose plans. Churchill, the inheritor of Britain's traditional policies, was aware of the importance of the Middle East but, refusing to accept the limitations of logistics, interfered with the plans which his generals on the spot had drawn up and demanded offensives or expeditions for which the British Army in the desert, for all the Imperial resources upon which it could draw, was too weak to undertake with any guarantee of success, at least until the middle of 1942.

Hitler, a central European, had little idea of the Mediterranean strategy and thus he had no detailed, long term plans for the German contingent which he sent to aid the Italians, except the vague concept of a southern pincer arm. What reason compelled him to support his weak ally? Hitler knew that the Italian Army and Air Force needed to be completely re-equipped if they were to play their part in a highly technical and industrial war, just as he knew that Italy had no natural mineral deposits and needed to import most of her basic raw materials. His Axis partner considered from an economic and military point of view was a broken reed and yet Hitler supported her. The answer to this question lies, perhaps, in the emotional debt which the German Chancellor owed to the Italian Duce. In 1938 Mussolini had stood apart when Austria was invaded and Hitler's telegram to his ally at that time 'Mussolini, for this I shall never forget you', found expression in later years when the need to help Italy arose. Hitler remained loyal to the Rome–Berlin Axis and was determined to maintain it even though his partner was a burden. This political line was echoed by his military subordinates who used the Führer's loyalty as an argument to defend political and military decisions which had been made. Even as late as December 1942, when it was clear that Italy was collapsing and that the whole area of the southern Mediterranean was passing under Allied control, Kesselring, the German Supreme Commander South, defended Hitler's decision. During a discussion with Buerker, commanding 10th Panzer Division, Kesselring was asked point-blank why the Tunisian bridgehead was not evacuated. Buerker pointing out that German-occupied Europe was proving too big to be successfully defended then asked what was so important about Africa that it had to be held at any price? Kesselring echoed Hitler's credo that to give up Africa would present the Italians with an opportunity to leave the Axis partnership.

Thus politics and not military sense dictated the orders, shaped the plans, and dominated the strategy which moved Rommel and his men like pawns. That commander saw with bitterness that as the war against Russia went increasingly badly the High Command relegated Africa to the status of a side-show denying to the Africa Corps and its successors those supplies of men and material which might have enabled it to win victory for the Axis. Only when the tide had turned did Hitler realise the danger and tried to reverse the situation by sending across the Mediterranean fresh men and arms. But he was too late; he was only reinforcing defeat. Those men and that material which survived the double gauntlet of the Royal Navy and the Royal Air Force, passed into Allied hands shortly after landing on African soil.

The principal battlefields during the years of war in the southern Mediterranean lay in the area between El Agheila and El Alamein, and through that region ran Via Balbia, the only all-weather coastal road. Possession of that highway dominated the fighting for the pattern of military operations was the same whether it was the Axis or the British who were attacking. The armour would come up out of the desert in an enveloping or encircling operation, while the infantry and the less mobile forces kept close to the Via Balbia, fighting to capture one of the three major ports into which would come the ships to nourish the next advance. The lack of originality in the strategy of the successive offensives was not due to the rigidity of military thinking but to the fact that neither side had the capability to mount a seaborne landing behind the enemy front.

Peculiar to the war in North Africa was the fortunate fact that for most of the time no great numbers of civilians were involved. The civil population was small and concentrated chiefly into a small coastal strip. The rival armies could, therefore, manoeuvre and fight in the southern deserts knowing that their destructive operations were not endangering the great mass of the native population. A second factor of the desert war was that this was the first completely mechanised war to be fought by both sides in the western hemisphere. Because of the enormous length of the battle zone – only those of the Soviet Union were greater in extent – and the absence of railways, movement had to be by mechanical transport. With the exception of the stallion, upon which Mussolini intended to ride in a victory parade in Egypt, a few mounted patrols, and mule trains which were used at times in Tunisia, there were no horses on active service in the African theatre of operations.

The third distinctive feature of the desert war was that no SS combat units fought there. A small SS security office was opened in Tunis but its personnel were not fighting troops and thus the area of the southern Mediterranean was spared the actions and reactions which were suffered in other places. German writers describe the fighting as chivalrous and this was not surprising for, although the war in the desert was hard, both sides had a common enemy, the desert itself, for this could be viciously cruel to the weak and helpless. A defeated enemy had to be helped to overcome the hardships of that region and thus there grew up the legend of the 'gentlemen's war'. Certainly it had pace, style, and, above all, colour. The men of all armies which fought there emerged with a certain flair and, *semper aliquid novi ex Africa* (as always something new comes from Africa), that continent was the fount of many new ideas on armoured warfare tactics, dress, and language which then gained currency and passed from the southern Mediterranean into other battle zones where war was a drab and unromantic misery.

1. The background to war

'I have eight million Fascist bayonets'
Mussolini, Bolzano, 1939

In the years immediately preceding the outbreak of the Second World War the political influence of Fascist Italy was at its peak and the period which Mussolini had spent in office had brought to the Italian people not only a certain stability and prosperity but also prestige, for in certain European political circles Mussolini's many years in office had given him the aura of a fairly young elder statesman, a role which he played to perfection during the Munich crisis of 1938. True, he had been responsible for a small number of short colonial wars in North Africa but these had been successful and had enlarged the Italian colonial empire.

Libya, the name given to the three territories adjoining each other in North Africa and all bordering the Mediterranean, was the oldest colony and had been conquered in 1912. Tripolitania, its most westerly region, was mostly desert and was consequently poor; its economic wealth was vested in two million date palms. Its greatest value lay in its strategic position, for it was only 250 miles removed from Sicily and thus could be regarded as a base from which an attack could be launched upon either the British in Egypt or the French in Tunisia. Marmarica, the eastern province, was also a poor desert territory. Only Cyrenaica had been extensively settled by Italian colonists and had, therefore, been subject to European influence in matters of agriculture, architecture, and attitudes. Running the entire length of the Libyan coastline was a thin strip of fertile land within which had grown up towns and harbours which were to be of greater or lesser importance to the future conduct of military operations.

Although Mussolini in the years immediately preceding the outbreak of war had seemed to be in a very strong position his blatantly aggressive attitudes, his intervention in Spain, and his formation of a political Axis with the even more aggressive Third Reich had so alarmed those countries which bordered on, or had influence in, the Mediterranean that they took combined measures against him. Thus when Italy entered the war in June 1940, the two most powerful nations in the Mediterranean, France and Great Britain through their naval and military bases – the British at Gibraltar and at Alexandria, the French at Toulon, Corsica, and Tunisia – held Italy encircled and confined; a prisoner in the central Mediterranean.

Even though France fell the Royal Navy and the Royal Air Force operating from the chain of British bases stopped supplies of arms and men reaching the Axis armies and thus starved them, for the deciding factors in the North African war were whose ships ruled the waves and whose aircraft dominated the skies. Until the middle of 1941 the Axis powers under the cover of the Luftwaffe and the Regia Aeronautica's air superiority had built up their armies almost unopposed, but from the last months of that year to the end of the war in Africa theirs was, for the greatest period of time, the inferior position. The bravest, most imaginative and brilliant commander leading an army in a theatre of operations overseas from his homeland is only as strong as his supply lines. Cut these and his brilliant, wide-ranging, strategic sweeps are halted: the tanks become static, immobile, and useless steel boxes; the guns, starved of shells, fall silent.

In an area as vast as North Africa losses of territory were not important and even casualties were relatively minor calculations in the military equation. The most important factor was which of the combatant powers had the resources to replace the losses and the ability to bring fresh men and supplies to the commanders in the field. The Axis powers were never able to increase significantly the numbers of men which they could put into action, neither could they equip them. The British, on the other hand, could and did reinforce their armies with new men and modern equipment even though the convoying of this material was carried through under the most difficult and dangerous conditions.

As a result of the Rome–Berlin axis which had been formed in 1939, Germany had been drawn, imperceptibly, almost against her will, and certainly against the inclinations of the Oberkommando der Wehrmacht (OKW) – the High Command of the Armed Forces – into Mediterranean affairs, and these were to have a profound influence upon the conduct of the war. It is a surprising fact that the Axis powers had not held joint consultations on military co-operation and in the only discussions which were held before the outbreak of war the Italians had requested not to be asked to undertake hostilities until 1943, by which year they anticipated that the expansion and modernisation of their armed forces would have been completed. The German delegation agreed, for their country too was undergoing a modernisation and expansion programme which would not be finished until the same year. The OKW hoped, rather naïvely, that Hitler would not embroil Germany in a war until that year. Thus both Axis partners, unprepared for war, went into hostilities without having had an exchange of ideas and certainly without having had discussions on joint military strategy, planning, or co-operation.

In August 1939, as if to underline the demand by the military for time to prepare the army, Mussolini declared that Italy would take no part in the war which had just broken out but that she would still remain in the Axis. This quasi-neutral position was abandoned during the campaign in France when Mussolini, fearful that Italy's influence in Hitler's new, restructured Europe would be too small, declared war. This declaration, made on 10 June 1940, a direct rejection of the advice given to the Duce by Badoglio, the Chief of the General Staff, that Italy could not sustain a long war against the western Allies, spread hostilities into Africa. As a result of the defeat of France, the French colonial territory of Tunisia had become a neutral power, Libya was no longer a buffer between the African territories of France and Great Britain and Mussolini could now turn the colonial might of the Italian empire in North Africa against the British in Egypt. The Germans, too, having defeated France could now concentrate upon the single enemy

Britain and, during July, von Brauschtisch, C-in-C of the German Army drew up a plan with five alternatives for future operations in the Mediterranean. Included among these alternatives was the seizure of Gibraltar and the despatch of a panzer unit to support the Italians in their war in North Africa. If both these operations were successfully executed then British influence in the Mediterranean would be destroyed and it was, perhaps, considered that Malta would then fall of its own accord for, surprisingly, no plan was put forward for an attack upon that island.

A far-seeing staff officer at Oberkommando des Heeres (OKH), Army High Command, had prepared a monograph on the development of the campaign in Africa in which it was proposed that a panzer Corps be sent to aid the Italians, and the OKH planning section was able to report that sufficient vehicles and military stores could be made available to form a Corps. Hitler had also been thinking along parallel lines and having studied the staff paper then asked certain questions, the most important of which was how soon such a Corps could be ready for action. OKH replied that the movement of troops, their transportation, acclimatisation, and the shipping of the necessary equipment would not permit the force to be used in combat operations before December 1940. Discussions at OKH then revolved around the intention to send a two-division expeditionary force to Africa.

Meanwhile in Libya the declaration of war by Mussolini had caught the Army off-balance. So sudden had been the Italian dictator's volte-face that the military was completely unprepared for the demands which were then made upon it and which were to be made at later dates – irrespective of whether these were defensive in character, that is to say, to halt a British attack or whether they were offensive, that is, to invade Egypt. Mussolini ordered an advance into Egypt overriding the advice of Marshal Graziani, the Commander-in-Chief in Libya, that an offensive should not be undertaken until the spring of 1941, by which time there would be an Italian Army capable of meeting the Duce's imperious demands for glory and victory.

The Italians thrust into Egypt on 13 September 1940 and had reached Sidi Barani on the following day. Here Graziani halted to prepare the next step of the advance which he anticipated would bring him to Mersa Matruh by December. In Germany Hitler had reconsidered the African venture proposing that it might be more advantageous to the Italians if units of brigade strength were sent and his proposals were passed to the Italian Military Attaché in Berlin.

When Hitler and Mussolini met in the Brenner Pass during October 1940, these intentions were discussed more fully and it was decided to send a small but powerful, armoured brigade to North Africa and that the men for this unit would be drawn from 3rd Panzer Division. It was also proposed that this unit together with VIIIth Air Corps would be placed under Graziani's command. On 24 October Hitler received a pessimistic report from General von Thoma whom he had sent on a fact-finding mission to Libya. The burden of von Thoma's memorandum was a statement which a succession of German military commanders were to repeat without avail to the end of the war in Africa, namely that a successful conclusion to operations in that theatre depended upon the ability to supply the forces in the field. He went on to stress that, as a result of British control of the seas and the poor harbour facilities in Libya, it would not be possible to supply a force larger in size than four divisions but that this was the minimum strength required to bring victory. Hitler rejected Thoma's appreciation and his counter proposal of a single division to be sent to Africa was in turn dismissed by Thoma who said that a single German division could not affect the situation. Hitler stated his belief in the ability of the Italians to maintain their position against the British and repeated that the whole purpose of sending a German contingent was to hold Italy loyal to the Axis, a statement of intent which was to be echoed by senior German officers in the Mediterranean theatre for the next two years.

In November Hitler ordered that the embarkation of 3rd Panzer Division was to be halted and that no movement of German troops was to take place until the Italians had captured Mersa Matruh in Egypt. A formal declaration of intent was expressed in *Instruction No 18*, issued by OKW, on 12 November 1940, which stated under the heading 'The Italian offensive against Egypt' that,

'German forces will be used, if at all, only when the Italians have reached Mersa Matruh and in the first instance these will be Air Force units for whom the Italians will have provided aerodromes. The Armed Forces are to prepare for the employment of their units in this or any other North African theatre of operations:

Army: The Army will hold ready for use in North Africa a panzer division.

Navy: The Navy is to convert ships lying in Italian ports into troop transports with which to convoy strong bodies of troops with best possible speed to Libya, or to some other place in North Africa.

Air Force: The Air Force is to prepare to carry out air operations against Alexandria or the Suez canal and to block the latter so as to deny its use to the British.'

During December while the euphoria of victory was yet with the Italians further discussions took place between the Axis Supreme Commands at Innsbrück, during which Graziani expressed Mussolini's intention of fighting the war in Africa without German help. In view of this declaration 3rd Panzer Division was stood down and plans for German intervention in Africa were no longer proceeded with.

The British forces, which were fighting against the Italians, were few in number and were spread over a 200-mile area from Sollum, on the coast, to the Siwa Oasis. The weakness of this force did not deter its commander General Wavell from undertaking an offensive and the mass of his Army of the Nile struck out of the desert and into the Italian flank on 9 December. Collaborating closely with the Royal Navy and the Royal Air Force, Wavell's 30,000 men defeated an Italian Army ten times its number. By 11 December, Sidi Barani had been recaptured, on 5 January 1941 Bardia fell, Tobruk followed on 23 January, and by February British and Imperial troops had occupied Marmarica, most of Cyrenaica, and much of Tripolitania. But then with his forces exhausted and his supply lines over-extended, Wavell halted the advance along the edge of the great Sirte Desert. Before him lay the remnants of the broken Italian Army whose remaining unshattered units were preparing to dig in around the capital city of Tripoli ready to fight the final battle. With the loss of Tripolitania the whole of Libya would pass under the control of the British who would then be able to turn upon and conquer the Italian Somaliland and Ethiopian territories piecemeal. It was, therefore, vital to the Axis war effort that a foothold be retained along the North African coast and this bridgehead expanded to form a firm base for future operations aimed at the recapture of the lost provinces and to prevent the British establishing a base from which to attack Sicily and the Italian mainland.

It was against this background of urgency and Italian despair – the defeat of Graziani's 10th Army coupled with the reverses which other Italian armies were suffering in the war with Greece – that Mussolini was forced to ask for that German assistance which he had declined. Hitler responding to his Axis partner's needs reactivated the plan to send a German force to Africa. The first results of this support was an air raid upon Malta on 10 January by machines from Xth Air Corps but help was needed more urgently on the ground and a memorandum to this effect, handed to the German liaison officer with Commando Supremo (Italian Supreme Headquarters) was forwarded to Hitler. His reaction was immediate and on 9 January he decided to send a blocking force to Tripolitania, outlining his intentions in *Instruction No 22*, dated 11 January. In the section which dealt with events in Africa he wrote:

'The situation in the Mediterranean demands that for strategic, political and psychological reasons Germany must give assistance . . . (to Italy) . . . and I order that a blocking force be raised by OKH which must be capable of supporting our allies against British armour in their defence of Tripolitania. Preparations must be concluded so that this unit can be shipped to Tripoli in conjunction with an Italian armoured and motorised division.'

The critical situation in which the Italians now found themselves as a result of the loss of Tobruk, one of their main bases, produced the urgent demand from General von Rintelen serving at Commando Supremo that a German unit strong enough to operate offensively and not merely as a blocking force be despatched without delay. His appreciation of the situation was shared by General Funck who had returned from a visit of inspection to Libya and who reported that Graziani's intention was to convert Tripoli into a fortified town. Funck proposed that a panzer Corps be sent to carry out an offensive to regain Cyrenaica. Hitler then entered one of those periods of indecision which bedevilled his relations with his commanders and his allies and could not make up his mind on either the necessity for, or the nature of, the German formation to be used in Africa. To the request to increase greatly the strength of the blocking force, OKH replied that such an increase would have to be taken from the forces being assembled for the campaign in Greece and that this in turn would weaken the forces to be used against Russia.

The OKW, proposed in turn that the blocking force be reinforced, in the first instance, only by a panzer regiment and that at later dates other components of a panzer division could be sent across to Africa. It was also proposed that the German and Italian mobile, that is motorised and panzer, units be under the command of a German Corps commander. Hitler weighed the disadvantages that would accrue from the loss of the Italian colonies against the advantage of successfully intervening in Africa, reached his decision, and issued instructions to begin embarking troops. But 3rd Panzer Divisions had been stood down and a new formation needed to be raised. Into this new division entitled 5th Light was incorporated 3rd Reconnaissance Battalion, 39th Anti-tank Battalion, a light artillery battalion, a panzer company, and a medical company. The special tropical service fuel and ammunition, water filtering equipment and water cans which had been assembled for 3rd Panzer was also taken over by 5th Light.

There were daily meetings and arguments with the quartermaster's department of the Army which was involved with preparations for the attack upon Russia and who, lacking other criteria, based their calculations for the requirements of the new force upon European campaigns with adequate water supplies and good roads. The division scale of transport was finally laid down at only two-thirds of the requirements which the divisional officers had demanded. Preparations were then made to ship the first units across to Tripoli, and these were to be followed by 5th Panzer Regiment which in turn was to be reinforced by a second panzer division.

On 6 February Hitler then gave instructions that the blocking line was to be as far east as possible – in the Sirte Desert – and also ordered that the role of 5th Light Division was, initially, to be one of aggressive defence. On the same day OKW issued its own orders to commence Operation *Sonnenblume* – the transport of German forces to Tripoli. The Africa Corps was on its way.

On the question of who was to command the Africa Corps Hitler selected General Rommel, who had been commander of his Escort Regiment during the campaign in Poland and on 7 February he briefed the new Corps commander on his tasks, the most important of which was to hold Tripolitania at all costs.

The German troops who disembarked in Tripoli on 11 February were followed by the first fighting units three days later. These men were the advanced guard of a force which was to be known by many titles, the one which it retained longest being that of Panzer Army Africa, but which is more famous for the name which it held only a relatively short time – Africa Corps.

The tasks, responsibilities, and duties of this formation had been worked out by Hitler and Commando Supremo and included within the terms of reference were the following:

(1) For tactical purposes the general officer commanding German troops is subordinate to the Italian Supreme Command in Libya. He is responsible to OKH for all other decisions.
(2) German troops may only be used as complete units . . .
(3) German troops may not be distributed in small groups along the front.
(4) In the event of the German commander being given an order which, in his opinion, could lead to his force being lost then he had the right and duty to ask for Hitler's decision, although he must inform the Italian High Command that he is making this appeal.
(5) The Xth Air Corps remains under the command of supreme commander Luftwaffe and is to collaborate with the Italian Air Force.

On 9 February 1941, a conference between Mussolini and von Rintelen led to Mussolini accepting Rommel as commander of the joint German/Italian mobile forces and on the same day came the announcement that Mussolini had replaced Graziani by Gariboldi, the former commander of the Italian 5th Army. The Axis leader confirmed Hitler's intention that Tripolitania was to be defended by aggressive defence in the Sirte. Rommel then flew to Rome on 11 February for a conference with Mussolini and, in the afternoon of the same day, went on to Sicily for a briefing on the situation in Libya by Xth Air Corps commander. By the following day Rommel was in Africa learning at first hand of the serious situation in which the Italian Army was placed.

He flew back to Germany and laid before Hitler his plans on the course of the operations which he intended to conduct in a counter-offensive to re-conquer Cyrenaica. He proposed to wait and to hold the blocking line until his two German divisions, 5th Light and 15th Panzer, had arrived and then together with the Italian armoured division Ariete and the motorised division Trento he would attack the British. Rommel was not aware and neither were his superiors at OKW nor Commando Supremo that Wavell had been ordered to give active military support to the Greeks and that, even as Rommel descended upon Africa once again, an expeditionary force drawn from the British desert army was preparing to leave for Greece, leaving only a thin screen to garrison the conquered territories and to watch the badly shaken Italian armies.

2. Conditions in the desert

'The desert: a tactician's paradise but a
quartermaster's hell.'
General von Ravenstein

The previous chapter has stated how 3rd Panzer Division was to be a nucleus in the Africa Corps organisation and that how, within six months, an expeditionary force had been selected, had been stood down, a new unit re-formed, despatched, and was ready for action. In view of the urgency there had been little time for preparation and the German Army in undertaking a campaign in tropical desert regions was entering very much into *terra incognita*. With the exception of reports based upon the experiences of von Lettow-Vorbeck's force, which had fought in equatorial Africa during the First World War, and upon the recollections of veterans who had fought with the Turks in Palestine, there were no first hand experiences upon which the staff could make their plans.

Not until after the armistice with the French did discussions take place on the subject of equipment and supply for units serving in sub-tropical or tropical climes and, once again, contemporary information was lacking. There were no French or British papers dealing with the tactics or employment of motorised or armoured formations in desert warfare and the Italian material had, generally, dealt only with the recently concluded war against Ethiopia. In the autumn of 1940 the Italians produced their first reports based upon the campaign against the British in Egypt but these papers were lacking in detail, were often inaccurate in report, and frequently as wildly false as the maps which their cartographic service had produced. Basic and sometimes vital details were omitted from the Italian reports so that the first German units were supplied with unnecessary or badly designed equipment.

A case in point was the fact that upon Italian recommendation the Germans sent no diesel engines to Africa, although in tropical conditions the diesel was a more suitable engine than the petrol motor. The Italians also forgot to add that they had themselves designed a successful, special tropical pattern diesel. With no advice forthcoming the Germans made no special preparations to protect vehicle motors from the scouring effects of sand and dust, so that in the early months the life of a German tank engine was between 800 and 1000 miles, that is about half that of a British vehicle. It was only when special filters were fitted that the life span was increased to equal that of British machines.

The adverse effects upon the efficiency of tank engines of the great heat during the summer campaigns could not be completely overcome by mechanical means and it was found that there were less troubles if marches were undertaken by night or the vehicles moved in the cooler hours of early morning or late evening. Of course, night marches demanded the ability to read the compass efficiently and all tank crews had to be trained in this skill. An added advantage of this training and one which was only later appreciated was that panzer operations could then still be carried out even in the artificial darkness of a sand storm.

Experience was to show that during a tank battle the onset of darkness usually brought an end to the day's fighting and the post-battle actions of the combatants are interesting. The British almost invariably drew back from the battlefield to laager, to rearm, and to prepare for the morrow. Thus, after the strain of battle British tank drivers still had to undertake a march and then on the next day had an approach march to battle. This voiding of the field by the British meant that vehicles which had fallen out or were only suffering from slight mechanical faults were left in German dominated territory for that army, by contrast, laagered on or very close to the scene of the fighting and thus spared their drivers the extra strain imposed in driving.

The German tank recovery organisation was first class and its units followed close behind each panzer company ready to carry out, under fire, local and immediate repairs. For the more seriously damaged vehicles there were low-loader trucks able to bear weights of up to 18 tons and thus able to remove such tanks from the field to the workshops immediately behind the firing line so that specialised repairs could be carried out on them. Such organisation, much improvisation, and as a result of such practices the Axis forces were able to overcome the numerical inferiority from which they suffered. They further reduced the superiority of their enemy by taking into their own service or by blowing up the British tanks which had been left unrecovered on the field.

The Italians were unable to give any details on camouflage, a difficult task in an area devoid of all natural cover, and the Germans tried many methods of concealment. The first vehicles to arrive in North Africa had been covered in standard European paint for the quartermaster's department had no paint suitable for desert conditions. To tone down the shades of grey and green the machines were first sprayed with oil and upon this foundation sand was strewn. The greatest need in all concealment is to break up the outline of the shadow which the vehicle casts and to do this extensive use was made of netting, sometimes set about with small tufts of camel thorn. The method which the infantry frequently used to escape detection was to dig slit trenches into the sides of wadis or if in the open desert then to spread a net across the trench opening and thus to have not only protection against detection but shade from the sun.

Not even by night were vehicles safe from detection for bright, desert moonlight illuminated them at considerable distances even from the air and it was necessary, therefore, for vehicles to move tactically dispersed when travelling in moonlight. In addition to camouflage against visibility, units concealed their locations and avoided being surprised during the hours of darkness or in periods of rest by practising wireless silence. Any message which it was essential to pass went out either on the ultra short-wave wireless frequency to avoid interception or by telephone, although this latter method was only used inside a laager during long halts or at night.

Very little information was available on the effect of tropical living upon northern Europeans although it was widely held at OKH that the summer heat would be too great to allow military operations to continue and that both armies would withdraw into summer quarters to await better campaigning weather, just as the armies had taken up winter quarters in cold climates in former days. Having no data the Germans made no special selection of men to serve in Africa, other than a simple medical examination. Nor was any special training given or, in the early days, any time spent in acclimatisation. By an unplanned piece of good fortune the first troops arrived in early spring and needed no period of acclimatisation before going into battle within weeks of their debarkation. Subsequently, reinforcements were sent to Bavaria or to Sicily to accustom them to the heat but still no special training or instructions were given other than a few lectures on hygiene.

These statements conflict with contemporary British newspaper accounts which described how hordes of blond stormtroops, the recruits for the Africa Corps, had been set to marching in vast glass, hothouses set up on Baltic beaches to prepare them for the great heat: the difficult, airless, and arid conditions under which they would live and fight in Africa. This legend of the highly trained supermen helped to salve British wounds inflicted when Rommel's small force beat the remnants of Wavell's Army, depleted by the removal of much of its strength to serve as an expeditionary force in Greece.

One of the most important requirements in the African campaign was the ability to identify quickly and at long range men or vehicles encountered in the desert and in this field, too, the Germans had to learn from experience. The effect of sun upon sand caused severe eye strain – a form of sand blindness – often produced mirages, and always shimmering heat waves. All or any one of these reduced the range of effective vision and thus the ability to identify vehicles with speed. In open desert vision was only slightly affected between the hours from first light to about 09.00hrs and from 16.00hrs to dusk. At those times accurate vision varied between 2000 and 5000 yards. As the day wore on and the temperature rose the effective range decreased to less than 1500 yards.

It should have been apparent to the German planners, but seems to have escaped their notice, that North Africa is, by and large, a treeless waste. Yet they made no attempt to supply fuel oil for cooking or for workshop firing and relied on wood which had to be brought from Italy thus reducing shipping space which could have been used for more vital supplies. They were also unaware that the desert terrain is not a vast series of sand dunes as a result of which the lorries fitted with double tyres for better traction in such conditions suffered from punctures caused by the infiltration of sharp stones picked up and wedged between the double tyres when the vehicles crossed the hard-going which constituted much of the desert's surface. Later during the campaign special wide tyres were fitted to the Volkswagen cars and thereby improved the cross-country performances of those vehicles.

By and large it can be said that the Italians did nothing to prepare themselves for a desert campaign and that the Germans were unable to do anything through lack of time and foreknowledge. But it must also be admitted that once there were experiences upon which to base conclusions or to make appreciations then Rommel's force adapted, improvised, and fought a good fight.

FOOD, HYGIENE, AND OTHER REGULATIONS

On the problem of food suitable for soldiers in tropical areas the Germans, again lacking first-hand information, drew very heavily upon out of date sources and upon theories. The dieticians issued instructions on the type and preparation of food that were completely at variance with available resources and showed little forward planning and even less imagination. They were convinced that potatoes, the German soldier's staple diet and bread, his other basic foodstuff, were liable to spoil and turn mouldy in the North African climate. Substitutes for these two basic foods were issued: beans in place of potatoes and biscuits in place of bread. The British Army which faced the same problem had solved the potato question by canning those vegetables, a solution which the German scientists seem not to have considered. In the event German field bakeries began to turn out a flat type of rye biscuit but then went over to baking real bread. Experiments were made using sea water, to economise on sweet water supplies, but these proved unsuccessful.

In view of the fact that butter or margarine melted in the heat, olive oil was used as a substitute and with the exception of small amounts of cheese and tinned beef there were no other ration foods available. The diet was monotonous and lacked not only variety but vitamin C.

With typical German attention to detail instructions were given on how to prepare freshly killed meat or game, on hygiene, on the fact that water should be drunk only during the cool periods of the day, on sanitation, and on relations with the local population. For the greatest part of the years they spent in Africa the German soldiers had little fresh meat, of game there was no sign, the hygiene instructions were commonsense, and it was difficult to establish relations with the Arabs. Those in the populated coastal areas avoided contact and there were few dwellers in the desert places. In later years, in Tunisia, there was such a rapport that native battalions were raised but these men had, perhaps, enlisted more as an anti-French gesture than as a demonstration of pro-German feeling. The Germans certainly made great efforts to win the friendship of the Arabs for their commanders knew that with such support they were assured of a freedom from guerrilla warfare, from partisans, and from sabotage.

UNIFORM

The uniform with which the Army in Africa is most closely identified – the long visored cap, the shorts, and high boots – was a development of a pattern of clothing of which the first issues were made late in 1940. The material was an olive-coloured cotton cloth and the cut was the same for all the ranks. The tunic was a lighter version of the standard European pattern garment and the breeches were intended to be worn with the specially designed leather and canvas high, lace-up boots. A sun helmet was covered with olive green canvas and was fitted with light alloy decals of the same pattern as that painted on the steel helmet.

Practical use showed the uniform to be badly designed. The jacket restricted movement and the breeches were too tight, the sun helmet was too bulky for front line use and gave almost no protection against head wounds. A second disadvantage with the sun helmet was that sand and dust entered the ventilation holes and matted the hair. Only the boots were practical and long lasting.

In the course of time the Germans became aware that it was possible to survive and even fight in the desert during the hottest months of the year so long as clothing was light, loose, and comfortable. The impractical uniform which had been issued was either discarded or amended. The sun helmet was the first item to go and to be replaced by the long-visored field cap, and the steel helmet was brought back for front line use. The tight breeches were discarded and were replaced either by slacks, paratroop overalls buttoning at the ankle, or by short trousers. These latter were not authorised wear in every unit for some regimental officers realised that long trousers gave better protection to the legs against small, accidental cuts and grazes which quickly and almost invariably turned ulcerous.

After long wear and frequent washings the German olive green uniform colour, tended to fade to the shade of khaki worn by the British and when in 1942 vast stocks of British uniforms were captured in Tobruk these were adapted and issued to German units so that on some sectors, except for the rank insignia and specialist badges, both sides wore the same pattern uniform. This use of enemy clothing was not a new phenomenon – equipment and vehicles in particular were often captured and put into service against their former owners. The British had in this fashion used Italian tanks captured during Wavell's offensive, Rommel's command vehicle was a British truck, and after the Mechili operation the captured British soft-skinned vehicles had been issued to the German units to give them a greater mobility. Under such circumstances it is not surprising that most soldiers had great difficulty in correctly distinguishing friendly from enemy units although to aid identification British vehicles in Axis service were frequently marked with a swastika flag and almost always painted with a German straight-edged, black cross.

TERRAIN

Mention has already been made of the fact that the Germans, in a false assessment of the terrain conditions, sent trucks with double sets of tyres to the African theatre of operations. It is a common fallacy, and one which was held by the OKH, that the whole of the North African desert was a vast sea of loose sand formed into rolling dunes.

There were, of course, large stretches of country in which this condition obtained but the desert also had more areas of firm going on which rocks of varying sizes were met and when in later years the Axis armies entered Tunisia they were climatically in an area akin to southern Italy with mountains, vegetation, and cacti. There was in Libya only one single, all-weather road, the Via Balbia, which traversed the country extending from the Tunisian frontier to Egypt and upon this tarmac surface traffic could move as swiftly as in Europe. The Via Balbia was one of the factors which determined the success or failure of an offensive and it followed very closely the line of the Mediterranean linking, in its west to east journey along the coast, the widely spaced towns and settlements of the Italian colony for there were no important inland towns. The distances between the towns was enormous and it was, therefore, upon a battlefield of vast lateral extent that the campaign was fought out. From Tripoli, the capital city, to Buerat on the eastern border of the province was more than 300 miles. To El Agheila, on the south-western edge of Cyrenaica, it was 470 miles, Benghasi was 650 miles away, and the Egyptian frontier was nearly 1000 miles distant.

Criss-crossing the desert were native tracks (trigh) with varying degrees of value as roads capable of bearing military traffic. Most of these trigh were on firm going but with constant use the hard surface rutted and the trigh widened as drivers left the original track to find smoother going or a less dusty surface. These tracks were useless in wet weather for rain washed away their surfaces and wheeled transport using them frequently bogged down. At a point where two trigh crossed there was usually some sort of landmark, a bir (well or cistern) or sidi (the grave of some Muslim saint). These track junctions played an important part in the fighting for they were landmarks or points of reference in a countryside totally devoid of distinctive features. Such strategically important places were usually held by a garrison or used as advanced supply depots.

A thin, fertile strip of land in which much of the population lived and which bordered the Mediterranean extended into the desert for only a short way and then, as the vegetation ended, the hard surface was met. Farther inland the going deteriorated and there were vast sand seas which were almost impassable, even to tracked vehicles. It was into these isolated and barren wastes that long-distance reconnaissance patrols were sent at infrequent intervals and it was the presence of these great impassable seas which prevented the deployment of masses of men and hemmed the combatants into an area extending inland from the sea to a depth of about 50 miles. Most of the battles and offensives which will be described in this book were fought out within this narrow strip of Libya. Rising above the level of the desert were escarpments (djebels), possession of which allowed some of the trigh and, in places, the Via Balbia to be dominated. At certain places along the coast the escarpments rose sheer out of the sea and at these points, as well as along some inland djebels, vehicles could not cross. But, in the main, most of the high ground could be conquered by tracked vehicles. Where the mountains ran almost to the sea the coastal plain reduced in width to form a narrow pass, ideal defensive positions across whose mouth a small number of defenders could hold off superior forces. Other defence lines could be constructed wherever there was a natural feature on the desert flank which could not be bypassed. The British position at El Alamein where the desert flank rested on the impassable Quattara Depression is a classic example of that type of defence line.

Climatically the best campaigning seasons were the spring and autumn although both these times of the year were periods during which the *khamsin* or *jibli* blew. These hot winds raced across the desert at high speed whirling the sand into the air and producing a sort of hot, gritty fog with the air as thick as soup and of an enervating closeness. Some storms were of such intensity that they lasted for days and halted all movement as men and machines tried desperately to prevent themselves being sanded in. The side which could attack under the cover of the *khamsin* had the advantage of approaching almost totally concealed from sight and sound. Of the other seasons the winter produced bad weather and often rain which washed away the trigh while, in the opinion of OKH, the intense heat of summer was likely to reduce operations to small-scale, patrol affairs. In fact this turned out not to be the case and there were summer offensives during both 1941 and 1942 although the strain which the fighting placed upon both men and their vehicles was quite severe.

Despite the terrible disadvantages the desert had a charm, almost a fascination, which affected most of them who lived and fought there. The vast distances, the deep silences, the tricks of light, even the spartan conditions had a profound effect upon the soldiers who were in this desolate wilderness thousands of miles from their homes. This nostalgia, this longing for the empty spaces was best expressed in a poem written by one Cockney soldier during a winter in Italy.

Give me a brew can and let me go, far away up in the blue
Sit in a laager and talk of the days of Medjez and Mersa Matruh
Sand in my teeth, sand in my hair, free from all worry, far from all care
And no redcap to check me for the clobber I wear; far away up in the
  blue

Because there were so few civilians and, thus few distractions the armies, German as well as British, turned in upon themselves and became such closely knit organisations that the word family best describes them. The desert and its ways produced in addition to peculiar ideas of dress the invisible but distinctive styles of comradeship, loyalty, and decency which were never found in any other theatre of operation. In Africa there were no mass atrocities committed as an act of policy against civilians or soldiers for the possibility of becoming a prisoner of war was a continual hazard in the ebb and flow of armoured warfare.

TACTICS

Tactics are defined as the art of handling troops in the field to gain a desired end easily and smoothly. Weapons determine tactics and to a very great degree it is the ability to recognise the potential of a new weapon which shapes the course and the outcome of battles. It was Rommel's flair for combining the new weapons of blitzkrieg, the tank and the dive-bomber with the classic foot and guns, which brought him tactical victories on so many occasions and, although his ability had been demonstrated as early as the French campaign of 1940, it was in North Africa that this military genius truly flowered.

He had come to Africa with tactical doctrines based on European experiences and then found that some of these had little or no relevance to the new theatre of operations. Faced by new problems the Germans applied themselves with their customary vigour and in the lulls between the summer and autumn fighting of 1941 produced tactics in which at first only the men of 15th Panzer Division were trained and these innovations having proved themselves in the winter campaign of 1941 and the spring campaign of 1942, they were developed as a battle drill and introduced into other panzer units.

Rommel's doctrine was that all arms – infantry, guns, and tanks – should fight as fully integrated parts of a whole and that thereby they would be able to bring down a maximum concentration of effort upon any chosen target within the shortest possible time. In the desert this chosen target was the British armour whose destruction was the key to tactical success. One of the first discoveries made by panzer men in the desert was that the force did not need to move in column, which had been the practice in Europe, for given firm going the advance could be made in line abreast. Out of this knowledge evolved the tactic of a panzer unit advancing to contact already formed for battle and not having to waste time in deployment manoeuvring. A whole panzer division could move forward as a series of 'boxes' or 'handkerchiefs', each box forming an individual battle group and echeloned with a depth four times that of its front. The various components of the division were usually located within the box in the same position. The armoured brow made up of a tank battalion with artillery support. Then followed the second panzer battalion with heavier artillery and engineers, all forming another box. On the 'enemy' side of the divisional 'box' ranged the reconnaissance detachments and the anti-tank guns while located in the centre of the box were the soft-skinned vehicles and divisional headquarters. Behind this mass of trucks there were the heaviest guns of the divisional artillery and at the rear the infantry component, the remainder of the artillery, and the tank recovery details.

The course of the desert war was marked by short but intense bursts of furious activity followed by longer periods during which the winning side consolidated its gains and built up its strength for a further advance while the losing army constructed defence lines and brought up fresh supplies of men and materials to replace the losses which had been suffered. Thus the fighting, when it took place, was of a fluid nature and it was the cut and thrust of armoured conflict which characterised it; actions in which the fortunes of war changed almost hourly. Nevertheless, the idea of tank versus tank battles was considered by the Germans to be a wrong application of armoured power. Rommel chose to use instead the 'bait' tactic which he had applied with such success during the fighting in France. In this the panzer force would advance to contact and then retire 'baiting' the British whose standard reaction was always to mount a charge. When this happened the tank men of 8th Army, their vision obscured by clouds of dust and sand thrown up by the with-drawing panzers, would thrust towards and then be impaled upon the fire of a screen of guns. This simple tactic seldom failed until Montgomery arrived in the desert and halted these heroic but futile assaults.

This gun-line tactic was effective only given certain conditions; and in North Africa these conditions obtained for many years. The first of these was that the British 'attacking front' did not exceed the 'gun density'. It must be appreciated that the most effective German tank destroyer was the 8.8cm gun and that this weapon could outrange every British tank gun. Thus one single gun could fight a battle with a squadron of tanks engaging the first tank at distances greater than a mile and would have had time to smash the other vehicles of an attacking wave before they could bring fire to bear. The British tank commanders unwittingly aided the German gunners by committing their forces piecemeal. Most tank attacks went as single regiments and it was rare that the 'attacking front' covered a two-regimental width. Thus the 8.8s could select their targets at leisure in the certain knowledge that their shot could penetrate 8.3cm of armour plate at a range of 2000 yards.

The second condition which made the gun line effective was that the British tank gun had a shorter range than the German gun which it was fighting. Until this situation changed the gun line remained the standard and most successful tactic used by the Panzer Army, for theirs was a concept of guns versus tanks.

The inclusion of the 8.8cm in their armoury ensured that the outcome of such a battle was nearly always victory for the artillery and so effective was that gun that it may be claimed with some accuracy that the German success at Gazala was built upon the forty-eight 8.8cm pieces which Rommel had under command. There were two other first-class anti-tank guns on the German establishment, the 5cm and the Russian 7.6cm, the latter considered to be the best anti-tank gun in the world.

Another of the advantages enjoyed by the Germans was that their anti-tank guns and their tank guns could fire high explosive as well as solid shot. Thus their guns could bring fire to bear upon the British anti-tank gun line and by high explosive shells destroy it or at least neutralise it. It was not until the summer of 1942 with the introduction of the 6-pounder anti-tank gun and the Grant tank gun, both of which pieces fired high explosive in addition to armour piercing shot, that 8th Army was able to deal effectively with the Axis anti-tank gun lines.

Against the three first-class German anti-tank guns the British could oppose at first only with the 2-pounder, a weapon of such poor performance that it could only be fired with hope of penetration against the thinner side plates of enemy armour at ranges below 200 yards. Being thus almost totally ineffective this weapon could neither support a British tank assault nor could it defend infantry against panzer attack. To act as an anti-tank gun the 25-pounder was pressed into service and weapons were taken from their main task, that of supplying protection for the foot soldiers. Being therefore without proper artillery support the British infantry relied for protection upon the armour and this restriction bred among the tank units the feeling that they were being prevented from achieving their prime purpose – manoeuvre – by being tied down to the foot troops. The infantry, on the other hand, was convinced that the armour deserted it in time of need.

The German armour depended upon the two main types Panzer III and IV and during the years of campaigning these were up-gunned and up-armoured so that their already great capabilities were enhanced and their effectiveness increased. Both of these types were capable of subduing any tank which the British could put into the field. On the British side the Matilda was a slow vehicle with a maximum speed of 16mph and a main armament of the 2-pounder gun; the Matilda was to all intents and purposes defenceless. The Grant tank which came into the battle at Gazala, during the summer of 1942, helped in part to restore the imbalance through its 7.5cm gun, but this weapon had only a limited traverse and was set too low in the hull. Thus the Grant could not take a 'hull down' position but had to expose itself almost completely in order to fire its main armament.

German attacks against British positions followed a battle drill. A preliminary reconnaissance would determine the sector to be attacked and an armoured thrust would be made to divert attention from the main thrust. This main effort would be made by several 'boxes' of tanks which would advance at a given speed with carefully regulated intervals between the individual tanks and the individual 'boxes'. The assault would roll forward and by a combination of fire and movement the position would be taken. Once this had happened a gun line would be formed to protect the flank while the panzers pressed the attack forward.

Reconnaissance was of the pattern common on European battlefields and in the early months Panzer II vehicles were used to screen the front and flanks of a battle formation. These lightly armoured and undergunned, obsolete vehicles were pushed forward of the main body about 8 miles, that is to the extreme range of their wireless sets. Up with the forward reconnaissance detachments was also a small but highly specialised group whose task it was to listen to wireless messages which passed between the British armour and its commanders, and to lay this intelligence before the divisional commander so that the direction and size of British thrusts could be countered.

The movement of Axis supply columns was made difficult by British patrols; one German report warned that not even the tracks behind their own lines could be considered as absolutely safe from enemy attack, and for a short time a convoy system was introduced. A continual problem had been the delay which occurred while the fighting group waited for its supplies of fuel and ammunition to catch up, and to overcome this a number of soft-skinned vehicles loaded with these essential supplies travelled with the battle group and were protected from attack by being held in the middle of the divisional box. An officer of the quartermaster's department was attached to tactical headquarters, forward with the battle group, and was linked by radio to the main quartermaster's department back at Corps.

In the fast-moving fighting on the desert battlefields the problems which usually confronted a military commander were increased and the difficulties of fighting a modern battle from the rear, which had been encountered even in the slow-moving days of the early campaigns in Europe, proved impossible to resolve in Africa. Situations arose which demanded immediate solutions. It was, therefore, essential that not only the divisional commander but the whole of his tactical headquarters, the forward observation officer for the artillery, and the panzer regiment's commander be well forward to control and to direct operations. The whole command echelon was carried in special armoured vehicles. It was also essential that the elaborate communications procedures which had obtained in Europe be simplified and for this purpose the divisional commander's vehicle was fitted with an ultra short-wave radio so that he could both listen in to the orders being given to the panzer regiment and give his own instructions direct, without going through the standard but time-wasting practices. The remainder of the leading group as well as all the other boxes listened in on the medium-wave band and were directly linked with the divisional commander. Thus he could deploy his forward units and co-ordinate the panzer assault with that of the supporting arms in the rear boxes. Between the divisional reconnaissance groups and headquarters there was a signals link mounted in an armoured vehicle. A simple system of set pattern orders made the transmission and execution of battlefield manoeuvres a speedier process than had been the case in Europe and constant practice of the manoeuvres as well as of other battle drills reduced time-wasting and in the artillery units enabled these to go into action with surprising speed.

The presence of generals, even of the Corps commander himself, upon the battlefield not only speeded up decision making but improved the morale of the fighting soldier for he could see for himself that the commanders were undergoing the same privations and sharing the dangers of battle with him. To the German front line soldier in Africa the generals were not shadowy figures in a headquarters miles removed from the fighting but were physically present upon the field of battle. This personal presence helped to produce a good *esprit de corps*. By contrast the Italian and British High Commands were remote and their decisions arrived at usually after staff conferences had often been overtaken by events leaving new crises to be resolved. It was not uncommon for Rommel or indeed any senior commander to take over the direction of a battalion in battle, a situation which may not have been very comfortable for regimental officers but did produce results. It is recorded that once, at Mechili, while flying over his advancing columns Rommel saw a unit halted for no apparent reason and radioed to the officer commanding that unless the advance was renewed he would land his Fieseler Storch and take over command. The unit moved on.

THE COMMANDER-IN-CHIEF – ERWIN ROMMEL

The personality of Erwin Rommel dominated not only the Axis armies but, indeed, the whole African campaign. As a young officer during the First World War he had been awarded the highest German decoration for bravery, the Pour le Mérite, for an action on the Italian Front and in the inter-war years he had produced a number of text books on infantry tactics. After serving as commander of Hitler's Escort Battalion in Poland Rommel had taken over command of 7th Panzer Division and in a most determined way had converted the minor role of his division into the spearhead of the panzer force which defeated the western Allies during 1940. Hitler had personally chosen Rommel to command the Africa Corps and was to have his faith justified.

If only Rommel's faith in Hitler had met with the same loyalty then, there is no doubt that the Axis powers would have been strategically successful in the fighting in Africa but Rommel was the victim of his superiors. The supplies which they promised him either never arrived at all or were reduced in number before they reached Africa. He was to see artillery pieces of new and startling power, which had been promised to him, sent to the 5th Panzer Army in Tunisia. His armies were halted when the flow of petrol stopped, the artillery ceased firing for lack of ammunition, the tanks he asked for were diverted to other fronts, and against all these breaches of faith he could make no protest for he was entangled in an extraordinary hierarchy of command.

Africa was an Italian theatre of operations and Rommel as commander of only the mobile forces of the desert army was subordinate to an Italian general. Then the person of Kesselring, the German Supreme Commander South was interposed and the Commando Supremo in Rome was often in accord with Kesselring's points of view. Between Rommel and Hitler there also stood the OKH and the OKW, not to mention Benito Mussolini who was not only the *de facto* Head of the Italian State but also a personal friend of Hitler.

Each and all of these layers of obstruction prevented Rommel from achieving the objectives which he had set himself and his men. He was a tireless soldier and demanded of his troops the same indifference to hard conditions and to privations that he himself had. He drove his men hard and his vehicles to the limits of their endurance, allowing his soldiers little time for rest and his panzers less than adequate time for maintenance. His whole attention was concentrated upon the objectives of fighting and winning the desert war. Not for him the problems of logistics and the difficulties of supply. His attitude to his desert quartermasters can be best summed up in the plea which Churchill made on another occasion, 'Give us the tools and we shall finish the job'. But for the greater part of his service in Africa Rommel was bedevilled by two factors which negated the victories which he won and prevented him exploiting the successes which had been achieved. The first of these was a lack of supplies and the second was the over elaborate command structure which allowed him no freedom of action or of manoeuvre.

Rommel led his men from the front and the charge that he neglected staff duties to direct operations personally is a valid one but the peculiar conditions of desert warfare demanded the presence of a taskmaster on the battlefield.

He was a poor subordinate and like Nelson preferred not to see – or in his case hear – the orders, warnings, and injunctions which his superiors at every level of command gave him on the conduct of operations. With the ebb of the Axis tide at El Alamein in October 1942 the Commando Supremo had its revenge upon the man who had come to the desert and had made it an area which bore the imprint of his military genius. Demands for his resignation were made each time his understrength armies were forced from one un-tenable position to another. And always he had to face the lack of supplies, the unkept promises, the demands to carry out some other task above the capabilities of his armies until at last he returned to Hitler to make one more desperate plea for supplies that would enable a bridgehead in Tunisia to be held. Flamboyantly, Hitler promised Rommel that he would lead an Axis army against Casablanca – so little knowledge of the true situation did the German leader have – and with that Rommel had to be content. He never returned to Africa and thus avoided seeing the Army which he had so often led into victories pass into the bitterness of final defeat.

THE ITALIAN ALLY

It is not the purpose of this book to dwell upon the defects of the Italian Army in general or upon the faults of those Corps and divisions, in particular, which fought the campaign in Africa. There can, however, be no doubt that the Italian service was weak, badly led, and poorly armed and equipped. Mussolini may have boasted that behind him stood eight million Fascist bayonets but this was oratory and not fact, for even had he had eight million men there would not have been the arms available to outfit them. Italy had prepared her Army in the early 1930s and when her infantry and tank arms went into battle against the British they did so equipped with obsolescent weapons and were fully aware of their inferiority *vis-à-vis* their enemies. For the Italian Army to have fought at all knowing of the British crushing superiority would have been sufficient; that they fought for three years is a memorial to their incredible endurance and bravery.

From the highest level down to that of junior commanders the structure was defective. The whole system of messing was completely wrong and the Germans were astonished at the disparity in ration scales between the Italian commissioned ranks and the men they led. The officers ate first and best; the men last, badly, and sometimes not at all. The officers lived almost at a peace-time level. There was even a mobile brothel in a large caravan. The comradeship of danger shared was missing; a sense of purpose was absent. The Italian Army lacked spirit and with the defeat by Wavell only weeks before the first German troops found the morale of their allies to be dangerously low. The Italians had such an inferiority complex about the ability of the British that many considered any attempt at defence to be worse than useless.

Whereas it was common in the German Army for commanders to be well forward leading their men, the Italian leaders seldom left their headquarters and thus had no direct and immediate influence upon the course of a battle. There was little, or as good as no, wireless or telephone communication between units and their commanders; higher echelons generally depended upon a system of liaison officers for the relay of orders.

The organisation of the supply system showed many defects and the whole edifice was predicated on the assumption that war in the desert would be a static campaign, although no effort had been made to erect proper and permanent defences. The Italians had been in Libya for nearly thirty years and had settled down into a comfortable routine of life which only an occasional campaign against tribesmen had disrupted. Against the poorly armed locals the Italians and their old-fashioned equipment had been adequate, but against the British they had not prevailed. When Wavell's forces swept over them and forced them out of the fertile strip to fight a mobile war in the desert, the Italian forces were completely unready. They had never had to fight against the desert; they had ignored it and had lived in the fertile area. Wavell coming up out of the blue of the sand sea had confounded them and it was this total inability to cope with two enemies – the desert and the British – that had led an Army ten times the size of its military opponent to be defeated so quickly.

Even with a supply system based on the expectation of a static war the Italians had built up no stocks. There was no pool of vehicles to create a mobile Army and this in a region where mobility equalled life and to be immobile was to be overtaken and destroyed. No properly equipped supply depots had been filled, no fuel reserve built up, no dumps of ammunition created and filled; there was nothing, in fact, which a modern Army serving overseas needed to sustain it. And then, too, the arms themselves were inferior. The field artillery's weapons were mostly pieces from the First World War, the anti-tank guns were incapable of dealing with British armour, and the Italian armoured fighting vehicles were so weak both in thickness of armour and in their main weapon that they were, to all intents and purposes, defenceless targets when set up against the British tank Corps.

Tactically the Italian Army of March 1941 was made up of two Corps. The first of these, X Corps had two infantry divisions Bologna and Pavia, as well as a mixed unit of all arms. In support of X Corps was the remnant of Ariete armoured division with at least 60 tanks. The XXI Corps was made up of Savona and Brescia infantry divisions as well as a mixed group formed from the remaining elements of other divisions which had been badly hit during the fighting in the desert.

THE BRITISH AND THEIR ALLIES

The armies which fought in the North African desert campaigns were initially made up solely of men from the United Kingdom, the Empire, and the Commonwealth. Many of those soldiers who had driven back the Italians during 1940 were professionals who had garrisoned the Middle East in peace-time and who had mapped the desert, plotted routes, explored the sand seas, and produced the splendidly accurate maps on which every important piece of information was marked.

Then in support of these veterans came the territorial and yeomanry units and then a greater number of men who had been conscripted to serve their country. But whatever the reason which had brought them to the desert for many of the years during which they served, their skill and bravery were wasted in offensives – ordered by politicians in London – using equipment that was at best unsuitable and at worst totally useless.

In artillery the British had one particular type of gun, the 25-pounder, which was a first-class weapon but the rest of the military ordnance was made up of pieces dating from the First World War. In anti-tank weapons the

2-pounder gun which formed the bulk of this type of artillery for the first two years of the war had been proved to be useless against German armour as early as 1940, but was still lauded as an effective panzer killer as late as 1942 although mainly by civilians who did not have to use it. Not until the 6-pounder came into service did the British Army have an anti-tank gun that could kill enemy tanks at a respectable distance, but this weapon did not arrive in the Middle East until early 1942 and ammunition which was able to penetrate the steel plates of the un-armoured panzers was not available until after the battle of Alam Halfa in September 1942. True the workshops of the Royal Army Ordnance Corps had tried to overcome the disability of unsuitable ammunition by converting 7.5cm shells into armour piercing shot, in time for the Gazala battles, but little of this ammunition seems to have been used.

The British armoured fighting vehicles were generally ineffective. The Crusader, whose weaknesses had been the subject of a parliamentary enquiry, was found to be not only mechanically unsound but also poorly armoured. Its highest cross-country speed was 12mph, but even this was twice as fast as the Matilda, which had been designed purely as an infantry support tank. The Valentine, like the two vehicles already mentioned, was armed with the ineffective 2-pounder tank gun which fired only solid shot and was, therefore, unable to engage and destroy the German anti-tank gun lines except by a direct hit. Not until the battle of Gazala and the introduction of the American Grant tank did the British Army in North Africa have a tank which combined the advantages of fire power, armoured thickness, and speed. The Grant was able to fire both high explosive and solid shot. Its 7.5cm main armament was a standard artillery piece and the turret-mounted 3.7cm high velocity gun fired armour piercing shells. Even this machine had a defect; the main armament was set low down in the hull and thus the whole machine had to be exposed to enemy fire whenever the main armament was used.

Although for much of the time the 8th Army had superiority in numbers the poor designs, weak armouring and armament of the armoured fighting vehicles reduced the advantage. Then, too, tank units were used incorrectly. There was no real understanding of the use of mass forces and regiments were allowed to carry out isolated and, generally, unsupported 'cavalry' charges against gun lines and not until Alam Halfa, when Montgomery had taken over command of 8th Army, were tank commanders restrained and forbidden to act as if the panzers were a sort of quarry, like a fox in some sort of mechanised hunt.

At the end of February 1942 there were certain changes made in the armoured units and an attempt was made to 'tighten up' the formations. The armoured brigade group became the standard battle formation and replaced the armoured brigade which had formed part of the armoured division. Within the brigade group establishment there were artillery and engineer units taken from the former support group which, with the new regrouping, had been scrapped. The anti-tank gun regiments which had been with 8th Army, were broken up and distributed among the field artillery regiments. Thus, each artillery regiment controlled not only three batteries of 25-pounder howitzer guns but also 16 anti-tank guns. To provide anti-aircraft protection the light anti-aircraft gun batteries were disbanded and the batteries allotted to each brigade group. It was hoped that these new all-round units would provide the cohesion and the dynamism which characterised the German battle groups but they failed, because they were never large enough to be effective against German armour moving in mass, nor was the British command structure sound.

The direct and immediate control of the battle, essential in armoured warfare, was lacking in 8th Army. The structure was too loose, was too far removed from the scene of the battle, and was too slow for decisions arrived at were usually the result of long discussions. At intermediate command level there was great freedom of action and at divisional level the group was quite firm. At brigade and in lower echelons there was a great deal of professionalism, determination to succeed, and tenacity. This was particularly true of the infantry formations which comprised the bulk of the Army. It is wrong to make comparisons between fighting units of the same army and in the case of 8th Army it is almost impossible for it contained such first-class units as 9th Australian Infantry, 2nd New Zealand Infantry, and the first class 4th Indian Divisions.

British military power rose from two divisions in 1940 to a strength of six by May 1942, and then to nearly a dozen by April 1943. When 8th Army entered Tunisia it linked with Anderson's 1st Army which had begun operations with only one infantry brigade and a weak Allied tank force but which ended the campaign with an Allied army made up of men of three different nations. For it must be remembered that in addition to the British and Imperial troops, American divisions, French units, Polish and Greek Brigades had also fought in Africa. When one considers the Allied battle line then one becomes aware of the terrible odds which faced the army of Erwin Rommel and its Italian allies.

3. The Germans come to Africa, February 1941

'The desert tracks are passable. I myself have flown over them'
Rommel before the battle of Mechili, April 1941

It is a military truism that supply services must be established, lines of communication laid out, and depots set up before combat operations can begin, for without these fundamentals a fighting force is restricted either to that which it can carry or to being forced to live off the land. The first German troops which debarked in Tripoli on 11 February 1941, were, therefore, supply specialists and water purifying teams who immediately set about establishing store depots, ration, fuel, and ammunition points, and generally preparing the area for the arrival of the fighting troops.

The German combat units which were despatched to Africa were the only Axis soldiers which could be considered as ready for battle and because the original task of the force had been foreseen as a blocking operation the group consisted principally of a number of machine gun battalions and anti-tank units. Artillery support was afforded by a single motorised artillery battalion and the services detachments were a signals and an engineer company. At a later date 5th Panzer Regiment was to come under command and this addition of light and medium tanks increased the force's potency. A battalion of self-propelled (SP) anti-tank guns which arrived during March at the port of Tripoli was not taken on strength of 5th Light Division but had an independent role.

From 13 February onwards the combat troops began to arrive regularly; at first elements of 3rd Motorised Reconnaissance Battalion and 39th Anti-tank Battalion and then, during the first weeks of March the artillery and armoured fighting vehicles were unloaded. Although Hitler's name for the new unit was Africa Corps, it was not organised as such until a much later date and for a long time there were neither Corps troops nor supply columns and the second German division, 15th Panzer Division, which would have raised the group to Corps level was not expected to arrive in Tripoli until the beginning of May.

The military situation in those anxious February days was that the British had reached El Agheila and their armoured reconnaissance units had appeared to the west of that place. The Axis command had to anticipate the British intention. Would Wavell go on to capture Tripoli and to destroy not only the Italian Army but also a major part of the Italian Colonial Empire, or would time be given to Rommel and his battle-ready troops to establish a defensive line in the desert south of the gulf of Sirte? The Italians anticipated an early resumption of the offensive by Wavell's army, which they estimated to contain two armoured and three motorised divisions. The German commanders were less inclined to this appreciation for they reasoned that any advance by the British from El Agheila to Tripoli would require that Army to cover a distance of over 400 miles, the greatest part of which advance would be through a waterless and empty wasteland.

The British offensive, which had just smashed Graziani, had covered more than 800 miles and the losses of men and material which would have been incurred during that operation would have to be made good before the offen-

Right: General Field
Marshal Erwin Rommel

Below: Field Marshal
Albert Kesselring, Supreme
Commander South, during
one of his many visits to
the North African theatre
of operations

Left: German armoured fighting vehicles drawn up in a street in Tripoli shortly after their arrival in North Africa. The machines in the foreground are Panzer IV—February 1941

Top: The first units of the German Army in Africa parade through Tripoli—February 1941

Above: Reinforcements were sometimes flown into the African theatre of operations in JU 52 aircraft

Top Left: Reinforcements on a desert airfield

Bottom left: A half-tracked prime mover towing an 8.8cm anti-aircraft tank gun

Top right: A Panzer I Ausf. B, mounting a 4.7cm Pak L/43 tank destroyer, driving through Tripoli

Bottom right: The face of the German infantry soldier in the desert

Below: German tanks enter an Italian fort in Libya

Left: Rommel's command vehicle was a captured British truck

Below: Panzer IIs on a desert battlefield. In the foreground a Grenadier searches a captured British position

Right: A young tank commander of the German armoured force

Below: A tank destroyer and infantry move forward

Bottom: A Panzer III passing a burning Honey tank

Left: During one of the pauses in the fighting there is time to write home

Below: The crew of an MG 34 on outpost duty during a reconnaissance patrol

sive could roll again. Then, too, there would be supply problems; for Wavell's lines of communication had been extended and any attempt to use the ports along the coast, in particular Benghasi, would be interrupted by the Luftwaffe whose Xth Air Corps was now operating in Africa against British targets and which had begun to bomb Benghasi as early as 12 February.

Rommel first sent his troops to positions in the empty desert of the Sirte where they gave backbone to the Italians in that area and prepared to delay any British advance. On 16 February, 3rd Reconnaissance Battalion travelled 360 miles along the Via Balbia, took up position east of Sirte, and sent out patrols which made contact and drove off the British reconnaissance detachments near En Nofilia. This successful clash showed that the British had still not reached that area in any strength. The reconnaissance battalion then advanced to reconnoitre at Arco dei Fileni, some 100 miles to the east, where the tactical headquarters of 5th Light Division was established and to which the divisional units were directed to advance, once they had debarked in Tripoli.

The Brescia and Pavia Divisions were set to build defences in the Sirte around which Rommel formed a blocking line, set along the high ground approximately 20 miles west of El Agheila. The right wing of these positions was touching a salt marsh but, to guard the wide open, deep southern flank, patrols were sent to occupy the Marada Oasis, 80 miles south of El Agheila and Ariete Division was also positioned to give greater strength to the southern flank.

At the beginning of March, 5th Panzer Regiment arrived in Tripoli, held a ceremonial parade to show the flag, and moved up to the temporarily stagnant front. The Africa Corps was now strong enough to act offensively and could plan for the recapture of Cyrenaica. Rommel's original intention, to wait for the arrival of 15th Panzer Division before going over to the offensive, was discarded and now he urged Gariboldi, his superior officer, to bring the Italian divisions forward. Reluctantly Gariboldi agreed and released Ariete, the armoured division and the partly-motorised Brescia. Rommel then took this latter formation and put it into the line to relieve his German units.

On 23 March, after discussions with both Hitler and Mussolini, Rommel grouped his Corps and on the following day sent a battle group in to attack 8th Army reconnaissance troops in El Agheila. There was a short, fierce fire fight and the British withdrew closely pursued by the Germans. The next objective was the Marsa el Brega gap between the sea and the difficult country to the south. Even at this early stage in his new command Rommel had shown an independence in the conduct of his operations which often conflicted with the intentions and even the orders of his superiors – particularly those of General Gariboldi, a militarily timid man. He had intended the Marsa el Brega operation to be only a reconnaissance to establish British strength in that area. The attack, he had told Rommel, must not go in without his approval and even OKH had stressed caution for it did not anticipate that the Axis forces would have sufficient strength to reach Agedabia, the principal objective, before May. Africa Corps commander had other ideas and planned to capture Marsa el Brega by a pincer operation. The stronger of two columns, containing the panzer regiment, 3rd Reconnaissance Battalion, 8th Machine Gun Battalion, and elements from the anti-tank gun detachment, was to advance along the Via Balbia supported by artillery. The second column, made up of anti-tank guns mounted as SPs, together with 2nd Machine Gun Battalion was to outflank the British positions from the south and through this threat speed the assault of the main column.

In the event only the main column came into action and when the attack opened on 30 March, it ran up against strong British defences manned by 3rd Armoured Brigade lying behind extensive mine-fields and supported by an aggressive Royal Air Force, which attacked and delayed the German advance. Not until the second day of the offensive, and in daytime temperatures of over 80°F, did the infantry and the panzer regiment, supported by 8.8cm guns firing over open sight and with Stukas dive-bombing ahead of them, break through and by pursuing the British closely allow them no time to form fresh defence lines. The southern column, meanwhile, had failed to reach the battlefield at all due to a combination of navigational errors and bad going.

The results of this minor affair were all positive: the British had been driven from the last good position blocking the south-western passage into Cyrenaica, German troops had proved themselves capable of fighting a desert campaign, and 8th Army was not as strong as Italian intelligence officers had believed it to be. Rommel began to consider whether he might not open an offensive, using the forces at his disposal rather than wait until the panzer division arrived from Germany. He knew that to carry out this scheme would flout the authority of his Italian superior, that he would be acting without Hitler's consent or knowledge, and that he would be ignoring the advance of OKH. He made the decision and ordered 5th Light Division to resume the advance upon Agedabia. On 2 April it drove up the Via Balbia, in a compact group with the reconnaissance battalion in the van followed by the machine gun battalion. The panzers were out guarding the flanks and from horizon to horizon the sky was filled with pillars of dust as the vehicles ploughed their way forward. British artillery fire forced the reconnaissance unit to deploy and to take up battle formation but no sooner had the unit shaken itself out for battle than the rearguard withdrew – a wearying tactic which the British used throughout the morning. Tanks from 8th Army were reported to be in position south-east of Agedabia and Streich commanding 5th Light ordered the panzer regiment, the anti-tank detachment, and the machine gun battalion to move east of the road. The machine gunners began to move into position but were halted south of the town. Rommel, up with the forward troops in his usual fashion, swung the reconnaissance battalion round the left flank; a move which brought it floundering in a salt marsh. The panzer regiment then struck at the British forces, feinting and withdrawing, and enticing the British armour on to the screen of 8.8cm guns which stood waiting. The 5th Royal Tank Regiment, true to cavalry tradition, charged the enemy and were brought under fire by the 8.8s at almost point blank range. Twenty-five of the British vehicles lay broken or burning in front of the gun line and then the 2nd Battalion of 5th Panzer Regiment swung back and drove the RTR, off the field and pursued them northwards. Meanwhile the Tower Hamlets Rifles, a London territorial unit, had come under attack and had lost a company. Only another tank charge brought the hard pressed British infantry relief from the German panzers.

This pressure against the British southern flank reacted upon the stubborn defence which was being put up against the machine gun battalion on the central sector. Thus, by midday the machine gunners had advanced across an area dotted with the palls of black and acrid smoke rising from tanks which 5th Panzer Regiment had 'brewed up' and vast clouds hanging in the sky above depots which 8th Army had destroyed before their withdrawal.

The reconnaissance battalion having dragged itself from the salt marsh pushed on to the town and joined forces with the machine gun battalion. Their combined strength brought the advance across the Tripoli–Cyrenaica frontier and onward to Zuetina. Nightfall brought a halt to the fighting and the divisional units, having laagered, made preparations to maintain the advance during the following day and to pursue closely the enemy who was withdrawing upon Benghasi. Rommel's firm order was to keep contact with the British forces. They must not be allowed to shake off the German advanced units. During the night the Italian divisions and the Santa Maria detachment closed up on the German spearhead.

The battle was proceeding to that date in the manner in which Rommel had planned that it should go. The Agedabia wells had been taken, the way into Cyrenaica was open, and air reconnaissance as well as ground observation indicated that the British were abandoning the province in some disorder and were withdrawing upon Benghasi leaving behind them huge masses of stores. The immediate threat to Tripoli had been averted and the objective which OKH had hoped might be accomplished during May was in German hands by April.

It was on the battlefield at Agedabia that Rommel decided upon his next and very controversial move. He realised that it was useless to drive the British before the German armour; the 8th Army must be smashed in open battle. It will be seen from the map which appears on page 80 that, starting at El Agheila, Cyrenaica projects as a huge bulge, the Bight of Bomba, into the Mediterranean and that the Via Balbia follows this coastline. Rommel reasoned that the British retreat would be by road and, if this were so, then a swift advance along native tracks and via Msus and Mechili to Derna, that is across the chord of the bulge, would bring his forces to the eastern border of Cyrenaica behind the British and thus cut them off from their bases. He expressed this intention to his allies and to his staff; most of them were horrified for he was suggesting that a major military grouping of limited desert experience should cross a 400-mile expanse of waterless desert. The Italians said that such an operation was out of the question. It required months of preparation; the danger that columns might become separated and lost in the almost trackless expanse was too great and, in any case, the sand seas and the mountainous djebel were both impassable. Rommel who had personally reconnoitred the routes from the air declared them to be passable. In any case the British had traversed the desert and what they could do the Axis troops could also accomplish. His own quartermaster's department pointed out that there would be problems with both water and fuel and that tyres would be cut to shreds in the rough, cross-country going. Rommel proposed the most draconian measures to overcome the fuel and water crises. The forward movement of all German and Italian fighting units was halted. Every available truck which could be taken, commandeered, or requisitioned was assembled and soon there was a lorried force of more than 800 vehicles.

Each lorry was to ferry fuel and water to the front line troops and when sufficient had been brought forward the trucks would be prepared for the trans-desert trip. With the fighting column's lorries would be 6 days fuel, 5 days water ration, 5 days food including two days hard tack, and only sufficient ammunition for one day's battle, for it was not considered that there would be any fighting during the approach march to Derna. In the supply columns whatever was the lorry's normal load would be halved and the balance made up of petrol. Rommel's intention was that his whole force would be a self-contained combat group. Within two days the whole scheme had been worked out and the fuel supplies had been brought forward. The great desert trek could begin.

The battle plan was straightforward. There were to be several columns. Those of the left flank — a German reconnaissance battalion and Brescia Division — who were to hold the British and slow down the pace of their withdrawal, were to advance along the Via Balbia and go on to capture Benghasi. This column would then divide and the main body would thrust towards the strategically important cross-roads at Mechili, while the second and weaker column from Brescia Division would continue up the road exerting pressure upon the British before going on to capture Derna.

All the trans-desert columns were to head, by various tracks, towards Mechili. One of the major columns would be divided to form a pincer movement aimed at the objective. One main group would form the outer left wing and 2nd Machine Gun Battalion, forming the inner wing of these two columns, was to advance to Solluch at which point a column of empty oil drums pointed due east marking the desert track to the objective and along which the machine gunners were to advance. The main, southern pincer led by the commander of 5th Light Division, was to move towards Mechili along the Trigh el Abd. This column was headed by 8th Machine Gun Battalion and followed by an anti-tank company, a panzer company, the Italian Santa Maria detachment, a motor cycle company, and a motorised artillery battalion from Ariete Division. Rommel's intention was two-fold: he was trying to create the impression that the Axis forces were stronger than in fact they were and, that the German objective was a tactical one – Benghasi – and not a strategic one, the destruction of 8th Army's field force.

A report written after the operation and dealing with the column of soft-skinned vehicles which followed the machine gun battalion is revealing for the details it gives of the difficulties of desert driving. As the convoys of trucks headed across the desert in pursuit of the tank columns, pillars of dust rose high into the air and obscured the column. Shrouded by the thick blanket of hot dust and with the vision impaired even more by the *khamsin* which was blowing, drivers moved their trucks out of line to avoid the dust of the main in front. Thus the convoy extended in width as the drivers moved almost in line abreast and the dust cloud which hung above it stretched for miles, giving the appearance of a whole armoured division on the move. Daylight navigation was by compass for no reliance could be placed on the Italian maps which had inaccuracies up to 20 miles. The most prized possession was a set of British maps which were not only accurately marked but also showed such vital information as whether the going was good or bad.

Radiators boiled as the trucks struggled up the steep slopes of the djebel, a high stony escarpment, and during the following day the going worsened as the column struggled forwards through seas of loose sand which bogged down the vehicles. That day, 4 April, was a day of despair at the slow going but three broken down tanks, abandoned *en route* were put into running order and taken on strength. The column commander drove through a fierce sand-storm which had halted his group and reached Mechili where he reported the arrival of his convoy. By evening the trucks had rolled in and a petrol point had been set up. There was sufficient food, water, and ammunition; only lack of petrol, the life blood of panzer operations, had caused some worry.

Meanwhile the divisional commander's column was still struggling towards Mechili. It had been delayed by adverse conditions – bad going, sand storms, and seas of shifting sand – and did not reach the objective until the morning of the 5 April.

Mechili was a trigh cross-roads settlement in which 8th Army had set up a dump and a strong point into which had been brought 3rd Indian Lorried Brigade. This unit had orders to halt the German advance upon Msus and presently added to its strength was the headquarters of 2nd Armoured Division, 'M' Battery Royal Horse Artillery, 3rd Australian Anti-tank

Regiment, and a small number of miscellaneous units. These had fled into the box for the protection of the major units. On the German side there was anxiety in the columns pressing towards the place for they were running low on fuel. Rommel had to seize Mechili before he could swing his Corps northwards to Derna and ordered that the objective be seized without delay. He had flown over his columns following their progress through the desert and landing where necessary to give them detailed orders. Other Fieseler Storch aeroplanes from the command went out to locate and to direct the widespread columns on to their target. During the night, guided by Verey pistol flares, by searchlights shone into the air, and by a number of similar devices the Panzer company was brought up to Mechili.

The most northerly column of the trans-desert group was made up of the panzer regiment (minus the company with the southern column), a motorised artillery battalion, the anti-tank companies, and parts of Ariete Division. At Bir el Gerrari the column turned on to the Benghasi–Mechili track but as a result of map error found that it was confronted by an impassable salt lake. Confusion piled upon confusion as the original error was compounded by poor navigation and, as a result of this, the whole column drove round in wide circles for some time and then ran out of fuel leaving the panzer regiment stranded in the desert.

On the Via Balbia the reconnaissance battalion fighting against Australian infantry and artillery rearguards captured Benghasi in the bright moonlit pre-dawn of 4 April. The town and its airfield were handed over to the advanced guard of Brescia Division and the battalion then swung towards Mechili to add strength to the panzer ring which was beginning to surround the 'box' there. Other small units which had been separated from the columns came in and Rommel led in 8th Machine Gun Battalion and then directed it to advance upon Derna and to cut the Via Balbia. Parts of the British force encircled at Mechili were ordered to break out towards Derna and by unlucky fate they encountered the machine gun battalion also heading for that town who flung them back into the Mechili box. But there were other delays to the machine gun battalion advance particularly around the Derna airfield and not until the reconnaissance battalion arrived during 7 April, to reinforce the attack and to bring it forward again, was it possible to cut the road. The town and the aerodrome fell quickly and more than 1000 prisoners were taken including two generals, Neame and O'Connor, and much equipment including several tanks.

The 8th Army reacted and established a series of blocking points. At nightfall on 7 April the 9th Australian Division supported by tanks had taken up position astride and thus blocking the Via Balbia. The Australian left flank was at Acroma, a town 15 miles west of Tobruk, and there was a small British force garrisoning the important box at El Adem to the south of the town.

The fighting around Mechili rose to a climax. Even though the Panzer regiment from the northern column was still stranded for lack of fuel other units of other columns had arrived to strengthen the encircling forces. During the night of 7/8 April the main attack went in. The Santa Maria detachment stormed from the east, the machine gun battalion from the north, and a group of 10 tanks of the southern column drove up to strike at the southern side of the box. Part of the British garrison thrust along the western track mounted on vehicles and armoured cars, but this escape attempt was brought under fire and was turned back by anti-tank guns and the machine guns of an Italian motor cycle company. Isolated small groups of British soldiers, which then struck to the south-east, broke through the ring but the main garrison stood fast and fought it out. The British and the Imperial troops battled on until the panzer company broke into the box and beat down all resistance. Five generals were among the prisoners but of more use to the Germans were the supplies and fuel which they seized, for these enabled their drive to continue. The 2000 prisoners brought problems for the northern column had still not arrived in force and the remaining German troops were thin on the ground. Not until the evening of the 8th had sufficient forces been gathered to renew the advance northwards to reach the coastal road and by the time that the Axis troops arrived at Tmimi the British had already evacuated it. The advanced guard of Brescia Division, whose task it had been to hold the British while the outflanking movement was carried out, had failed in this and did not arrive at the objective until 8 April.

With the seizure of Tmimi the province of Cyrenaica had been recaptured, the British had been thrown back, some of their principal commanders captured, and their armour beaten in battle. But the Australian Division had withdrawn in good order towards Tobruk and thus, although the Axis forces had gained a tactical victory, they had not defeated the British in the field.

There were other gains both in strategy and morale. Strategically the British Army fighting in Greece was now aware that its rear communications were threatened by the German victory in the desert. In the matter of morale Axis prestige rose, not only in the Arab countries but also among the people of Italy and in the Italian Army, for that force began to regain much of the confidence which it had lost as a result of earlier defeats.

All this had been accomplished with only a small loss of men and, although the fall-out of armoured vehicles was quite considerable, due to the long and exhausting march through the desert, the German recovery service was able to return most tanks to their units. Losses in soft-skinned trucks were made good from stocks captured from the British.

The greatest praise must go to Rommel for his incredible ability, energy, and resource. He seemed to be at every part of the front, leading an attack here, guiding a column there, and it was due to his fierce drive that the offensive succeeded. He was now supremely confident. He had grasped the secrets and the tactics of desert warfare. Not only did he have the measure of the terrain but also that of his enemies. Now with adequate supplies he could advance and he made no secret of the fact that he planned the final objective to be the Suez canal.

On 9 April orders were issued to continue the pursuit of the British towards Tobruk with all possible speed, and 5th Light Division, with the reconnaissance battalion in the van, stormed eastwards leaving the Italians to carry out security duties around Mechili.

4. The advance upon Tobruk and the first siege, April–May 1941

'Panzer rollen in Afrika vor'
('Tanks are rolling forward in Africa')
German song of the Second World War

With the first offensive concluded Rommel considered his next move and saw that this must be the capture of the port, fortress, and fleet base of Tobruk into the protection of which a great part of the hard hit but undefeated mass of the British desert force was undoubtedly moving.

There were only two alternatives. Either he could obey the orders of his superiors and go over to the defensive along the eastern borders of Cyrenaica, there to await the arrival of the main of his Army before undertaking further operations, or he could continue his pursuit of the British enemy in the hope of bringing them to battle and of defeating them in the field before undertaking the advance into Egypt. Rommel considered the alternatives and the factors which would affect his decision and then came down on the side of the offensive. He would pursue the British and in a race to Tobruk might either enter the town and seize it from its weak garrison or enter it simultaneously with the British and in the resulting confusion capture the place. But if he was to act offensively then he must act quickly and obtain men for this operation.

The mass of 5th Light Division was widespread across the desert's dusty face and some of its units were still lying stranded for lack of fuel in the desert south-west of Mechili. The Italian divisions had not yet caught up and, of 15th Panzer, only the motor cycle battalion and the anti-tank battalion were on their way to the front while the main of that division was still unloading at Tripoli.

With the decision to pursue the offensive, orders went out and behind a German advanced guard the main of Brescia Division left Derna on 8 April in an advance upon, and with the intention of, capturing Tobruk. Behind this advanced group the rest of 5th Light followed and then, in succession, the Ariete Division and those elements of 15th Panzer which had been able to join the column. By 9 April Gazala had been reached although strong British rearguards had frequently caused the column to halt, to deploy, and to take up attack positions. The advance continued all through the day and by evening had reached the 'White House', some 25 miles west of Tobruk. By now the pattern of life which the desert compelled upon those who lived in it had established itself. The interval between daylight and complete darkness in this climate is a very short one. Combat operations in the desert were usually halted, therefore, some time before the onset of darkness so that the troops could be fed, the vehicles serviced, defence positions allotted, and preparations for the morrow put in hand.

Those hours of darkness between the night of 9 and 10 April, had been used by the British to concentrate their forces on the approaches to Tobruk so that the German advance during the morning of 10th met determined and increasing resistance which brought it to a halt about 14 miles west of the town. Rommel, up with the forward troops and determined not to allow the tempo of the advance to falter, ordered the leading elements of Brescia Division into an infantry assault to clear the road but the attack failed in the heavy defensive fire which crashed down upon the two Italian battalions. During this unsuccessful assault the remainder of Brescia had closed up and Rommel, who had ordered the attack to be resumed on 11th, cancelled this when he realised through a personal reconnaissance how strong the British defences were around the town. Brescia then took up investment positions along the western front of the fortress between the coast and the high ground south of the road.

It was quite clear that until his reconnaissance Rommel had had no idea of how strong Tobruk really was and he seems not to have considered that the British would have improved upon the Italian fortifications and converted the town into a first-class defensive position. The British would find the supply problem less difficult to resolve for the Royal Navy controlled the seas, and the reinforcement and adequate provisioning and equipping of their troops in Tobruk could be carried out without too much interference from the Luftwaffe.

Tobruk had been designed by the Italians to be held by a garrison of divisional size but the population had risen to more than 36,000. It must be stated that more than two-thirds of that number were made up of non-combatant Corps and army troops, Arab refugees and prisoners of war. The actual fighting strength was between 10,000 and 12,000 battle-hardened veteran soldiers who were determined to hold out and to conduct an aggressive defence.

The physical defences of the town were two perimeters each defended by a belt of barbed wire and an anti-tank ditch. The confidence of the past months had allowed gaps in the wire and the ditches to remain open and therefore vulnerable although Australian infantry battalions had undertaken the task of preparing the defence and repairing the evidences of past neglect. The outer defensive belt extended nearly 30 miles across from west to east and nearly 9 miles inland from the sea. A double row of strong points were set within the perimeter, laid out like a chess board and capable of giving mutual supporting fire. Most of these strong points had been prepared for infantry garrisons armed with machine guns and light anti-tank weapons. They were usually concreted with covered communication trenches and were hard to detect for they were not pill boxes standing upon the ground but sangars lying on, or just below, the surface.

The inner defence line was a small version of the outer and within the inner perimeter there were five miniature fortresses. The whole area was extensively mined and to aid the defence there was an airfield.

The battles to capture Tobruk fall into three phases. There were the reconnaissance probes on the 11 and 12 April, followed by the attacks from the southern front on 13th and 14th, and then from the south west on 16th and 17th.

When Rommel became aware of the strength of the place he realised that his troops helter-skeltering towards the town might dash themselves against the fortress and be destroyed piecemeal. He determined to throw an iron ring around the town quickly and intercepted the reconnaissance battalion and the anti-tank battalion as they headed eastwards. He switched them southwards and ordered them to pass round the British positions and to try to find a weak spot on the flanks. East of Acroma, artillery fire and extensive barbed wire defences brought the advance by the German troops to a halt. Rommel then gave orders to General Streich to swing further south and to advance upon El Adem. At that point there was a road up which his forces could drive and thereby enter Tobruk from the south. Streich pivoted his troops behind Brescia and moved to carry out his orders but sand storms and the usual inaccurate maps, together with poor navigation, so delayed his advance that he did not reach his objective until 11th. Local successes were scored against British patrols throughout the day but the main intent – to advance up the southern road – failed and the newly arrived panzer regiment, which then tried to force a passage on 12th, was brought to a halt by gun fire and an anti-tank ditch.

The first of the phases of the battle of Tobruk had opened. Rommel next changed the direction of his attack and flung a machine gun battalion to the east of Tobruk but that assault, too, failed in the face of heavy and accurate artillery fire which the defenders summoned up to defeat the Axis assault.

German troops had now thrown a cordon around the town and, although they were still too weak to carry out a major assault, it was felt that they had sufficient strength to defeat any break-out attempt by the garrison. The danger lay more in an offensive to raise the siege which British forces outside Tobruk might make.

The 8th Army had a screen of weak but mobile columns operating around, or holding certain strategic areas to the east of Tobruk, notably at Halfaya Pass, Sollum, Bardia, and Sidi Barani. This open eastern flank now became Rommel's immediate worry for it was from the east, along the Via Balbia and the desert tracks that the Matildas and the other British armoured fighting vehicles would storm in a massive counter-offensive. It was important that, even if the Axis forces did not have the strength to defeat an all-out blow, the British advance should be obstructed for as long as possible and their movements impeded. To achieve this it was essential to seize and to hold the ground running south from Bardia to the Halfaya Pass. If this area could be secured then the British forces attempting to move westwards could not use the Via Balbia but would be condemned to a wide and fuel-consuming drive via Sidi Omar. Such a deflection would not only break up their concentrations and betray the direction and strength of their thrust, but also allow time to prepare against it.

In order to know the significance of this eastern sector its topography must be understood. From the town of Sollum an escarpment, generally impassable to vehicles and difficult even for infantry, runs inland on a south-east line for about 50 miles. Only at Sollum and at Halfaya, 8 miles to the south-east of that place, were there passes permitting the escarpment to be crossed without difficulty and it was for the possession of those passes that the battles of the eastern flank were to be fought.

So that the reader is not confused with the fighting which then went on at the western flank around Tobruk and that which was conducted on the eastern front around Halfaya, this latter will be recounted separately, for the battles were, in a sense, only the seizure and consolidation of an outpost and, in that sense, a subsidiary to the main effort which was being made around Tobruk.

Rommel then removed from his beleaguring army a small detachment and sent this in a thrust to the Egyptian frontier with orders to take the vital positions in the Sollum–Halfaya area. The battle group was to act as a blocking force and as an outpost from which would come early warning of any relief operation against Tobruk. On 13 April, the specially reinforced 15th Motor Cycle Battalion and 3rd Reconnaissance Battalion reached the frontier and went on to capture Bardia, Fort Capuzzo, and Sollum from the weak British garrison which then withdrew into Egypt. But 8th Army still held Halfaya Pass and the Germans, too few in numbers to force the issue, made no serious effort to take the pass but contented themselves with consolidating the gains which they had made. On the following day, the 15th Panzer Division was entrusted with control of operations along the frontier and took command of all Axis troops in the area, for now one of Trento Division's motorised battalions, Montemurro, had been brought forward and placed in reserve.

Weak British counter-attacks to capture the lost ground were launched on 15 April and during the following days they became more frequent, larger in number, and more difficult to beat back. The Axis forces were hard pressed and were being forced back under pressure from British armour and infantry, from the Royal Air Force which attacked their positions with low level machine gun attacks and high level bombing, and from the Royal Navy which took part in the operation by sending a monitor to bombard the positions in Sollum. But then on 17th came reinforcements with the arrival of a mixed flak battalion whose two light and three heavy batteries were soon in action against British tanks. Stukas of the Luftwaffe, sent into aid the embattled ground forces, dive-bombed and sank the monitor. Rommel was determined that the eastern enclave would hold.

Fighting flared or sank until 26 April, with the German and Italian troops maintaining their positions but on short commons because their ration truck convoys were intercepted and destroyed by British armoured car patrols. On 24 April the 15th Panzer Division decided that its forces were strong enough to strike for Halfaya and, aware that the British tankmen frequently mistook the Volkswagen cars for Panzer I, bluffed their opponents as to the actual number of armoured fighting vehicles which were under command.

Rommel had been informed of the forthcoming attack and, anticipating victory, had already issued orders that elements from 15th Panzer would be withdrawn to the Tobruk front once Halfaya Pass was safely in German hands. The vehicles for the assault formed up ready to move forward but then came disaster as the Luftwaffe bombed its own troops and caused a postponement of the attack until 26th. To replace the losses and to strengthen the assault the positions held by German units north of Capuzzo and in Sollum were taken over by the Italians and Rommel's men were disposed on either side of the fort. At top speed the advance roared forward into the pass but was halted abruptly by extensive and sophisticated mine-fields. Against fanatical resistance the German point units clawed their way, until by nightfall they had captured the British trench line. Immediate and heavy thrusts by 8th Army's armour flung back the main body of 15th Panzer Division to Capuzzo leaving only infantry outposts to hold the Pass. During the night of 26/27th reinforcements from 3rd Reconnaissance Battalion, the Montemurro Battalion, and a German motor cycle company were sent up to thicken the line and the local commander now considered that he had sufficient strength to force the pass. The elements of 15th Panzer were returned to Tobruk to help in the assaults on that town, while a battle group struck again into Halfaya pass and overran the British defenders who withdrew south and east to the line Buk Buk–Sofafi. The pass had been captured and with the positions consolidated the motor cycle and the reconnaissance battalions returned to the Sollum sector and passed into reserve. The eastern flank was firm and a German enclave, although isolated from the main body of the panzer group and surrounded by British forces, was firmly in position along the Egyptian border. To the west of the outpost was the mass of the Axis forces investing a British enclave at Tobruk.

On 14 April Rommel had decided that he would assault Tobruk frontally with the forces at his disposal, hoping to catch the defenders not fully prepared. Against a garrison of unknown strength he could pit only 100 tanks, a machine gun battalion, an artillery battalion, an engineer company, and elements from Ariete Division, together with parts of an anti-tank battalion.

The plan was for the panzer regiment, with the men of the machine gun battalion riding into battle on the outside of the vehicles, to penetrate the outer line of defences during the hours of darkness and then to press on into the heart of the fortress, towards the objective, Point 187, a place some 4 miles west of the El Adem–Tobruk road where the ground suited a tank attack. The positions from which the attack would begin were held by the Ariete who had been on that sector since 12 April. Before the armour advanced the Engineer

Company was to blow a gap in the wire, the panzers would pass through this and Ariete would seize the strong points on either side of the gap. The attack would go in under artillery fire and bombing attacks by Stuka aircraft. The whole operation was to begin at 04.00hrs on 14th – a delay of 10 hours from the original zero hour – to allow the panzer regiment's men time to rest after the long approach march from Mechili.

There was no time for discussion of the plan nor for adequate reconnaissance and thus the units were attacking in the dark and into an area with which they were unfamiliar. Improvisation was the order of the day and an engineer officer was given the task of hand-guiding the panzers through the gap in the wire. The noise and evidence of the preparations warned the Australians of 2/17th Battalion of the impending assault and, even as the attack opened, artillery covered the approach routes with a fierce and prolonged bombardment. The engineer officer lost his way and misdirected the tanks so that they were nearly 'bellied' in the anti-tank ditch before he found the gap and the penetration could begin.

But by this time dawn had broken, the German defensive fire plan had come to a halt, and a concentrated barrage of infantry and artillery fire was being directed upon the advancing panzers and their infantry. The armour advanced slowly thrusting through the crash of shell fire and the hail of machine gun bullets, vision reduced by the dust which the explosions and their own movement had raised, and gradually they penetrated the outer defence line. The advance suddenly halted. Immediately in front of the tanks lay the inner defence line based upon the Solaro and the Palastrino forts. The British fire rose to hurricane force driving the panzers back through the gap in the wire. The infantry who had already jumped from the tanks to engage the British infantry had suffered severe losses and small groups began to move back to the start line only to find that the way was blocked by Australian troops who had driven back the Italian Ariete. The Italians had been unable to take the strong points and British infantry had recaptured and now dominated the ground between the gap and the retreating Germans. Bitter, and in some cases hand to hand, fighting took place as the German machine gunners tried to force their way back. A few isolated groups battled their way through to the start line where they came under more intense fire from British horse artillery batteries as well as from the uncaptured strong points on either side of the breach. The panzer column, too, suffered as it drew back through the gap in the wire.

By 10.00hrs the attack had obviously failed but Rommel ordered the panzers to go back in again to rescue those machine gunners who were still holding out inside the perimeter wire. Bending to the pleas of the divisional commander he cancelled his order and admitted, thereby, that he had suffered his first setback in Africa, although he could assure himself that now he had a good idea of the strength of the fortress. This knowledge had been bought at a high price in men and armour for 5th Panzer Regiment's loss of 16 vehicles represented 20 per cent of its effective strength in medium machines and with the virtual destruction of three-quarters of the machine gun battalion the infantry strength of 5th Light Division had been reduced by nearly 50 per cent.

In view of this set-back the question was raised again whether it would not be better to withdraw the Axis forces back to Cyrenaica and certainly Gariboldi, the Commando Supremo, and the senior German sources tried to influence his decision but Rommel determined to hold his position and to renew the attack once his strength had been made up. Indeed he pressed for more Italian divisions to be brought up and to invest Tobruk so that he could withdraw his German units and use them offensively. Gariboldi sent forward the motorised division Trento which had landed in Tripoli only a short time before and promised other units, but retained Pavia and Bologna Divisions for use along the Cyrenaican frontier. All these Italian units were sent as separate detachments, that is to say they did not combine to form Italian Corps as one would have expected, but remained as individual units under Rommel's direct control.

By the middle of April Tobruk was completely surrounded. Brescia held the western front, Ariete the south-western line, the 5th Light was on the southern sector, and the Santa Maria was on the south-eastern sector. Manning the eastern line was the bulk of Trento Division with one battalion at Sollum. But the line around Tobruk was so thin that in many places it was nothing more than a series of posts from which to observe the garrison. Then, too, the Axis front line was so far distant from the British defensive positions that an attack could be brought under fire before it had shaken out into correct formation.

British attacks which came in after the middle of April against the Italian-held western and south-eastern sectors met with such a great measure of success that they produced crises. During one attack a whole battalion of 800 men was taken prisoner and on Trento sector the Italians gave up ground which enabled the British to enjoy first-class observation and to direct accurate and heavy artillery fire upon the Axis lines of communication. These British successes, although local in area and small in scale, demonstrated to the 8th Army the weakness of the Axis beleaguring forces and encouraged the garrison commander to increase the size of his assaults upon the weaker Italian units in the full and certain knowledge that these would almost certainly meet with success. Rommel's problems were lightened, however, on 23 April when a rifle battalion and an artillery battalion, both from 15th Panzer Division, reached Tobruk area and Rommel put them straight into the line to plug another hole which had been punched in the front of Brescia Division.

Back on the mainland of Europe there had been two differing reactions to the successes which Africa Corps had achieved. At public level there was admiration and even, perhaps, a little hope that, in place of the colonies which Germany had lost after the First World War, Rommel might carve out a new and bigger colonial Empire. At the sober and coldly intellectual level of the military high commands there was a completely different reaction. It must be understood that the German High Command, already burdened with details for the forthcoming attack upon Russia, had suddenly had off-loaded upon them a Balkan campaign to rescue Mussolini and the Italian Army. Now, on the African front, there was a general who, with limited resources, had achieved a certain measure of success but who might go on to demand more troops, tanks, and guns. Rommel had caught the public imagination and he had been Hitler's personal choice for the African command. If he were to go on to fresh victories then the drain upon Germany's manpower resources might lead to strength needed for the main Russian front being siphoned off to a side-show operation; a military cul-de-sac. In any case, Rommel had gone against the instructions of the OKH. He must be brought to heel.

Accordingly on 27 April, von Paulus, the representative from OKH arrived on a tour of inspection to assess the chances of Rommel conducting a successful defence of the Italian colonies, to discover his future intentions, and to advise him of how few were the manpower and material reserves in Germany. Impassively the trained staff man listened to the commander in the field and refused to countenance the future and strategic plans that Rommel had drawn up.

With the arrival of 15th Panzer Division units the critical manpower situation in front of Tobruk had eased slightly and Rommel had decided to reduce the fortress by mounting another attack. This would come in from the south-west, would pass through the Brescia Division, and thus from a direction completely unexpected by the British. The ground was suitable for panzer movements and a successful initial assault would gain observation points from which artillery fire could be directed during the subsequent phases of the battle. There were already large gaps in both the wire and the anti-tank ditches. May Day was the date set for the attack and by that time Rommel hoped to have gathered the strength necessary to fight a successful battle. To build up his forces without delay he requested OKH to airlift the remaining infantry component of 15th Panzer Division.

The orders for the new offensive were that on the Sollum front there were to be demonstrations and movement to give the impression that the attack would come from the east. On the Tobruk front a mixed infantry, tank, and anti-tank group of 5th Light Division would assault and seize the south and south-western faces of Ras el Mdauar during the night of 30 April and at dawn a panzer attack would continue eastwards towards Fort Pilastrino. The left flank neighbours, mainly an infantry group of 15th Panzer, would take out the strong points on the north of Ras el Mdauar and cut the ridge running eastwards from Acroma. At daybreak this group would advance on both sides of the Acroma track towards Pilastrino and attack towards Tobruk harbour.

One battalion of 115th Infantry Regiment was to send out storm troops to take the strong point along the combat sector and then launch a night attack which would carry them into the fortress. The actual assault group, a regiment made up of all the other divisional troops, would enter the captured areas during the night and at dawn would go through the positions won by the battalion to conduct the final assault. To soften up the defences before the attack began, artillery and Stuka bombardments would be carried out at last light and two Italian divisions, one on either side of the main infantry and panzer groups, would roll up the British line and take out strong points.

When these orders had finally been issued, von Esebeck commanding 15th Panzer lodged an immediate protest against the time of the assault and against the plan of attack. His troops which had been brought by plane from the mainland would arrive tired and without their equipment and would have to take part in an attack unrested and hungry not knowing the terrain for Rommel, in overruling the protests, forbad any pre-battle reconnaissance.

The offensive opened on 30 April as planned with a heavy artillery barrage falling upon the breach area and at other points to confuse the Australian defenders of 26th Brigade as to the direction and point of assault. The first troops moved out followed by the machine gun battalion and 115th Regiment's Battalion and soon the first optimistic reports came in that many of the field defences had been captured according to plan. These reports proved to be untrue for the attacking troops, expecting European-style pill boxes standing above the ground, had not been told that the fortifications in Tobruk were sangar-type strong points at ground level and, therefore, had not captured them. The situation at midnight was so unclear that 15th Panzer Division's commander asked whether the assault regiment should take up position within the perimeter and, having received the confirming order, sent in the men at 02.00hrs. Immediately the regiment came under British fire. By first light the situation in the gapped area was still unresolved and remained so until 08.00hrs when early morning fog lifted and the commanders could see for themselves how intricately jumbled were their units and that those which had reached the target areas had suffered severely.

A number of British strong points had still not been taken and these were firing into the backs of the 15th Panzer infantry. The armoured fighting vehicles headed through and across the positions held by the machine gun battalion and the German infantry rose out of their shallow holes to follow the assault. Suddenly the tanks swung to the east and not to the south-east as had been ordered, for they had been instructed to help forward the attack of the Ariete Division which, like that of Brescia, had failed to make any headway against the determined British defence. The whole assault was grinding slowly to a halt; the troops had had most of their officers killed, the units were mixed, and the objectives unclear. The commander of 15th Panzer, who came up about 09.00hrs ordered the attack to be halted and for the troops in and around the breach to go over to the defence. He refused to countenance a withdrawal back to the original start line for it was hoped to revive the attack when fresh troops were brought up.

Throughout the long May day the British artillery shells crashed down upon the German troops in slit trenches, scraped hastily in the rocky ground, around the gap in the wire. The bombardment was aimed not only at destroying them in their positions but of preventing reinforcements from reaching them or allowing them to withdraw from the breach. But even under the barrage, units were sorted out, regrouped, fed, and issued with fresh ammunition. The ground was prepared for defence and all things made ready. At last light British attacks supported by heavier barrages came in and were beaten back. For days 8th Army's guns thundered a cannonade to which the German artillery could make no adequate reply because ammunition, already in short supply, had been almost totally consumed on the first day. Infantry reinforcements from 15th Panzer took over from the front line survivors.

The breach in the defences which the Germans still held was more than two miles deep and, although it held the British attention and tied down part of the garrison, the same restrictions applied to the German troops for they, too, were held fast in that sector, unable to move. As a result of this offensive the strength and weaknesses of the Tobruk fortress were assessed and the German troops became accustomed to the type of fighting in which they were engaged in the African theatre of operations and to the difficulties of life in the desert. The battle enabled the German commanders to produce new tactics and to improve upon old ones and their Italian comrades-in-arms increased in confidence as more and newer weapons were made available to them.

All the troops had been subjected to strain but those who had come by air to fight at Tobruk had suffered the most. Immediately upon landing they had been taken by lorry towards the town, had been debussed, and marched up the line carrying all their kit, weapons, ammunition, food, and water. Tired and hungry they had then put in a night attack across ground completely unknown to them. Due to the battle conditions and to certain administrative blunders during their first few days in the line they had neither been fed nor given water. That these men, with their leaders dead, themselves hungry, thirsty, and totally exhausted, still had the determination to go forward again and again into local attacks to storm the British positions demonstrated their military ability and a high degree of soldierly courage.

Von Paulus made his report to OKH, and in it set out the supply priorities suggesting that the lines of communication were the most important feature of the campaign. The principal task, as he wrote, was for the Axis to hold Cyrenaica. There was to be no more talk of an advance to Suez.

5. The tank battle of Sollum, June 1941

'Advance upon Halfaya and destroy the enemy there'
Battle orders 17 June 1941

From the 1 May, while the main of Africa Corps was making great efforts to break into Tobruk, the weakness of the eastern flank was again causing concern, for a British attack in that sector was inevitable and imminent. To defend this weak sector Rommel proposed to withdraw 15th Panzer Division from its positions around Tobruk and to replace his offensive armour with static Italian units. But then in the middle of May came news that a British assault was being made against Sollum and Capuzzo. Giving ground under pressure from superior forces the garrison commander withdrew his perimeter to a line running from Sidi Aziz to the road south of Bardia and, during this contraction, some of his Italian units were lost to swiftly moving British units.

The commander-in-chief then ordered the construction of a defence line along the high ground at Gazala, to the west of Tobruk, in the event that he would have to withdraw as a result of a British offensive and with work on this in full progress, then regrouped his forces. To support the eastern flank he formed a battle group from 8th Panzer Regiment and a battery of 8.8cm guns and ordered it to thrust with best possible speed towards the Sidi Azeiz–Capuzzo line but in that sector aggressive defence had already thrown back the British tank thrusts forcing Wavell to put in more men and machines to force a conclusion. Capuzzo fell to the British and was recaptured, Sollum was won back, and Halfaya seized. With no successes to record Wavell withdrew his forces and called off the offensive. The eastern flank outpost to the investing forces around Tobruk was secure.

The relative peace along the eastern enclave was short lived and during the night of 15 June German reconnaissance patrols reported that 8th Army's advanced guards had crossed the frontier wire and were driving across the desert towards the Via Balbia. In Rommel's eyes this was the big attack and it had been expected for Luftwaffe reconnaissance had told of the forming up of strong armoured and lorried columns behind the British front. Intelligence appreciations indicated that 8th Army's advance was being made in three columns. The right wing would move against the garrisons in the Halfaya Pass from the east, the central column would move against Capuzzo and go on to attack Sollum, while the third column, undertaking a march across the desert, obviously had the intention of cutting off, surrounding, and then destroying the Axis forces south of Bardia.

Rommel moved 5th Light Division to a point south of Tobruk there to act as a mobile reserve and sent orders to 15th Panzer Division, in position around Gambut, to prepare to move eastwards. His simple battle order read 'Halfaya will be held and the enemy beaten'. To support the assault Ariete was ordered forward but reported that its Santa Maria detachment, having neither fuel nor rations, could not undertake the mission. Until the direction of the main British thrust became clear 15th Panzer was held in position to await developments. The whole eastern flank was embattled: Capuzzo fell to a massed tank attack; at Sidi Omar the outnumbered garrison was fighting for its survival; but at Halfaya all the British assaults had been repulsed and the German battalion then won back the ruins of Fort Capuzzo. Another wave of heavy British tanks swept up to the fort and rolled over the defenders. Capuzzo was lost again.

Rommel unleashed his panzer division and it roared across the desert towards Capuzzo. In the afternoon of 15 June the armoured forces of both sides clashed and the 8.8cm gun proved itself as a first-class tank killer. A single battery of three guns in line held position with some 8th Panzer Regiment vehicles and took under fire a wave of Matilda tanks as they rumbled forward. Eighteen of them were destroyed. By sunset the outcome of the battle was still unclear and conflicting reports were reaching the headquarters of 8th Army and of Africa Corps. But one thing was clear; the speed of the panzer reaction had held Wavell back from reaching his objective and he had lost, according to German reports, more than 60 tanks.

At first light on 16 June the panzer division renewed its attack against Capuzzo. On the British side the armoured might of 7th Armoured Division had been concentrated into a giant steel fist and was striking westwards. The two forces met in a head-on collision and the impetus of the British assault forced 15th Panzer Division to give ground. It lost heavily in the battle and was soon reduced to a strength of only 35 vehicles. The 5th Light Division was ordered forward and came into action against the British flank by striking out of Sidi Omar. This was a day of crisis for both sides and there hung over the battlefield the unresolved question – would Halfaya Pass be captured? If Wavell's forces could seize the pass then they could reinforce the battle with fresh supplies of men and armour. Against this flood of material the whole eastern enclave would be able to offer no long resistance and the Axis armies, weakened in the battles around Halfaya and Capuzzo, would be crushed against the rock of Tobruk.

The fate of the German and Italian enterprise in Africa depended, for a short time, upon the ability of a heavily outnumbered German garrison to hold its ground. The first attack came in and the British and Indian troops were driven back. A drum-fire of shells was poured upon the defenders and then, during the afternoon, covered by another barrage the second assault came in, was repulsed, came in again and again, and was flung back again and again. Not only did the German battalion hold its positions but counter-attacked whenever possible.

In the south, at Sidi Suleiman, 5th Light and 15th Panzer Divisions were ordered to smash forward in a combined attack against the flanks and rear of Wavell's Army but 5th Light struck heavy opposition and only weak elements were able to struggle forward to reach the Sidi Omar area. The main of the division was caught by the British artillery and dispersed. The 15th Panzer stood waiting for the arrival of its sister division.

At midnight on 16 June a simple battle order was given to both divisions –

'Advance upon the Halfaya Pass and destroy the enemy there', and after first light the panzer boxes moved out to battle with an enemy against whom the tide of fortune had turned. The delay in capturing Halfaya Pass was having a serious effect upon the British conduct of operations and on the Egyptian side of the pass still lay the convoys ready to rush forward the reinforcements which Wavell and his depleted armour needed to maintain the tempo of the attack. The 7th Armoured Division had suffered crippling losses and its tanks were running short of ammunition. Wavell was faced with a crisis but this intelligence was not known to the German commanders and Rommel, concerned at his own weakness in the Halfaya area, demanded that divisions in position around Tobruk be sent to support the Bardia garrison and to strengthen the Sollum front. The Libyan High Command released Pavia Division and sent it forward.

Then a wireless intercept picked up messages from 7th Armoured and from these Africa Corps knew that a striking victory lay within its grasp. Revivified, the combined panzer power of 5th Light and 15th Divisions struck at Wavell's force intent upon the killing blow. So impatient were the soldiers of the Africa Corps to join battle that ahead of the panzers drove the gun line of 8.8cm weapons to take the British under fire at close range and by a storm of gun fire to force Wavell's tanks back eastwards in headlong flight. The first thrust cost 7th Armoured Division a further 14 of its armoured fighting vehicles, but the British were not beaten and put up such resistance to the assaults of 5th Light Division at Sidi Suleiman that their defence could only be beaten down with Stuka dive-bombing.

Other wireless messages were intercepted at 11.00hrs reporting that the 7th Armoured Division's tanks had fired off all their ammunition. They would be forced to withdraw. During the afternoon of the 17th the German columns met and joined forces in an approach march upon Halfaya where they linked with the garrison which, having been supplied by air-drop, was still busily engaged in beating off the attacks of 4th Indian Division. The 15th Panzer Division then moved forward with the still aggressive Halfaya garrison in a final counter-attack which brought the main fighting to a close. Only a sweep and search operation needed to be undertaken in the Sollum, Capuzzo, Sidi Omar, and Bardia sectors to round up the scattered survivors of the British divisions.

The great three-day Sollum tank battle was at an end and like all the battles in the desert it had been a mêlée having no properly defined front lines or rear areas, but had been a confusion of noise and destruction. It had, however, been the mightiest armoured engagement to date in the African theatre of operations. More than 200 British tanks were left behind on the battlefield and 7th Armoured Division went back across the wire with only 24 runners. The 15th Panzer Division lost 15 of its tanks and 5th Light had 10 of its vehicles destroyed. But strength returns for Africa Corps on 20 June reported the figure of 136 vehicles. The recovery and repair sections had once again shown their ability.

The losses in men from the start of the campaign to 5 June were reported by Africa Corps to be 513 killed in action, 1689 wounded, and 1015 missing. During the period from 15 to 20 June the numbers lost, including the figures for the Tobruk front, were 95 dead, 355 wounded, and 235 missing.

The results of the Sollum battle confirmed the suspicion which most Germans had had in their minds from the very first days, namely that they were no longer just supporting the Italians – the Africa Corps was the only Axis fighting force in Libya. The defects in the Italian Army did not allow it to stand against the British and if 8th Army made simultaneous attacks on the eastern front, then to withdraw more contingents of German troops from around Tobruk would invite the aggressive garrison there to smash the Italian troops investing the town. It was, therefore, essential that the number of German divisions in Africa be raised if North Africa was not to be lost by default. The German High Command had already appreciated the point and was preparing to send reinforcements. The only difficulty lay in the supply position which had begun badly and which had never improved. The fuel supply was so inadequate that on occasions staff officers had been unable to undertake journeys to the front. Vital supplies, including the heavy artillery which the Africa Corps needed, were held in Tripoli for lack of petrol and trucks to bring it forward. There were whole units without their lorries and others for whom only the most basic equipment and transport was available. The Italian Navy, to whom German ships were subordinate, was not prepared to sail into those North African harbours close behind the Axis front even though the use of such ports would have reduced the long road haul and the consequent waste of valuable fuel. The most important harbour, so far as the Italians were concerned, was Tripoli nearly 800 miles away from the front line.

The Axis armies and their leaders underwent yet another reorganisation as a result of which Gariboldi was replaced as Italian commander-in-chief by Bastico. A Panzer Group Rommel was formed out of the amalgamation of the old 5th Light, 15th Panzer, and an Africa Division, a conglomeration of units serving in North Africa. An Italian Corps also came under command of Panzer Group Rommel.

The attack upon Tobruk which the German commander-in-chief had been pressing to undertake and which had been proposed for August was then postponed until November but Rommel, who had been warned by his Italian superiors to be cautious, was determined to keep the operational initiative in his hands for, if he did not, then the British would grow in strength and their offensive operations would become more numerous and heavy. But in September patrol activity gave no indication of a British build-up for an offensive and secure in this knowledge Rommel increased the tempo of his preparations to reduce Tobruk. As a result of the knowledge which he had gained from personal reconnaissance and with the experiences of earlier battles upon which to draw he changed the plan of attack. The new thrust line would be from the south-east and to distract the attention of the garrison while the main attack went in, 'Chinese' assaults (decoy attacks) would be launched. Two German and two Italian divisions were to carry out the actual attack and this was to be supported by 200 guns. The supply situation deteriorated again and this was one of the excuses advanced by Commando Supremo which caused the date of the opening of the Tobruk offensive to be postponed. The non-arrival of an Italian motorised division was the principal reason given for the postponement but Rommel decided to make his attack with or without the promised Italian support. He knew that his own units were under-strength and that the Luftwaffe, forced by Hitler's direct order to protect the merchant marine convoys, could not spare aeroplanes to carry out air bombardments of the town but nevertheless he was determined to go ahead.

As examples of the shortages which he was facing one division of the Africa Corps was 4000 men short of its war establishment and for the whole Corps no less than 11,000 men were needed to bring the units up to strength. Losses to convoys were enormous and losses of 50 per cent were not uncommon. It is not surprising, therefore, that the artillery establishment of Africa Corps was 66 per cent of its total and that reinforcements were not reaching the combat units. In one two-month period only 7640 men were disembarked, of whom 2640 came by air.

Determined to reduce Tobruk, Rommel then put his troops through a period of intensive training and by mid-November the preparations had been completed. The heaviest concentration of Axis artillery seen in the desert to that time, no less than 461 guns of all calibres, were in position around the town. With the troops trained and the battle plan drawn up, the artillery fired-in, and the tanks fuelled the Africa Corps and its Italian allies waited in the cold winds and rainy days of November 1941 for the attack to open.

Meanwhile, to the east Rommel's greatest fear had been realised; 8th Army had prepared itself for battle and had struck the first blow. Auchinleck, successor to Wavell as Commander-in-Chief had opened Operation Crusader.

6. Rommel deflects Operation Crusader, November 1941

'A tank man needs the courage to fight
in the unknown.'
Guderian

It was the plan of General Cunningham, commander of 8th Army, to recapture Cyrenaica and thereby to raise the siege of Tobruk. This operation, codenamed Crusader was to be carried out by 30 and 13 Corps. The task of the former, the westernmost placed, was to advance from south of the Trigh el Abd in a north-westerly direction towards Tobruk, while 13 Corps, on the east, was to skirt the Halfaya Pass, Sollum, and Bardia, to cut off the Axis forces and then to engage them in battle. A third British force, 29th Indian Brigade, was to swing wide on the deep southern flank, advancing across the desert towards Gialo to drive behind Panzer Group Africa and to threaten its rear and its lines of communication.

The British line from east to west had 4th Indian Division south of Halfaya and investing that place. In reserve on that sector lay 1st Army Tank Brigade, south of Sidi Omar. South-west of the Army Tank Brigade was 1st New Zealand Division, whose principal task it was to ascend to the line of the Via Balbia and then to move along that highway towards Tobruk. These units constituted 13 Corps.

The most important division of 30 Corps was 7th Armoured which was held in position around Gabr Saleh. Farther to the south of the armour was 1st South African Division and even deeper in the desert was the Indian Brigade. The British reserve forces were 2nd South African Brigade, 22nd

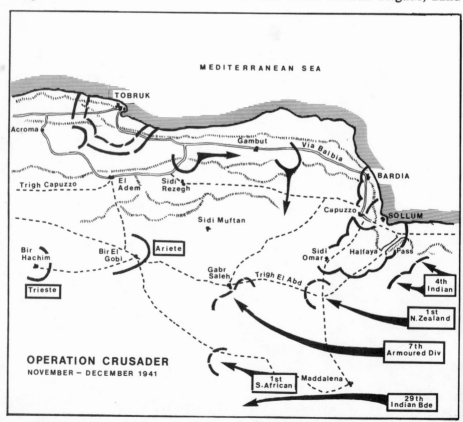

OPERATION CRUSADER
NOVEMBER – DECEMBER 1941

Guards Brigade, and 4th Indian Brigade. Inside beleagured Tobruk there was a garrison made up of a whole division plus two brigades.

The 8th Army's approach march began on 12 November and continued until D-Day for the operation, 18 November. Cunningham's force drove westward in stormy and rainy weather which produced the uncalculated advantage that low cloud prevented Luftwaffe reconnaissance and the British build-up went undetected so that the attack when it came, although expected and although defensive preparations had been made to meet it, was as a tactical surprise.

Rommel had also had an offensive plan in mind. Aware that one day 8th Army, massively reinforced and equipped, would come storming out of the desert in a drive for victory the German commander's only hope for his command was to strike a pre-emptive blow. Every hour was precious and only by concentrating and then striking to the east would there be a chance to defeat the British. But first the ulcer of Tobruk would have to be taken out and then, with Cunningham's force defeated, the advance upon the Suez canal could begin. Bastico, the local commander, approved the plan but made the proviso that the offensive was not to begin until forces, sufficient in strength to guarantee success, had been built up. During the second week in November the strength of Panzer Army Africa and that of its ally had reached that peak

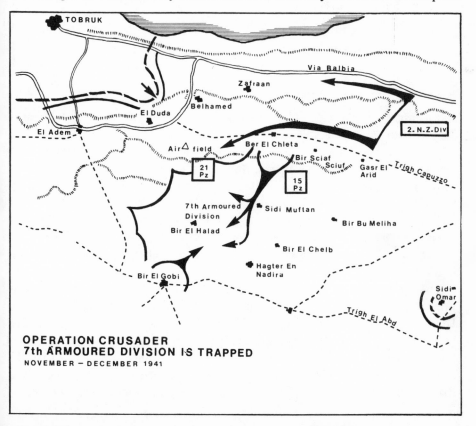

OPERATION CRUSADER
7th ARMOURED DIVISION IS TRAPPED
NOVEMBER – DECEMBER 1941

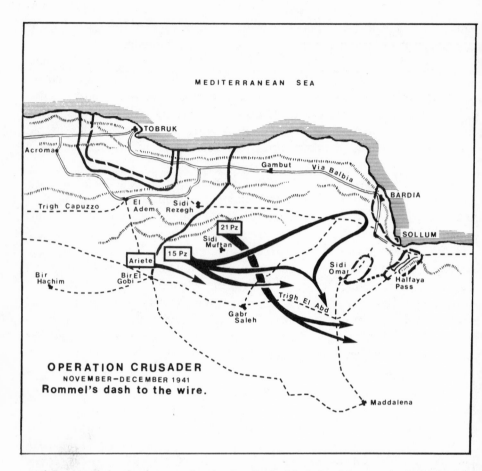

MEDITERRANEAN SEA

TOBRUK

Acroma

Gambut · Via Balbia

BARDIA

Trigh Capuzzo · El Adem · Sidi Rezegh

21 Pz

SOLLUM

Sidi Muftan

Ariete · 15 Pz

Bir Hachim · Bir El Gobi

Sidi Omar

Halfaya Pass

Trigh El Abd

Gabr Saleh

OPERATION CRUSADER
NOVEMBER–DECEMBER 1941
Rommel's dash to the wire.

Maddalena

and Rommel, beginning to plan in detail, decided that his attack should begin on or about 21 November.

The Axis forces held a battle line which had, in the east, an enclave that reached from the town of Bardia down to the Halfaya Pass and included within the perimeter the town of Sollum. The whole area was garrisoned by Savona Division and two German units. The Axis forces investing Tobruk, on the western flank, were mainly Italian: Brescia, Pavia, Trento, and Bologna Divisions; with the German Special Services Division, which was to be retitled during the fighting and which has passed into military history as the 90th Light Division.

The 15th Panzer Division was moved from its holding position near Tobruk to a forming-up area on either side of Sidi Belafarid. The 21st Panzer Division (the new name for the old 5th Light Division) held the middle ground, along the Trigh Capuzzo, midway between Tobruk and Bardia. To the south-east of the 21st Panzer the 3rd Reconnaissance Battalion and to the south-west the 33rd Reconnaissance Battalion, screened the desert against a British move. Protecting the south of the Axis line, at Bir el Gobi, was Ariete

Division while in deep echelon, either as a reserve or as a counter-attack formation was Trieste Division, in position around Bir Hachim.

To protect the Panzer Army's forming-up area, should 8th Army's expected assault come in early or even meet the advance of the Axis force head-on, 21st Panzer Division would intercept east of Tobruk and once that fortress had been taken the whole Axis army would crash like a giant fist towards and across Egypt.

Lacking aerial reconnaissance reports the Germans were forced to build up a mosaic of British intentions and strengths through the reports of their own weak and scattered armoured car reconnaissance patrols, but these were neither enough in number nor sufficiently widespread in area to enable the staff to assess accurately British intentions. By 16 November there had been patrol clashes and during 18th the Africa Corps headquarters had been sent a report that a British column was moving northwards from Giarabub, but this manoeuvre was dismissed as a mere reconnaissance and the build-up to the Tobruk assault was maintained. German patrols had not located those units from 8th Army which had reached the heights between Sidi Omar and Gabr Saleh and reports that German patrols had clashed with British armoured cars along the Trigh el Abd seem neither to have been received at headquarters nor, if they were received, to have been acted upon.

The British offensive opened under a massive air umbrella and the men and tanks of 8th Army crossed the frontier wire and began to move upon Tobruk. Operation Crusader was opened by an advance of the armour which struck in a three-pronged drive across the area from Gabr Saleh (4th Brigade) and Bir el Gobi (22nd Brigade). These two brigades also had flank duties – that of 4th Brigade to guard the 13 Corps wing, while 22nd Brigade was to secure the open southern flank. The 7th Brigade, in the centre, had as its objective the area of, and around, Sidi Rezegh. This wide open formation held the seeds of the severe losses which the British were to suffer in the next few days for the columns were too far apart to give each other mutual support, and that direct and immediate command system under which the panzer formations were controlled was missing. The British brigades were to be flung piecemeal into battle and destroyed piecemeal although, in the initial stages of the operation, the wide front over which they were dispersed had the advantage that the Germans thought themselves to be facing stronger armoured forces than was the case, and, also, they were not able to identify immediately where the main British thrust would come.

On the British eastern flank 4th Brigade's 3rd Royal Tank Regiment reached to within 15 miles of Gabr Saleh and there, meeting elements from 3rd Reconnaissance Battalion, engaged these and drove them northwards. The 7th Brigade struck towards Sidi Rezegh and met little or no opposition *en route*, but then having reached its given objective, halted and consolidated. During the afternoon of 19 November a group of 60 tanks from 22nd Brigade in the area of Bir el Gobi met, struck, and drove off the Ariete Division, smashing the obsolescent tanks with which the Italian Armoured Division was equipped. Five British tanks fell victim to the Italian artillery.

At midday on 19th the battle situation was still unclear to the Axis commanders. The British had achieved a complete tactical surprise and it was to be 48 hours before Rommel knew the might and direction of the assault, although a prisoner from 4th Indian Division had been interrogated and had given his captors full details of the British plan. The hitherto unknown fact that 7th Armoured Division had crossed from Egypt into Libya was supplied to the Germans but this accurate information was not believed by Panzer Group, which was still of the opinion that this was no major offensive but a raid in strength despite confirmatory evidence. The 33rd Reconnaissance Battalion had reported that an armoured force, estimated to be in divisional strength, was heading towards Tobruk and an air reconnaissance had confirmed three British columns, part of 1st Army Tank Brigade and 1st South African Division, between Giarabub and Bir el Gobi.

The 21st Panzer Division was ordered to attack and to destroy the British units which were believed to be reconnaissance forces and located in the area between Sidi Omar and Gabr Saleh. The 15th Panzer which had moved up during that afternoon, to the west of 21st Panzer, moved in a four-column formation to take up position in the area west of Gambut and had reached its specified area by 21.00hrs.

To undertake the mission of destroying the so-called British reconnaissance forces the 21st Panzer Division formed Battle Group Stephan. The armoured brow of the battering ram which would scatter the weak enemy group was made up of 110 tanks from 5th Panzer Regiment and artillery from 2nd Battalion 155th Artillery Regiment as well as 3rd Battalion of 18th Flak Regiment. This advance guard was closely followed by the main of the division. Moving forward in a solid phalanx the battle group drove at a fast pace across the desert and at about 15.30hrs crashed into 4th Tank Brigade at a point some 5 miles north-east of Gabr Saleh. This attack by the divisional battle group was a calculated risk for it was advancing deep into the British flank with its own flanks unprotected.

As the armoured forces clashed the crews of the powerful 8.8cm guns formed a gun line and took the British tanks under fire at ranges greater than those at which the Stuart tanks could retaliate. Under the double punch of the high velocity 8.8cm and the 5cm and 7.5cm tank guns, the British brigade was hurled back across the Trigh el Abd. But the British armour reformed and came on again, again, and yet again. In the fighting which lasted until dusk 42 Stuarts were destroyed or fell out for the loss of three of the panzer force. The German tank recovery teams were soon in action and even in the heat of battle began to recover some of those Stuarts which had been abandoned. At last light the British withdrew from the battlefield and thus out

Top: A light field howitzer with its half-track prime mover on the coast road

Above: Flies were almost a permanent feature of life in the desert. Here German soldiers wear nets to keep them away

Left: The Arco Fileni on the Via Balbia marked the border of Cyrenaica and Tripolitania. German tank transporters pass through the arch on their way up to the front

Above: The German view of the desert fighting

Right: Rommel in an armoured wireless command vehicle (SPW) watches infantrymen planning an attack

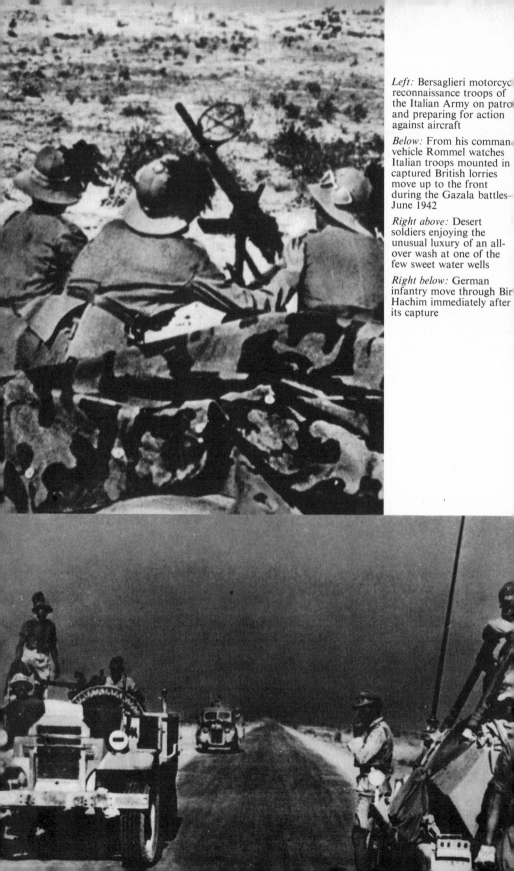

Left: Bersaglieri motorcycle reconnaissance troops of the Italian Army on patrol and preparing for action against aircraft

Below: From his command vehicle Rommel watches Italian troops mounted in captured British lorries move up to the front during the Gazala battles-June 1942

Right above: Desert soldiers enjoying the unusual luxury of an all-over wash at one of the few sweet water wells

Right below: German infantry move through Bir Hachim immediately after its capture

Left above: Dusk in the desert and the Panzer Army is formed in battle position

Left below: Rommel in his armoured command half-track together with vehicles and men of his escort company in the area around Tobruk—June 1942

Above: A Luftwaffe Volkswagen throwing up clouds of dust which were visible for miles

Right: Grenadier Halm, one of the youngest winners of the Knight's Cross of the Iron Cross awarded for his bravery during the battles of First Alamein—July 1942

Above: Infantry assaulting under cover of a smoke screen during the battle of Alam Halfa—1942

Left: The 8.8cm anti-tank/anti-aircraft gun in action

Below left: An infantry assault moving across the soft going of sand dunes at Mersa Brega—1941

of contact with 21st Panzer, leaving that unit laagered east of Gabr Saleh.

During the day 13 Corps had gone into the attack to the east of 30 Corps and patrols from both sides clashed along the line of advance of the New Zealand division, while during the late afternoon and far to the south the advance from Giarabub had been driven to within 25 miles of Bir Hachim and against this wide flanking movement the Axis command was helpless, for there were no ground reserves which could be sent to stem the Indian brigade's advance.

Even by nightfall the situation was still unclear to the commanders of both sides. The Germans still had no idea of the strength or the direction of the British thrust and Rommel, without accurate intelligence, decided to turn against the British armour and to crush each armoured formation in turn starting with those between Sidi Omar and Tobruk and then those units around Bir el Gobi. Cunningham had no inkling of German defensive power nor of the offensive abilities which had been improved by the new battle tactics. But the British command could feel slightly confident; the advance upon Sidi Rezegh had brought the British armoured spearheads to within 12 miles of Tobruk and the forward movement was to be continued on the morrow. The Imperial troops regrouped and prepared to drive off the inevitable counter-attacks.

With first light on 20 November Rommel began to concentrate his forces in the area around Sidi Omar and in the early morning moved 21st Panzer Division firstly towards Sidi Aziz and then swung it southwards; but the panzers had not driven far when they ran out of fuel and were forced to halt. Not until the evening did the supply trucks reach the area in which the division was stranded and then there was further confusion when a column, sent out from the main group to find 5th Panzer Regiment and to refuel its vehicles, was prevented only at the last moment by a search unit equipped with wireless from driving into a British laager. The 15th Panzer Division was moved from its position north-east of Sidi Rezegh and was sent roaring along the Trigh Capuzzo in a search and sweep operation, looking for the British armour supposed to be attacking the German reconnaissance battalion. It found neither. South-west of Gasr el Arid the division then swung in a great arc southwards and then south-westwards towards Sidi Aziz to support 21st Panzer. At 15.00hrs 15th Panzer attacked Gabr Saleh having the panzer regiment as point unit, closely supported by the field and flak artillery, and with 15th Infantry Brigade to the right rear and 200th Regiment on the left rear. In the course of its advance it came up against 80 British armoured fighting vehicles of 4th Brigade, but these could not halt the advance and by dusk the leading elements of panzer regiment were on the Trigh el Abd. British counter-attacks came in on the western and then on the south-eastern flanks but the fighting died away and the German group lay with the British tanks, forming a half circle around them and at some miles distant.

By the time that darkness halted the fighting of 19 November, the 4th Brigade had lost another 55 vehicles so that the 165 tanks with which it had begun the offensive had been reduced to only 68 runners. To support the 4th Brigade in the battle it had been fighting against 15th Panzer, the High Command had ordered 22nd Brigade from Bir el Gobi back to Gabr Saleh but it was dark before the appointed area was reached and not until dawn on 21st had the whole unit regrouped north-west of its objective. Help to the struggling 4th Brigade had been offered by the New Zealand division but this was refused under the terms of the Army Operations Order which decreed that 13 Corps was not to be involved in tank battles.

The 20th began and continued as a day of mounting crisis for the Germans, particularly for those defending Sidi Rezegh, for they were fighting desperately to prevent the breakthrough to Tobruk. The battle swayed to and fro as the tank attacks swept down upon the infantry of 90th Light Division and were repulsed time and again by a screen of anti-tank and 8.8cm guns. During the afternoon the Luftwaffe sent in fighter planes and Stukas to attack and break up the British tank spearheads; splitting up and driving these back to the heights at the southern edge of the airfield. The hard-pressed German infantry had a short respite. To the south of Sidi Rezegh the Ariete Division defending Bir el Gobi was coming under increasing pressure from the advanced elements of 1st South African Division and could not prevent that unit from advancing north-westwards. On the eastern flank, in 13 Corps sector, a two-pronged assault to capture the Halfaya Pass came in but the New Zealanders, now aware that on their left flank hovered the menace of the panzer divisions, moved slowly northwards to reach the Trigh Capuzzo. The move was a slow one for the New Zealand division needed to be certain that the panzers had been drawn against 30 Corps before a more rapid drive upon Tobruk could be made. In truth the British armoured presence had drawn upon it the German panzer force and it had suffered as a consequence, although it was still strong enough to pose a threat.

During the evening of 20 November Rommel worked out, in closer detail, the plan to concentrate the Africa Corps and to use it to destroy the isolated and unsupported British armoured groups one by one. The tone of Africa Corps orders for 21 November, that an attack was to be launched into the rear of the British forces advancing from Belhamed, anticipated the urgency which was shown in wireless messages which went out at 04.00hrs ordering the attack to be put underway immediately. The British intentions had at last been assessed and it was anticipated that an advance from Sidi Rezegh would be made in conjunction with break out attempts from Tobruk.

All through the night of 20/21st the fighting around Sidi Rezegh flickered and burst into fierce action. The infantry of 90th Light was forced farther and farther back from the southern edge of the high ground near Sidi Rezegh until it found that it was fighting back to back with the Pavia and Bologna

Divisions. The Germans were defending themselves against the assaults of 7th Armoured Division while the Italians were seeking to stem the blows from the Tobruk garrison. Attack and counter-attack followed in a series of bloody, little battles. Slowly the 90th Light gave ground under pressure but then, to prevent the danger of an encirclement of Africa Corps, the 3rd Reconnaissance Battalion was ordered out of Army Group reserve and brought forward to the left flank of Africa Regiment of 90th Light. The reconnaissance troops roared forward in a desperate charge and drove back a British tank unit from the ground which it had won. For the moment, but only for a moment, there was a relief of tension.

To the east in 13 Corps area there was a disengaging movement and the Germans shook off the hold of 4th Indian Division and of 22nd Armoured Brigade which had moved up in support. Hidden by the rain and the poor visability of a cold November morning the Germans withdrew and left only rearguards to obstruct and to delay the advance of the Imperial troops.

The German panzer divisions now stood as a solid mass of armour between 13 Corps to the east and 30 Corps to the west and the whole battle line from Tobruk to Halfaya can be seen as an eight-layered battle. An encircling ring of Axis troops lay without the British defenders of Tobruk. At Sidi Rezegh was a layer of Germans and Italians facing the thrusts of 7th Armoured Division. Then came the might of the two panzer divisions and to the east of that concentration there was 13 Corps advancing northwards towards the Trigh Capuzzo. Other Axis troops held the embattled perimeter from Bardia to east of Sollum and on the eastern side of that beleagured place lay the last layer of the front – the 4th Indian Division.

A similar layered battle was being fought on a north to south axis, that is from Tobruk to Bir Hachim. The British inside the perimeter were surrounded by the investing forces, other elements of which were facing the British around Sidi Rezegh. Then came a layer of Italian troops of Ariete Division around Bir el Gobi facing the South Africans. Lastly came the layers formed by elements from Trieste Divisions striking out from Bir Hachim against the Indian Brigade thrusting towards Gialo.

The seriousness of the situation in which the British had been now placed was not at first realised and, indeed, did not become apparent until both panzer divisions began to roll up 7th Armoured Division from east to west. For the assault 21st Panzer Division took the right flank with Belhamed as its objective, while 15th Panzer Division on the left moved via Sidi Muftan towards Sidi Rezegh. The wide, armoured front of the two panzer divisions advancing side by side and followed closely by the batteries of 8.8cm guns, moved rapidly forward and drove before it scattered British units which it encountered. By midday the heights south of Sidi Rezegh had been reached and 7th Brigade's commander, appreciating the sudden danger, broke off his own attack and swung his force to meet the onrushing panzers. The defence of

Sidi Rezegh airfield was then passed over to Support Group. The British tanks observed the panzer force passing across their front and firing from hull-down positions struck deep into the German flank. Once the shock of the first contact had passed a general mêlée developed and bitter battles were fought out between tank and tank, and tank and guns. Before long the British had settled down, had taken up all around defence against the Germans, and had prevented them from seizing the airfield. During the afternoon tanks encountered German trucks as they were replenishing their fuel and ammunition stocks and attacked these causing much panic and alarm. Night fell and the fighting tailed off leaving only the burning vehicles to illuminate the blackness of the night. The opponents drew back from each other. The two panzer divisions tired from the strain of fighting and of night driving, hoped to laager for the night but then came orders for them to change their positions and 15th Panzer Division was moved to Gambut while 21st Panzer Division proceeded to Zaafran.

During 21 November the pressure upon the Italians at Bir el Gobi had forced the Italian Corps commander to bring forward elements from Trieste Division from its position around Bir Hachim and to counter the advance of the Indian Brigade, on the deep southern flank, Rommel ordered his only available force – planes of the Luftwaffe – to bomb the Indian vehicles. On the far eastern front the New Zealand division reinforced by more than a hundred tanks struck across the Trigh Capuzzo.

The situation on the evening of 21st was that a link-up attempt by forces within and without Tobruk had failed, but only just, and that day was the first high point of the British offensive. Only at the last gasp could the attack towards Tobruk be halted by the Africa Corps striking for the first time in that offensive in a unified movement. The panzer mass between two British tank brigades had the opportunity to defeat these separately before either British Corps could intervene and by evening the important high ground in the area of Belhamed was again in German hands and formed a line from which future operations could proceed.

Nevertheless, in view of the serious difficulties with supply columns and a shortage in tank ammunition Rommel was compelled to order that for 22nd the Africa Corps would go over to the defensive. Rather surprisingly Corps did not act upon that order but to an earlier one which had given instructions to regroup. The two panzer divisions then moved out: 15th to a point south of Gambut and 21st descending from high ground, reached the line Belhamed–Zaafran, north of the Trigh Capuzzo.

That night supply columns once again had difficulty in finding their units but had reached them during the morning and the panzer force began to fill the empty shell racks with ammunition and the empty petrol tanks with fresh fuel. During that day a serious situation developed when it was realised that the depots around Tobruk which had been laid out to supply the investing forces had also been drawn upon to provision, refuel, and re-arm the attacking units and that this double drain had completely exhausted the stocks. In future the haul would be to depots farther back in the rear areas and would take not only more time but consume more fuel, and the convoys would be, over the longer route, more vulnerable to British air assaults.

At Sidi Rezegh the 4th and 22nd Brigades had fought their way through to the aerodrome and 5th South African Brigade, forming the spearhead of 1st South African Division, had struck out from Bir el Gobi into the flank of 155th Regiment defending Point 178, but against determined resistance it could only gain ground at a slow pace. During the morning both sides took the opportunity to regroup and the British who were ready first re-opened the battle by resuming the break-out attempts from Tobruk and combining these with armoured assaults launched towards the town by 7th Armoured Division. All these furious sorties were beaten back and in the ensuing lull the panzer divisions once again began to refuel.

During the afternoon of 22nd Rommel decided to take up the offensive once again and this move produced for the Germans the conditions for the opportunities, which were to be presented in the following days, of attacking the flanks and rear of the British forces.

Rommel placed himself at the head of 21st Panzer Division and led an armoured phalanx towards Sidi Rezegh. With artillery support and with the flanks of his advance protected by 90th Light Division, the panzer group struck down from the north. The 5th Panzer Regiment on the Axis road, south of Tobruk, drove towards El Duda in a two battalion box formation with 2nd Battalion in the van, reached the Sidi Rezegh aerodrome, and then turned eastwards. The panzer attack met the fighting vehicles of 7th Armoured Division; large and fierce tank versus tank battles were fought around Sidi Rezegh. Under German pressure 7th Support Group was slowly driven back from the airfield and late in the afternoon it began to withdraw southwards to link up with 7th Armoured Brigade. To support its sister brigade, the 22nd Armoured then thrust up from the south in a desperate counter-attack but the gallant advance was held by the front, while panzer forces swung round the British flank and smashed the brigade. Throughout the short, winter afternoon the battle raged but at last light the panzer drive thrust through the 22nd Armoured Brigade and, having knocked out 45 from a total of 80, scattered the remainder, leaving the British unit now only a rump to withdraw upon the main of 7th Armoured Division.

During the afternoon Rommel had compounded the British defeat by flinging the 15th Panzer Division from its positions around Sciafsciuf into the 7th Armoured Division's rear eastern flank, where was located much of that unit's weakly defended 'tail'. The heavy blow, carried out at top speed, met very little opposition as British soft-skinned trucks and isolated tank groups from 8th Hussars and 4th Brigade were surprised, overrun, or dispersed. This scything sweep cost the British units 35 tanks, the whole of the armoured car strength and all the guns.

Suddenly, or so it seemed, the tables were being turned and Rommel had in a few short days destroyed at least half of 7th Armoured Division's armoured force: had smashed 4th Armoured Brigade, had beaten off the assaults of 22nd Armoured Brigade, had flung back the assaults out of Tobruk, and had decimated through air attack the Indian Brigade advancing on the southern flank. Against this tally of victories the single British success had been the capture of some positions on the Sollum front and the westwards advance by the New Zealanders against determined opposition put up by 3rd Reconnaissance Battalion on the Via Balbia and by 33rd Armoured Reconnaissance Battalion along the Trigh Capuzzo.

The total successes claimed by Panzer Army Africa during the four days of the fighting had been 207 British tanks destroyed and to this total must be added the 50 claimed by the Italian Motorised Corps. The strength of the British tank brigades had been savagely reduced – only 10 runners were with 7th Armoured Brigade, 22nd Brigade had only 40, and there was a further handful with 4th Brigade.

As night fell the German divisions settled down on the battlefield with 21st Panzer Division on high ground south of Sidi Rezegh and 15th Panzer Division south-west of Sciafsciuf. To ease Rommel's administrative and command problems Mussolini placed the Italian troops in the Marmarica under his authority. It remained the intention of the German commander to encircle and to destroy the British south of Sidi Rezegh and his orders for 23rd were that Ariete Division was to move at 08.00hrs upon Gambut. An hour earlier the German panzer forces, combining once again to form a solid armoured block, had also begun to move upon Bir el Gobi. By strengthening his left wing Rommel intended this to have sufficient force to encircle his opponents. To avoid the confusion which would arise through Ariete having British vehicles under command, the order was given that two white signal flares would be fired as the Axis recognition sign.

Some parts of 21st Panzer Division were retained to hold back the break-out attempts from Tobruk, while the remainder joined forces with 15th Panzer in its assault against Bir el Gobi. To form the western and northern sides of the ring the two Italian divisions Trieste and Pavia stood fast in their positions while to the east the German and Italian armour flung a noose around the British.

During the night, 5th South African Brigade attacked along the Trigh el Abd to the north of Bir el Gobi, while 13th Corps, in the course of its northern pincer drive moved a second New Zealand brigade up the Via Balbia towards Tobruk and, this force coming across the tactical headquarters of the Africa Corps, attacked it dispersing part of it and pinning down and isolating other sections temporarily from the main battle.

Sunday, 23 November dawned cold and very foggy, causing certain confusion among some of the units of 15th Panzer Division as they headed uncertainly in the poor light into what was the day of climax of the whole offensive. Within a few miles of the start of 8th Panzer Regiment's drive British tanks and vehicle concentrations had been met but the panzer group avoided a confrontation with these and struck south to take the British force in the flank. The 2nd Infantry Brigade and its anti-tank weapons were dropped off to form a gun line and to hold fast the British front while the mass of 15th Panzer Division carved its way southwards. It drove into a zone of artillery fire from guns which held position all round but, bursting through the hail of explosions, the columns concentrated, moved in towards the centre battalion, and, combining into a steel fist, struck at and through the British flank and rear areas, encountering and destroying in succession a supply column with its light armoured escort, 7th Support Group, and then 3rd Royal Tank Regiment which was on its way south to regroup.

Then the German front spread out again to cover a wider area and to drive before it, and, thus on to the guns of the other encircling units, the British formations which it met on its way. But the British were neither panic stricken nor incapable and flung in one armoured attack after the other in gallant, but un-coordinated assaults against the lunging German unit. From flank to flank the German anti-tank gunners were switched to hold the whole line of advance as 15th Panzer Division's left wing swung in a great steel scythe around the British flank and rear at Sidi Muftan.

Losses on both sides mounted as the British commanders realised the danger to their formations and flung in more units to hold back the German pincer. In the Bir el Halad area, held by 7th Support Group, the British commander formed a defence of successive anti-tank, tank and gun lines to defend his southern and south-eastern flank, and this aggressive defence forced 15th Panzer Division to swerve away and to seek a weaker spot along the flanks. From the east thrust the Germans and from Bir el Gobi the Italians, sending out armoured probing fingers. One of these found the boundary between 1st and 5th South African Brigades. The panzer group tore a gap between these Imperial troops through which reconnaissance detachments and armour poured, destroying as they advanced more British soft-skinned columns, then rolled up the flanks of the South African brigades and destroyed with artillery fire the concentration of British tanks which were assembling for fresh assaults.

But the helter-skelter advance of 15th Panzer Division had strung that force across the desert leaving it in isolated and unsupported groups. A halt was called to regroup; a short rest and then, towards midday, the attack rolled forward again still pursued and accompanied by British artillery fire. Just after midday at a point only 10 miles north-east of Bir el Gobi, white Verey lights shone in the sky to indicate that just ahead of the German panzer units lay the armoured fighting vehicles of Ariete Division. The ring, however loosely fitting, had been closed and imprisoned within it was the mass of 7th Armoured Division.

At 15.00hrs and from the south came the main thrust upon the strategic Point 179 to drive 8th Army's armour on to the waiting gun lines of 21st Panzer Division. For the attack 5th Panzer Regiment was on the right and 8th Panzer Regiment on the left. These were reinforced with field artillery, whose principal task it was to support the infantry together with 18th Flak Regiment and their deadly 8.8cm guns, and followed by infantry from 90th Light Division. The German box poured up from the south but Ariete, which should have taken position on the left flank of the advance, arrived too late on the battlefield and took no active part in it.

The giant wedge of German armour hurtled across the desert raising clouds of dust in its advance but was then struck by a hurricane of artillery and anti-tank gun fire which the British poured upon it. As the range decreased casualties inside the German box began to mount and on the sector where the anti-tank gunners of 5th South African Brigade held post the first wave of panzers was almost upon the slit trench line before the order was given to open fire. Then the Boer gunners, working their pieces with frenzy, drove back the armour of 15th Panzer Division but it regrouped out of range and then came on again; but this time against a weaker sector of the line and forced a breach. Forward into the gap poured the riflemen of 115th Regiment but the Imperial infantry inflicted upon their officers and NCOs such losses that the attack halted and then receded as the German riflemen flooded back. The commanders and the staff officers reformed them and brought them forward again, up to, into, and then through the gap. The fighting became general and confused: infantry fought against infantry, tank versus tank, artillery battery against artillery battery. Attack was followed by counter-attack and then another attack as fighting swung first to the advantage of one side and then to that of the other. In vain did 22nd Brigade swing a left hook from the south-east; it was held, caught, and deflected with terrible loss. Carving its way through the British positions the 8th Panzer Regiment's 1st Battalion had, by 17.00hrs, forced a salient 8 miles deep and then upon the aerodrome at Sidi Rezegh linked with the advanced elements of 21st Panzer Division. This was the killing thrust but the British and Imperial troops, fighting for their very existence, battled on. To the east vehicles of 5th Panzer Regiment then carried the advance forward to link up with 21st Panzer's left wing and then the intensity of battle began to die down leaving only 2nd Battalion of 8th Panzer Regiment still involved in beating back counter-attacks which were still being mounted against it.

By 17.30hrs British resistance began to weaken and as darkness fell the whole area south of Sidi Rezegh was seen to be dotted with the fires of burning tanks and trucks. Explosions and shell fire lit momentarily the darkness under whose cover individual British vehicles and units were trying to storm their way through the Axis ring or to slip away and to make good their escape. The hours of darkness were used by both sides to regroup – a task made more difficult for the Axis troops than for their opponents for no wireless link had existed between Africa Corps headquarters and its subordinate units since the time that the New Zealand attack had dispersed it.

Only in the night as the regiments reported and as the exhausted soldiers unwound from the strain of battle did the realisation come that the Africa Corps, and indeed the whole Axis force, was fought out. The German units were jumbled up, fuel supplies had been totally consumed, ammunition had been fired off, and, when at last the supply columns were ordered forward, the confusion in which the units were mixed made the replenishing a long and exhausting one. Although some units had been refuelled and re-armed before midnight it was dawn of 24 November before the trucks had arrived in other areas. Workshop companies laboured all through the night repairing damaged tanks so that at 09.00hrs the 21st Panzer Division could report itself as ready for action, a claim that 15th Panzer could not make until midday.

The German victory had not been without grave losses. The 15th Panzer had suffered particularly heavily; 8th Panzer Regiment had suffered unusually high losses in senior officers and at the end of the day had only a handful of tanks as runners. Of the 36 Panzer III with which it had entered battle on 23rd, only 10 were still ready for action. Only 3 of the 7 Panzer IV were still runners and only 6 of the 18 Panzer II. The 115th Infantry Regiment had lost most of its senior officers and all its personnel carriers. The battle report from 5th Panzer Regiment gave its losses as 2 Panzer III and 1 Panzer IV, leaving that unit on the evening of 23rd with 11 Panzer II, 16 Panzer III, and 2 Panzer IV, although this number was increased by the repairs which were carried out. The 5th Panzer Regiment claimed in its report to have destroyed 32 British tanks, 2 scout cars, 18 anti-tank guns, and 3 batteries of field artillery as well as having taken over 500 prisoners together with much booty.

The plan to surround and to crush 7th Armoured Division in the area south of Sidi Rezegh had succeeded by the evening of 23rd and the victory was the fruit of a number of fortunate decisions and measures. The thrust by 15th Panzer into the area of Gasr el Arid gave the opportunity of a flank thrust and the decision to continue with that drive destroyed the British numerical superiority and thus by 23rd it was possible for the Germans to meet their opponents on a relatively equal footing. Although the fighting on 22nd had destroyed parts of the British armoured division, by the following day not only 7th Armoured but also elements of the South African Division had been defeated with a loss of 3000 prisoners, 120 guns, and 80 tanks. One brigade of 7th Armoured and one of the South African division had been totally destroyed, together with nearly all the guns of the armoured brigade, many lorries, and so many tanks that by evening it had only 40 machines ready to

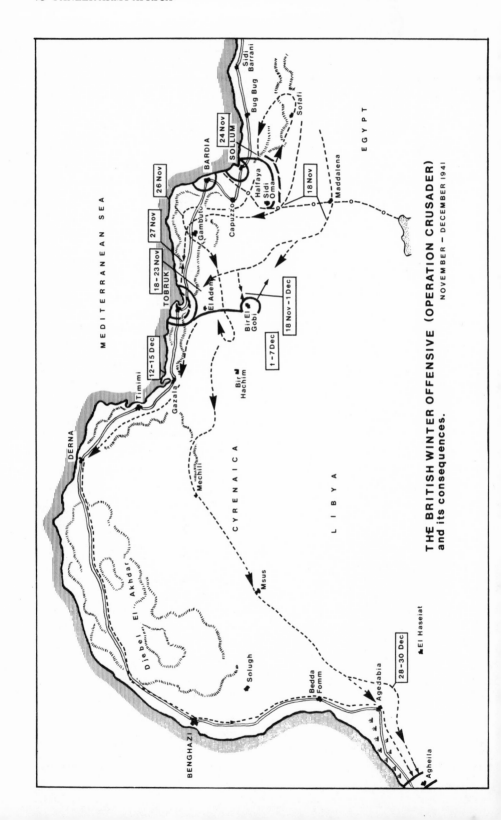

THE BRITISH WINTER OFFENSIVE (OPERATION CRUSADER)
and its consequences. NOVEMBER – DECEMBER 1941

continue the fighting on 24th.

While on the western front 30 Corps was bleeding and wounded 13 Corps had been making slow but steady progress and the pressure which its troops were exerting was beginning to make itself felt on the battlefield. The advance by 6th New Zealand Brigade against one German regiment brought its leading elements close to the eastern side of Sidi Rezegh airfield, other elements had captured Gambut while the main of the division had captured Bardia, had struck along the Trigh Capuzzo, and other 13 Corps units had captured parts of Sollum against strong resistance. On the Tobruk front break-out attempts had captured several strong points from the Italians and the Indian Brigade had at last reached Gialo against severe Italian resistance. The first part of the British offensive was closed on 23 November with a victory for the Axis. The British plan to crush Rommel had failed.

Lacking a clear picture of events and influenced by the results of the fighting of 23 November, Rommel formed the impression that 8th Army was defeated and this confidence permeated to regimental level. As an example the verbal orders given to 5th Panzer Regiment by commander of 15th Panzer Division said that the beaten enemy was withdrawing to the south-east and that the divisional task was to pursue the British via Gabr Saleh and Gasr el Arid, to break through to the frontier and to reach the area south of Sollum. Shortly thereafter the order to move off at top speed was given and even though the battle group had not been formed, the advance began.

Despite his losses and the exhaustion of his troops the German commander-in-chief thought he could scent victory and determined to go all out to achieve this. But the Panzer weapon which he was now wielding had lost much of its edge, for on the morning of 24 November the total number of armoured fighting vehicles still ready for action with Africa Corps was only 80. The British armour, shrunken but still a potent force, regrouped along the Trigh el Abd and then formed square around the forward supply depots upon which its whole existence depended.

Another day of crises and battle followed on 24 November and the statement in this book that war in the desert was decided by the side which could reinforce continually with men and machines is seen to be proved for the British were falling back upon stocks of supplies and reinforcements, although the new men to fight the tanks were often without battle experience. Against this continual and short haul replenishment the Germans had a long and arduous drive from rear depots hundreds of miles removed and only their superior tank recovery and repair service was able to keep up the strength of the army in the field.

Crüwell, Africa Corps commander, reported on the course of the battle and his appreciation of the situation reinforced Rommel's own mistaken belief that 7th Armoured Division had been destroyed as a potent fighting unit. Rommel then decided upon a long range penetration from Sidi Rezegh to Sidi

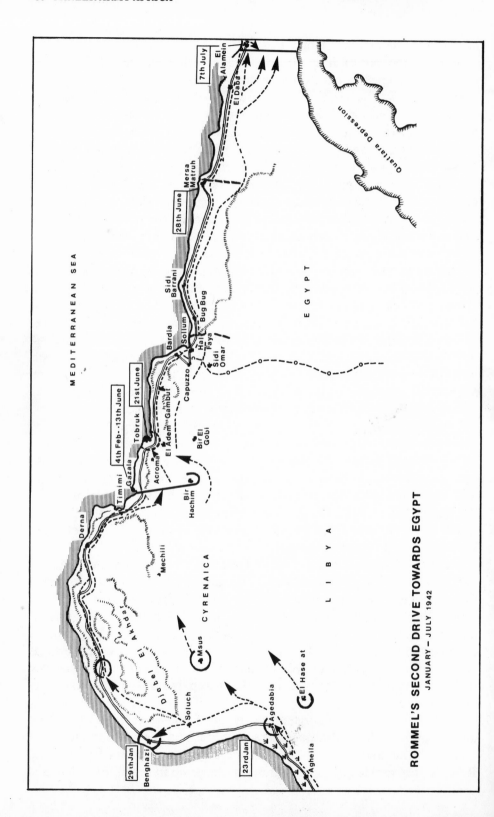

ROMMEL'S SECOND DRIVE TOWARDS EGYPT

JANUARY – JULY 1942

Omar and to Halfaya. His intentions were to raise the siege at the latter place, to build up his eastern flank for an advance into Egypt, and to spread a net to intercept and catch the British forces as they retreated from Sidi Rezegh. To carry out this 'dash to the wire' he would have to move the greatest part of his force and leave only minimal strength positioned around Tobruk. Battle Group Böttcher, a force made up of two battalions from 155th Regiment, one battalion of 361 (Africa) Regiment, engineers and artillery had the task of holding Belhamed and thus protecting the southern flank. The remainder of 90th Light Division was to hold the Via Balbia against all attacks from the east and to halt the break out attempts from the town.

The trans-desert group was despatched with great haste and with orders that there would be no halt for battle *en route* to the intercepting points; speed was of the essence. At 10.00hrs having had little time for rest or maintenance, 21st Panzer Division led by Rommel and with the reconnaissance battalion in the van, advanced as a single box towards Sidi Omar. Then followed 15th Panzer, to take up position on the right flank of the thrust and then, at 13.00hrs, the Ariete Division moved out. There was to be no thought of flank protection during the advance – no care nor concern for what was happening on the left or right wings – the thrust was everything and nothing must be allowed to impede it. Weak British units were overrun and stronger forces were avoided. As the panzer boxes advanced 8th Army artillery and tank assaults accompanied them, but against these latter self-propelled guns were used and the lines of 8.8cm flak upon which the British tank commanders were again seduced into making piecemeal attacks.

The sudden presence of panzer units so far in the British rear produced panic and rumour among the non-combatant echelons and as these headed south to escape the panzer clasp the stories they spread created uproar in the area through which the panzers were thundering. By the afternoon German armour stood at the Egyptian frontier. In the advance the panzer force had had to skirt Sidi Omar, for that place had been captured by 7th Brigade of 4th Indian Division, across whose 'tail' the panzers had driven.

At the frontier wire 5th Panzer Regiment halted and at 16.00hrs began to consolidate and to concentrate its units south of Trigh el Abd. The main of 21st Panzer Division pressed on eastwards into Egypt without the panzer regiment for it had run out of fuel and ammunition. The German wireless sets, already defective before the offensive had begun, had virtually ceased to function. Communications between the two panzer divisions had been lost and from Corps headquarters there was silence. Out of contact with its sister units and its main headquarters the armour of Africa Corps was moving blindly into the unknown. In an effort to establish the true picture, patrols were sent out by both panzer divisions to regain contact, a difficult task this as the last armoured car belonging to 33rd Reconnaissance Battalion had been destroyed that day by a Royal Air Force air attack. At 22.00hrs 15th

Panzer patrols not only brushed with British armour 20 miles south of Sidi Omar but also found 5th Panzer Regiment. Then came the intelligence that Ariete had not advanced past Gabr Saleh.

Fortune favoured the British during the night when 8th Army's carefully camouflaged but otherwise unguarded main store depots lay within a few miles of 21st Panzer Division as it lay halted on the battlefield waiting for its supply trucks. The presence of strong German forces within a few minutes drive of the stores which, if captured, would enable Rommel to forge strongly ahead caused the British command many anxious hours for there were no troops which could have been sent out in time to protect the depots from assault and capture. But Rommel had his eyes fixed firmly on Maddalena and Mersa Matruh and it was upon these places that he was directing his forces. He was aware that his position was not a strong one. Although he stood deep in the British flank, was in touch with the garrison at Halfaya, and was athwart the British lines of communication, it was equally true that his troops were widely scattered, had no communication with each other, and that British troops were across *his* lines of supply. To protect the soft-skinned vehicle convoys, prey to the roving bands of British armoured car patrols during the dangerous journey across the desert, Rommel ordered that they be escorted by any available fighting vehicles and this temporary expedient eventually became a standard battle procedure. Rommel's thrust eastwards was the turning point of the battle. German defensive tactics had proved themselves and the ring around Tobruk still held; 30 Corps had been badly mauled and the remnants of 7th Armoured Division were not at that time in a position to resume offensive operation. The New Zealand Division was isolated and should have been withdrawn back to its start lines.

Operational orders for 25 November commanded that the British forces in the Sollum–Sidi Omar areas be destroyed. In anticipation of the retreat which he was convinced 8th Army would have to make from the stricken battlefield of Sidi Rezegh, Rommel left his panzer divisions in a position to intercept the fleeing British columns. Ariete Division was out of the battle as it was still engaged in fighting the South Africans around Gabr Saleh. The main interception was to be made by 21st Panzer Division south of Halfaya. To clear up the battlefield and to prepare it for another intercepting force 8th Panzer Regiment was ordered to attack across the Trigh el Abd, to drive along the left side of Sidi Omar, then to swing eastwards to cut off the garrison in that place while 5th Panzer Regiment attacked from the south-east and captured it. The pincer operation failed for, soon after it started, it struck the main of 7th Indian Brigade and elements from 2nd New Zealand Division supported by tanks whose task it was to protect the positions around Capuzzo and Bardia. The 5th Panzer Regiment made no appreciable gain of ground and 8th Regiment came up against severe opposition and the growing strength of 8th Army. As the German panzer wedge rolled along to the west of Sidi Omar the

British artillery opened upon it a drum fire under cover of which 7th Armoured Brigade was hurled against the flanks of the advance. But the British tank guns were outranged by the 7.5 and 5cm pieces with which the German vehicles were fitted and in one attack 8th Panzer Regiment destroyed all of a 16-tank wave which went in against it. The Royal Air Force struck repeatedly at the panzers as they stopped to refuel but failed to halt their forward movement so that by evening a spearhead had reached Trigh Capuzzo, west of Sidi Aziz and 15th Panzer Division had partly encircled both Sidi Omar and Capuzzo.

The 5th Panzer Regiment had, however, failed to capture British strong points south of Sidi Omar and suffered heavily in the bitter and close fighting which marked the course of the afternoon. A summary of the battle entries for 25 November is interesting.

'. . . the enemy in the defensive line opened a terrific fire. The regiment charged this line of guns and after hard fighting silenced two batteries and six anti-tank guns. We . . . lost five Panzer III. More enemy batteries and anti-tank guns on the left flank of regiment now entered the fight and we lost another Panzer II and two Panzer III. The regiment then tried to bypass the enemy on the right . . . (but he) brought up anti-tank and field guns . . . and extended his line. The regiment was now running short of ammunition and was forced to deploy to the right and to move away south to break off the action. By 12.30hrs attempts to regain wireless contact with division had still been unsuccessful. The regiment, now in position 8 kilometres north-east of Gasr el Abd had only nine tank guns in action. At about 13.00hrs the C-in-C ordered an attack upon the enemy columns south of the frontier to break through on a wide front and to halt in sight of the frontier wire. The regiment had been reduced to the strength of a reinforced company and had little petrol or ammunition. Three immobilised Panzer III and IV were taken in tow to increase the fire power.

'Regiment then met enemy tanks and eventually clashed with enemy forces which were occupying position about 12km wide along the frontier. It was fired upon and five of our tanks were knocked out, two of them on fire. Regiment then turned west and opened fire upon the enemy to its front and on its left flank. Two more Panzer III were set on fire. Orders to turn south, regroup, and stop could not be passed because shellfire had shot away the aerials on many tanks, including those on the regimental commander's vehicle. The 2nd Battalion thereupon carried on through the wire south of Sidi Omar. Wireless contact with that battalion was not restored until 27 November.

'The rest of regiment now had only 3 Panzer II, 5 Panzer III, and 2 Panzer IV; only three of which had their guns in working order. On 27

November one of the Panzer IV had to be cannibalised to make the other tank battleworthy. During the night of 25 November further attempts were made to establish contact by wireless, or by any other means, with a higher HQ or some German unit, but without success. The regiment also received no supplies of petrol or ammunition because a higher HQ had directed our trucks to another unit in order to stimulate an attack.

'In the attacks of 25 November – carried out with no artillery or AA (anti-aircraft) support – the regiment lost 9 Panzer III and 1 Panzer II as total losses. Hit and, therefore, abandoned were 1 Panzer II, 1 Panzer III, and 1 Panzer IV. Two tanks fell out and were abandoned: a Panzer II and 1 Panzer III.'

In that dramatic report can be seen the steady draining of strength which marked the battle from the German side and 8th Panzer Regiment had only 53 runners during the afternoon of 25 November. Once again the wide dispersion of German units across the length and breadth of the desert and the failure of wireless communication led to a situation where lorried convoys ranged far and wide and search parties from battle-exhausted units had to go out to locate and to guide in the supply and fuel columns.

Still convinced that the British around Sidi Rezegh no longer posed a threat Rommel concentrated on clearing up the eastern flank and ordered that the attacks from the south of Halfaya and Sollum were to continue with the objective of reaching Bardia. Rommel ignored the threat presented by the New Zealand brigades, although these were moving steadily but very slowly along the Via Balbia, presenting the danger of his being outflanked from the north and, more immediately, that of their linking up with the defenders in Tobruk. During 25th attacks had come in from the garrison in the town and on either side of Belhamed, from New Zealanders supported by tanks, against defenders who were seriously short of anti-tank weapons. Only the intervention of the Luftwaffe slowed down the assault. There had been an increasing build-up of British strength south-east of Tobruk but because of the failure of signals communication this dangerous state could not be brought immediately to Rommel's attention. When, at last, the intelligence reached the commander-in-chief he realised how vital was the need to reduce Sidi Omar and Capuzzo before he could strike westward once again and prevent a break-out from Tobruk. On that sector New Zealand forces captured Belhamed during the night of 25/26th and the Tobruk garrison made a sortie shortly after first light which captured El Duda. A corridor which had been driven, against all the efforts of the Böttcher Group to contain it, had been closed by the Germans and a Bersaglieri Battalion during the evening and in savage fighting losses to the British cost them a further 26 tanks. Attacks were carried on all through the night to smash a corridor through to Tobruk.

With signals messages either failing to reach their destination or being garbled in transmission the Operations Department of Panzer Army, unable to warn Africa Corps of the dangerous situation around Tobruk and acting upon its own initiative ordered 21st Panzer Division to return to the Tobruk sector and directed 15th Panzer to attack the New Zealanders in the Bardia area. In its move 21st Panzer recrossed the rear of 4th Indian Division and left a trail of blazing vehicles. The division skirted the Halfaya garrison and passed through the surrounding mine-fields before going on to engage 5th New Zealand Brigade, while other divisional units linked with 15th Panzer and reached Bardia there to refuel, reprovision, and to re-arm. The creaky supply situation already overloaded, began to fail and not all units received their full quotas. The 115th Regiment was sent in to take Capuzzo and despite severe British defences and bitter hand-to-hand fighting the German infantry pushed forward until its leading sections were only half a mile from the place. But then a surprising order from Rommel halted the forward movement and brought the infantry back to the start line. Meanwhile, Ariete continued its slow move forward and had reached a point only 24 miles west of Bardia.

Rommel, not completely in touch with his headquarters, had halted the infantry attack upon Capuzzo and suddenly realised that 21st Panzer was not where he had believed it to be and could not, therefore, participate in a plan which he had worked out. Gradually he became aware that the reducing strength of the Africa Corps, the increased difficulties at Tobruk, the supply situation, and British air superiority were factors which would prevent his plans reaching fruition. One factor of which he was certainly unaware was that 8th Army had gained its second wind and was preparing to renew the battle not to break it off. The British in the area south of Sidi Rezegh had regrouped along the Trigh el Abd and had re-equipped their units with fresh supplies of tanks. A newly driven corridor through to Tobruk, although narrow was firm, and British pressure had forced the Axis units back; but in hand-to-hand fighting 90th Light Division on the northern wall of the corridor and Böttcher Group along the southern prevented the gap from being widened.

The British received the news that 21st Panzer Division was swinging westward again; 30 Corps used 2nd New Zealand Division to guard its back against the panzer units now roaring towards it and took up a defensive posture in the Gambut–Gabr Saleh sector. The fighting which had flared up around Tobruk increased in intensity and threatened the German units with complete disintegration as British pressure began to roll up their flanks.

At dusk on 27 November the 21st Panzer Division moved from Bardia to Gambut and 15th Panzer Division, acting on its orders drove along the Trigh Capuzzo on the left flank of 21st Panzer, overrunning in its advance, 5th New Zealand Brigade headquarters, and capturing 500 men and 6 guns. The mass of 15th Panzer then reached the Trigh Capuzzo and headed for Tobruk against moderate opposition. But as the unit drew near the town opposition stiffened and the British tried everything to hold the Africa Corps' return from the Sollum front. The 4th and 22nd Armoured Brigades went in – part of 7th Armoured Division which had now been reinforced to a point where it was now nearly as strong as the panzer units of the whole Africa Corps – but in the event 15th Panzer proved strong enough to cope with the situation. By evening the panzer force had driven to the area west of Gabr el Arid and had laagered south of Sciasciuf, there to await the arrival of 21st Panzer. The Ariete Division lay south of the Trigh Capuzzo and the whole armoured might of the Axis army, extended across the desert south-west of Gambut, was facing the British.

To the west of Sidi Rezegh there was the Böttcher Group and the Italian Divisions, to the north the 90th Light Division, while from the east there was the growing pressure of the two panzer and one Italian armoured divisions. But not until he contacted his headquarters did Rommel know that far from being beaten as he thought the British might still gain the upper hand through their better supply position for they were still able to renew their strength with fresh men and tanks while theAxis forces had reached the end of their tether.

During the period from 24 to 27 November the fortunes of the Panzer Group Africa can be seen to have changed alarmingly and by 27th the situation around Tobruk had become critical. The ring round the town had been split, the Axis forces driven back and at the end of their strength. The 30 Corps had been massively reinforced and was again posing a serious problem south-east of the town. The supply system, already bad, had become critical and there were grave doubts expressed whether Corps had the strength to restore the situation.

The rainy morning of 28 November saw 21st Panzer Division encountering heavy resistance around Zaafran but not only had part of it held the eastern pressure out of Tobruk but other elements made contact with 90th Light and, on the southern flank another column of the division passed Bir el Chleta and headed for Sidi Rezegh to which sector 15th Panzer Division was also heading. That formation put its main on the important high ground south of Belhamed and drove off the counter-attacks to the south which 8th Army had launched. During the day and despite the poor light a collaboration between 15th Panzer and Ariete Divisions encircled a number of British tank groups. The German commanders now were obtaining a clearer picture of the situation and their speedy regrouping allowed them to begin operations aimed at defeating the New Zealand and British forces.

One thing was very clear to the German command; although British material losses could be speedily replaced the restoration of confidence in the tanks and in the leadership would take much longer to build up. This point was borne out in Kippenberger's book *Infantry Brigadier* where he claimed that throughout the 8th Army there was a most intense distrust, almost a hatred of our, that is to say the British, armour. Suspecting this feeling Rommel reasoned that 8th Army must be beaten before it had fully recovered for he knew that already British forces were regrouping and reforming without let or hindrance along the Trigh el Abd, an area now empty of Axis troops.

The question which Rommel had to decide that day was whether to drive the British and Imperial forces, positioned around Sidi Rezegh, back into Tobruk or to cut them off from the town and to destroy them in the field. He decided on the latter course. The 21st Panzer Division held position and was involved in fierce fighting on both sides of the Trigh Capuzzo while 15th Panzer drove past the New Zealand flank to thrust back South African counter-attacks eventually to link up with the Böttcher Group and XXI Italian Corps. A short rest and then 15th Panzer swung northwards gaining in strength as it picked up other Axis fighting units from the area through which it passed before it went on to attack and to capture El Duda from the Tobruk garrison. So fast had been the pace of the advance that the infantry had become separated from the panzer spearhead and armoured personnel carriers had to halt their advance to go back and to porter the troops. The losses suffered that day were more than usually heavy and regimental strength of one infantry regiment had been reduced to 150 men by the time that El Duda had been taken. At that place, determined in spirit but weak in number the Germans took up all round defence but strong British infantry assaults drove back the German infantry from their positions and in the fighting more than half of them were taken prisoners of war.

Ariete and 15th Panzer Division then came under a series of heavy but unco-ordinated attacks launched by 7th Armoured Division and 1st South African Division on the southern flank trying to break through to the New Zealand Division but on 21st Panzer Division's sector the aggressive defence put up by the New Zealanders forced the Germans to commit its last few reserves. During the afternoon an attack by 4th Armoured Brigade hit the Böttcher Group but was deflected while the 15th Panzer Division swung through the intervals in the Axis line and struck north towards El Duda. The Africa Corps battle report recorded the destruction of 20 British tanks from a group of 100 which had begun an attack and these severe losses forced 8th Army's leaders to order a withdrawal south.

On the far northern flank of the battle 90th Light made strenuous efforts to close the narrow corridor but despite its struggle and the intervention of an anti-tank company no firm link had been made with 15th Panzer by that evening. Panzer Group had now concentrated and surrounded the main of the New Zealand and elements of 7th Armoured Division. The corridor was narrowing in width, British attacks on the southern front were weakening and were being beaten off, only on the far eastern Sollum front had there been defeats. The garrisons at Bardia, Sollum, and Halfaya were once again surrounded and cut off. The decisive attack against the New Zealand Division went in on 30 November but it was not co-ordinated because 15th Panzer Division arrived late at its start line, for as a result of false orders it had been given its units had had to spend the night in a fruitless desert march. To hide the direction of the main Axis thrust feint assaults were made against a number of points, particularly at Sidi Rezegh. Although the German assaults began well the Royal Air Force attacks soon halted the forward movement for the British High Command, realising the desperate situation, had brought every arm to bear to aid the encircled troops who were defending themselves with the utmost tenacity. Particularly did the strength of the British artillery distinguish itself during the fighting and the panzer forces gained a healthy respect for its accuracy and its punch.

In the early afternoon 15th Panzer Division, having rested after its night drive, came roaring up, made its first strike to the north, swung wide of Sidi Rezegh and then turned east to encircle the main British force from the west. This now had the 90th Light to the north, 21st Panzer to the east, Battle Group Mickl, a new formation chiefly artillery in composition, and Ariete to the south-east.

When the German units were in position Mickl Group, supported by a machine gun battalion and 8th Panzer Regiment, began to exert pressure upon the New Zealanders. Then the British corridor into Tobruk came under fire. Fresh, unsupported, and unsuccessful British attacks to rescue the trapped colonial troops were made from the south but these were thrown back by the combined strengths of Mickl Group, Ariete Division, and the left wing of 21st Panzer Division. British armour then probed for a weak spot in the German ring and Axis reconnaissance units reported that enemy forces were in movement from Bir el Gobi in the west. The 21st Panzer came under pressure from British forces outside the encirclement. During the night of 30 November/1 December, the South Africans made an unsuccessful assault to break the German noose and the New Zealanders were then ordered to break out south-eastwards.

In the foggy light of 1 December the 15th Panzer made its killing thrust from the north of Sidi Rezegh. The battle group was made up of 8th Panzer Regiment with elements from 90th Light, 200th Regiment, a machine gun battalion, 15th Motor Cycle Battalion, and two battalions from 33rd Artillery Regiment as well as a 21cm howitzer battery. Heavy resistance by 8th Army at first delayed the advance but by 10.40hrs the encircled Imperial troops had been captured while outside the ring 4th Tank Brigade and other British units mounted a series of fierce assaults on Mickl Group and 21st Panzer Division to ease the pressure upon the trapped New Zealanders.

By late afternoon of 1 December it was nearly all over. The 15th Panzer and 90th Light Divisions had overcome the British defences and by linking hands had cut Tobruk off again, although the garrison of the town had lengthened the perimeter by a further 8 miles and held the strategic height which dominated the Axis supply route.

As the December daylight faded the remaining New Zealand units were destroyed one by one and by 2 December, after five bitter days of battle the fighting died away. Two thousand prisoners had been taken, together with more than 40 guns and a mass of equipment. The last two days had truly been a battle of attrition and at the close of the fighting foe and friend alike sank exhausted to the ground. Operation Crusader had ended.

Although 2 December marked the end of the Crusader offensive the campaign continued and the immediate post-battle interlude was used by both sides to regroup their forces. Each side had at least one division which was still ready for action. For the British this was 4th Indian which in the days after Crusader sealed off once again and even more strongly the Axis garrisons in Bardia, Sollum, and Halfaya.

On the German side 15th Panzer was still fit for action but the strength return of that formation gives an indication of how hard had been the battle. On the evening of 1 December only 11 Panzer II, 24 Panzer III, and 3 Panzer IV remained. The Africa Corps report for 3 December stated that more than 167 of its tanks and armoured cars were a total loss. The Italians had lost more than 90 of their armoured fighting vehicles but the British had suffered the destruction of over 800 machines. In personnel the German casualties were 600 killed, 1900 wounded, and 2200 missing. The Italians suffered less as the bulk of their forces were not so deeply involved. The British and Imperial forces had lost heavily and more than 9000 of 8th Army had been taken prisoner.

Most battles have a tactical and a strategic outcome. Strategically the British won the day for they were able continually to reinforce their Army and go on to push the Axis forces out of Cyrenaica. The Germans had gained a tactical success and had used mobility, the speed of attack, and the greater range of their tank guns to reduce the numerical superiority of their British opponents. When attacking they struck at the weakest part or element of the 8th Army line with the strongest possible force and, when forced on to the defensive had fought aggressively. Their intention had been to destroy the British force; mere possession of ground they saw was unimportant and could under certain conditions be a burden. They had, therefore, been prepared to give ground temporarily to conserve strength in order that, at the appropriate time, strength would be available for them to make a counterstroke and to regain the territory which had been lost.

Against the new British attack which opened on 8 December and which had come up from Bir el Gobi the Germans had no more strength and as the Italian motorised Corps could not be ready in time to take up its defensive position, panzer group ordered the withdrawal to begin. The Axis troops fell back upon the Gazala line but so closely did the British pursue them that they reached the Gazala positions at the same time as the Italians.

Cyrenaica was indefensible. Rommel recognised the truth of that thesis or, to qualify the thesis, it was indefensible with the forces which he had available. Wavell had been the first to prove and Rommel had gone on to show that the deserts which lay to the south of the great curve of the Gulf of Bomba presented no obstacle to the determined commander. Although he resolved not to give ground without a battle and was prepared to offer the most determined resistance whenever possible, Rommel's decision to withdraw from the province was completely misunderstood in Rome, Berlin, and, even by his superior, Bastico. This latter set his face absolutely against the evacuation of territory until Rommel offered him the alternative of either agreeing to give up ground or of trying to hold Cyrenaica without German troops, for Rommel was quite prepared to leave the Italians to fend for themselves if his plan was not followed. Kesselring, the Supreme Commander South, intervened and together with a number of German and Italian officers opposed Rommel's intention for they considered the loss of Cyrenaica would have political repercussions for Mussolini. Rommel dealt with their objections point by point and convinced them that, in view of the continuing and omnipresent problems of insufficient men and supplies, there was no other choice.

A new British thrust on 16 December threatened the panzer force with encirclement but Rommel ordered that battle be avoided and that his troops break out. He knew the true weakness of his command and that if it were to stand and fight then its strength would be reduced to a point where Tripolitania could no longer be defended. Nothing but defeat could be gained from fighting.

The Axis forces flooded westward withdrawing past the fortress of Tobruk and giving ground in the face of 8th Army's pressure. By Christmas Benghasi had fallen, although at a high cost to the British in men and material, and still the rearward movement continued until the whole Axis army had moved back to take up the new battle line in the prepared positions which ran from Marada to Marsa el Brega. By 7 January this move had been carried out and, with a shorter line to defend, Rommel could now begin to build up strength again to mount an offensive which would capture Cyrenaica and drive forward to the Suez canal. Hundreds of miles to the east Halfaya still held out, unsupported and without hope of reinforcement. It was to continue its resistance until 17 January but then when its water supply was cut the garrison surrendered.

Rommel's counter-offensive opened on 19 January and under cover of a sand storm the Panzer Army made a surprise thrust towards El Agheila. Two days later an infantry and a machine gun Battle Group Marcks, was led in person by the German commander-in-chief through the mine-fields east of

Marsa el Brega while the main of Africa Corps moved south of the Via Balbia. Agedabia was captured and immediately the Stuka squadrons occupied the field and from this front line position came into action against British tank forces. If the offensive had shocked the British it had come as a complete surprise to Rommel's superiors in the OKW and in the Commando Supremo, for Rommel had allowed no word of his intentions to be known.

The advance continued on 24 January when 15th Panzer with the 21st Panzer Division on its left flank swung south from Antelat opening a broad front as the advance was made towards Maaten Giofer. The Battle Group Marcks and an Italian unit continued to drive eastward to close a ring around the British and by midday of 24th these had been cleared from the area south-east of Agedabia and had lost 117 of their tanks in the severe fighting. Some British units escaped through a corridor between the Marcks Group and 21st Panzer Division but the main was surrounded and destroyed. On the morning of 25 January the panzer group moved forward again and attacked Msus, the main British supply depot, from which the Axis troops obtained no less than 600 trucks, 127 guns, and 280 armoured fighting vehicles.

The next move was to regroup and to form four battle groups which were to move upon Mechili and on 25th, while the bulk of the Africa Corps rested in the Msus–Antelat area, reconnaissance detachments and motorised infantry carried the advance eastwards. The Marcks Group, which Rommel led in person and in pouring rain throughout the long cold night, brought the assault forward until in the grey dawn of 27 January he had reached El Regima. By the afternoon that place had fallen and with it the airport of Benghasi. An infantry battle group cut round behind the town to block the Via Balbia and to seal within the city the British troops still fighting there. Once again the booty captured served the Axis forces well for more than 1300 trucks were captured together with food, equipment, and petrol.

There was no time for rest and once Ariete had taken over security duties east of Benghasi and Trieste Division had begun to carry out the same tasks in the Gemines sector the German reconnaissance in force continued at a mad pace. The coastal towns along the Via Balbia were taken one after the other defeating or throwing back the mainly Indian garrisons until at last Derna was reached.

Then began the final stages of the German advance to the Gazala positions and at first these were to be occupied by the reconnaissance detachments only while the bulk of the Africa Corps stayed in Benghasi. The Italian XXI Corps was ordered to move up to secure the area between Benghasi and Agedabia. The first new mine-fields were begun on 3 February, the start of belts of such defences which reached deep into the desert from the coast for a distance of over 150 miles.

In the relative peace which the efforts of the strenuous campaigning of the past months then forced upon both sides, the Germans and their Italian comrades strengthened and improved their positions. The Gialo Oasis was occupied and thereby the southern flank of the Axis line was secured. Behind the main Gazala mine-fields others less extensive in area but dominating important sectors were also laid and anti-tank gun positions sited. The next months were taken up with resting, training, and preparing the troops for the forthcoming offensives of the summer.

7. The pre-emptive blow at Gazala, June 1942

'We have time to prepare for the offensive against Cairo'
Rommel, February 1942

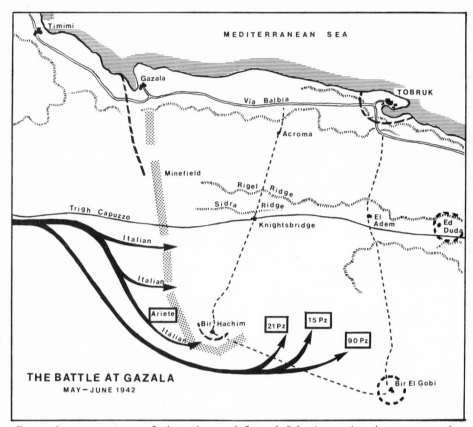

THE BATTLE AT GAZALA
MAY – JUNE 1942

Cyrenaica was now safe but the undefeated 8th Army lay just across the desert and the conviction that British resources were seemingly inexhaustible, revived Rommel's fear that thousands of British tanks would one day come storming out of the desert. He decided to strike a pre-emptive blow which would capture Tobruk and then go forward to the Nile delta. But the genesis of the German summer offensive had been an OKW order issued on 30 June 1941, which laid out a grand strategy in which a southern pincer would drive through Egypt to link up with two northern arms, one of which would advance from Bulgaria through Turkey and the other from the Caucasus through Iran. The success of this giant pincer movement was predicated upon the capture of Tobruk for Hitler refused to seize the Tunisian ports through which the army could have been more easily reinforced and supplied.

Cavallero, of Commando Supremo, planned to establish a giant depot at Agedabia from which the Axis troops could be nourished during their advance, but as an undefeated Malta remained a base from which Axis convoys could be attacked then Malta would have to be taken out. Discussions at the highest level authorised Rommel to mount an attack upon Tobruk but added that he was to halt at the Egyptian frontier to allow the maximum support to be given to the Malta undertaking. The timetable for the operation was the end of May to mid-June and Rommel was directed that if Tobruk did not fall then a withdrawal back to Gazala must be made.

The strain of battle had reduced the unit strengths but not the confidence of the Africa Corps but then convoys arrived bringing across reinforcements and equipment to fill out the shrunken units and to rearm them. In addition to individual tanks whole companies of fresh men and machines came in and 5th Panzer Regiment of 21st Panzer Division which in February had had less than 70 panzers, had, by the end of April, been reinforced to a strength of 165, an establishment which the regiment had never had before nor would ever reach again. There was still a shortage of soft-skinned vehicles so that some units had only 60 of their official strength of 400 trucks. There were 12,000 men fewer than establishment for the whole of the Africa Corps, whose total strength, including supply troops for rear elements, was only 36,000 all ranks, the most acute shortage being in infantry.

Rommel then began to prepare the men of his command for the battle ahead. During May individual training gave place to company schemes and to collaboration with armour both by day and night. Special emphasis was laid on attacking prepared positions and permanent fortifications. Storm troop units were formed and these worked with combat engineers and tanks so that all-arm co-operation would be at a high peak of efficiency when the attack went in. By the end of May there were large-scale, divisional manoeuvres.

The 21st Panzer Division had been carrying out extensive patrol activity against severe British opposition and then the whole Africa Corps advanced into 'no man's land' at the south-eastern corner of Cyrenaica. This move fulfilled the purposes of thickening the battle line, of providing the maximum strength should 8th Army attack, and, lastly, of forming a firm jumping-off point for the panzers in the forthcoming battle. Officers were taken on secret reconnaissances to familiarise them with the terrain over which they would be fighting, forward fuel depots were built up, and slowly, so as not to arouse suspicion, the number of shells fired was reduced to allow stocks to be gathered. On 12 May Rommel briefed the divisional commanders and then began the last minute preparations; traffic control points were established and the second echelon details sent back. To equip the fighting troops, orders were issued that all weapons, including those in training establishments and detachments, were to be handed in. The Africa Corps had girded itself for battle.

The 8th Army's defensive positions at Gazala stretched from the sea to Bir Hachim, a distance of some 45 miles and along the length of this very strong line defensive positions, known as boxes, had been laid out. These were usually sited on high or broken ground and capable of all round defence. They were intended mutually to be supporting and each of them had a strong garrison usually of brigade or equivalent establishment. To the west, that is the enemy side, lay extensive mine-fields of considerable depth and, in some areas, this sea of mines had been laid down on the eastern or 'friendly' side of the boxes.

To hold the forward, static defences Ritchie, 8th Army commander, put in 13 Corps. In the north, at Gazala, was 1st South African Division, then to the south 50th Infantry Division and 3000 men of 1st Free French Brigade holding the left flank box at Bir Hachim. This left wing was extended and strengthened by putting into a hastily prepared box, south-east of Bir Hachim, the newly arrived 3rd Indian Motor Brigade. At certain strategically important points along the southern flank and extending eastwards there were other boxes of which Knightsbridge, held by 22nd Guards Brigade, and El Adem were the most important. Behind the infantry boxes to give immediate support were 1st and 32nd Army Tank Brigades and behind this, located west and south of Tobruk, was the armoured mass of 8th Army, formed into 30 Corps. The 1st Armoured Division lay aside the Trigh Capuzzo and controlled the central sector while 7th Armoured Division was positioned farther south to deal with any threat from the direction of Bir Hachim.

The strengths of the two armies gave the British superiority. In armour there were 742 British tanks to 360 German and 210 Italian. In artillery there was a three to two superiority – 500 to 350 – a seven to five superiority in aircraft – 700 to 500 – and a larger number of men – 125,000 to 113,000.

The German commander-in-chief was faced with the choices of a frontal assault which would not only have robbed him of the element of surprise but would have allowed the mass of British armour to concentrate against him. The second alternative was to drive round the open flank at Bir Hachim and by a pincer operation from east and west of the Gazala position destroy 8th Army in the field. Rommel chose the second plan which had the advantages that the element of surprise would be maintained and that a successful assault would divide the British Army in two and separate the infantry from its armour. The divisions holding the boxes in the Gazala position would not be able to release men to aid their comrades farther back because their whole attention would be needed to defend the western mine-fields. Neither could the Tobruk garrison spare forces and reduce its strength for then the town might fall to a *coup de main*.

Rommel's battle plan was for a diversionary attack to be mounted upon the northern, Gazala sector by X and XXI Italian Corps together with the non-motorised brigade of 90th Light Division. This force, known as Crüwell Group, would attack during the afternoon of 26 May and its aggressive moves were to hide the main thrust and to convince the British that the mass of German troops were on the northern sector. Instead, these would be concentrated in a second, mobile group. This would comprise the Africa Corps and the Italian XX (Motorised) Corps which, led by Rommel, would sweep round and behind the southern flank of 8th Army. Part of this group would strike northwards via Acroma and attain the coast thereby cutting off from the main of 8th Army the divisions in the Gazala sector. A pincer movement going in with the Crüwell Group from the west would then destroy the British and South African divisions. Another part of the outflanking group would strike the British positions along the Gazala line in the back and to protect the flanks of this and the northern advance the motorised elements of 90th Light Division together with the reconnaissance battalions would drive eastwards towards El Adem and threaten Tobruk.

The final preparations had been made. The routes forward had been marked with lamps, stores depots had been filled, a seven-day ration of food and water issued to all ranks, and, to aid in the deception plan, decoy convoys were sent out in the direction of Crüwell Group. The most difficult move in the opening stages of the operation would be the night drive by the outflanking force. This would be made over a vast distance and through unreconnoitred country by two Corps, neither of whom had even carried out such a manoeuvre at divisional level. Special measures were taken to ensure that distance and direction were maintained. The convoys were to move at exactly regulated speeds, 8 miles per hour in bright moonlight, on compass bearings which had been precisely worked out and the Luftwaffe was to drop flares throughout the night over the French held positions at Bir Hachim.

During the afternoon, with their movements hidden by the veil of a sand-storm, the divisions of the outflanking force moved to a point some 13 miles south-east of Rotondo Segnali there to rest and to refuel. At 17.00hrs on 26 May, the code 'Venice' was flashed; the battle for the Gazala line was on.

The attacks by Crüwell Group produced no reaction from the British. The Italian assault had been so weak and had been so well concealed by the *khamsin* that the 50th Division's boxes had not been aware that the attacks had taken place. At last light the fighting died down on the northern flank and Axis attention was directed southwards to where the outflanking group was marching through a brightly moonlit light towards Bir Hachim. A short distance ahead of the main body were the advanced guards of 15th Panzer Division followed by the 'boxes' of the panzer regiment, the artillery and divisional headquarters, the motorised infantry, engineers, anti-tank, and other services. Between the two panzer blocks of 15th and 21st Divisions marched Corps headquarters. When it is considered that a panzer division's vehicles on the move covered an area of 11 square miles then it is possible to gain an idea of the impressive might of the Africa Corps and the Italian Corps as the divisions moved towards the British flank.

British armoured car patrols met *en route*, withdrew in the face of this armada signalling to 8th Army headquarters news of the desert march. At 04.00hrs on the morning of 27 May the great armoured mass, having marched 32 miles by compass bearing all through the night, halted south of Bir Hachim and there rested and refuelled before shaking out into attack formation. The strike force of the Axis army was now in position ready to carry out the next part of Rommel's plan; the northern strike. But 8th Army which had received the patrol reports had dismissed the movement of the out-flanking group as bluff to draw attention from the centre and the north.

Dawn on 27 May lit the armoured mass of Africa Corps positioned east of the Gazala mine-fields and facing towards the sea. The 90th Light Division was already on the move towards El Adem; immediately to its left 15th Panzer Division. On the left flank of 15th was 21st Panzer and on the extreme left flank Ariete Division. Towards 07.00hrs 15th Panzer Division was struck by a group of 60 British tanks who brought the panzers under fire from distances which were greater than normal. This sudden blow halted the German advance on that sector and the reason for the shock was due to the fact that the division was advancing without its usual screen of armoured cars. These had been detached from both panzer divisions to strengthen the right wing where 90th Light was operating and without this advanced guard the Africa Corps was moving blind into battle. The British 4th Armoured Brigade, which had received advanced warning of the panzer thrust, stood in 'hull down' position waiting for the German tanks to come within range. The guns of the Grant tanks with which the British armour was now equipped struck the Germans and destroyed three of them forcing the others to with-draw upon the artillery which had been left behind in the speed of the advance. The Corps commander brought out of Corps reserve an 8.8cm battery and put it into action supporting a flank thrust by a panzer platoon and part of 33rd Reconnaissance Battalion. Under this double thrust the 8th Hussars and 3rd Royal Tank Regiment were driven back and almost destroyed. The remnants of 4th Armoured Brigade fell back upon El Adem.

The 3rd Indian Brigade's box lay in the path of 21st Panzer Division and the two armoured blocks of the panzer battalions swept down upon the weakly armed defenders. For forty minutes the out-gunned brigade held 5th Panzer Regiment back but then a blow was delivered under which the defenders were crushed and the panzers swept across the now-silent position, heading northwards. During their advance they encountered 7th Motorised Brigade in the 'box' at Retma and swept across that unit destroying and dispersing it. The Ariete Division struck at Bir Hachim. The first attack went in at 09.00hrs when a force of 50 M 13/40 tanks stormed forward and ran into a mine-field. The Italian attack halted within range of French anti-tank guns but then a small, determined group smashed its way forward and into the positions held by the French Foreign Legion. The tanks were destroyed in close-quarter combat. Then a second assault came in at 09.30hrs but this lacked determination; the tenacity of the small, French garrison had baffled the efforts of a whole Italian armoured division.

Towards 11.00 hrs the 44th Royal Tank Regiment was ordered to advance and to intercept the panzer spearheads and the graphic words of one of the officers of the reconnaissance detachment convey the morale effect of mass armour, 'On topping a rise we could see on the eastern skyline a solid mass of vehicles stretching southwards into the haze as far as the eye can see'. This was the 21st Panzer moving on to Trigh Capuzzo and in the battles which then followed the anti-tank gun line of 21st Panzer Division destroyed 18 British tanks from concealed positions in a wadi.

By 10.00hrs the Africa Corps was driving northwards with its flanks protected by 90th Light Division which had encountered British armoured forces west of Bir el Gobi. The Italian XX Corps delayed by the determined resistance of the Bir Hachim garrison had to skirt round the French 'box' and had only reached a point five miles north-east of Bir Hachim, where it regrouped.

The panzer spearhead of the Panzer Army Africa was under attack from east, north, and north-east for although 8th Army had suffered from the initial assault it had pulled itself together and had begun to launch counter-attacks. The 15th Panzer's move just after 15.00hrs was struck in both flanks by artillery and tanks and one British attack at 16.00hrs caused alarm when the 60 tanks which struck at the flank threw back the panzers and the impetus of the British thrust being maintained overran a motorised infantry battalion. Then the armour was among the panzer division's lorries dispersing them in disorder and cutting off from their armoured spearhead the follow-up units. This severing produced a critical situation both at divisional and at Corps level. The commander flung in his headquarter defence unit. This battle group made up of a battery of 8.8cm guns, a panzer platoon, and a light flak company was joined by 16 other 8.8cm pieces from 1st Battalion 43rd Flak Regiment and the whole formed a defensive flank against the armoured assaults, while 15th Panzer Division forced its way northwards. The German guns stood at bay immobile but powerfully armed against an opponent less heavily gunned but with mobility. As the tanks charged forward the guns spoke and the barrage drove back the British machines. On came the tanks again and yet again; each time they were driven back but still they moved into the assault until 12 of their number were destroyed or burning. They then drew back out of range and stayed immobile until nightfall. With one flank covered by a gun line but encountering opposition which demanded that she fight every step of the way 15th Panzer reached a point 9 miles south of Acroma where both 21st Panzer and Corps Headquarters closed up to her. To the east 90th Light Division and its satellites had reached to within 8 miles of El Adem but were locked there in battle with 7th Armoured Division. The Italian Motorised Corps was echeloned deep in the left rear and the situation around Bir Hachim was quite alarming for aggressive French patrols had intercepted and destroyed German supply columns. The German and Italian troops of Crüwell's Group were still halted awaiting developments but mine-clearing teams had begun to gap the fields.

Although the panzer army's main objectives had been gained the ulcer of

Bir Hachim, together with the ungapped mine-fields, had forced Rommel's supply convoys to make a wide detour round the open southern flank. The British tank attack, which had carried past the southern flank of Africa Corps and which had cut off the panzer units from their supply columns, affected the future of Rommel's plan for neither fuel nor ammunition was reaching the forward units. Seen from the British side Rommel's position was untenable. His panzer force had been mauled: 21st Panzer Division had only 80 runners, and 15th Panzer only half that number. After initial successes the Africa Corps was dispersed in packets across the desert surrounded from the east, west, and north and short of the two basic requirements of desert warfare: petrol and ammunition.

At 05.15hrs on 28 May the two Panzer Divisions were ordered to advance; 15th Panzer upon Acroma and 21st Panzer upon Eleut el Tamar, but 15th Panzer was unable to comply with the instructions. There was a shortage of tank and artillery ammunition and the petrol tanks were dry. The division's chronicle of woe included the fact that its armoured strength was down to 29 runners, that one of its infantry battalions had been destroyed, and that its artillery had suffered heavy loss. The 21st Panzer Division went in alone at 07.30hrs and had captured Eleut el Tamar and the heights at Point 209 some 90 minutes later. During this sweep the 21st had cut a destructive swathe through the British units in the area. First it had met a mobile column code-named 'Stopcol' and had destroyed it. Tanks from 8th Royal Tank Regiment had been encountered and crushed and then the panzers swept over a defensive box at Commonwealth Keep (Point 219) and had taken that out. Although the 21st Panzer units had reached the escarpment there was no route down from the summit to the Via Balbia and division halted there.

The situation at last light on 28th was that the Africa Corps was still surrounded and that strong British forces were driving along the Trigh Capuzzo towards the trapped divisions. On the Bir Harmat front the 90th Light was slowly giving ground and XX Corps had sent forward the Trieste Division to gain touch with Africa Corps in response to the urging of the Army Commander. There was a slight improvement in the supply position when a number of lorries and tanks which had been dispersed by British attacks rejoined the main body. Then, too, Rommel had made his own reconnaissance and had found a route which his supply columns might use without much difficulty during the following day.

British commentators on this battle describe the 28 May as a quiet day but it is more accurate to describe it as a day of wasted opportunities. The 8th Army had expected Rommel to maintain his northward progress and had gathered strength to take the panzers in flank but the comparative inactivity and the inaction of the British units had allowed Rommel to continue with gapping the mine-fields and to reconnoitre routes for his supply trucks.

The battle order for 29 May was 'The Africa Corps will take Acroma in an

Previous page: The infantryman's view of battle. Armed with a 98 Kar. and hand grenade this Grenadier waits in prepared positions in the Alamein line—1942

Above: Gunners man-handling an 8.8cm gun into position in Tunisia

Left: Armour to reinforce the Africa Corps being unloaded at Tripoli

Right: General Bismarck of 21st Panzer Division observes the battle from the turret of a Panzer III

Above: An example of
Allied air superiority—an
Axis airfield after an Allied
bombing raid

Left: A gun line of 8.8cm
guns in defensive positions

Right above: A French
15.5cm GPF gun used by
the Germans in Libya,
here being towed by an
SdKfz. 7 prime mover

Right below: A Panzer IV
speeds past a knocked out
Bren carrier during the
attack upon Bir Hachim
—May 1942

Left: Junkers aircraft fly in supplies and petrol to Tobruk aerodrome—August 1942

Top: Rounding up British prisoners of war during the Gazala battle—May–June 1942

Above: Gunners examining the damage caused to the turret of a Matilda tank by their 8.8cm guns

Following page top: Italian infantry towing the 47/28 anti-tank gun during a march past.

Following page bottom: Panzer IIs moving up the line for the Gazala battle

attack to begin at 09.00hrs' and in an effort to draw the British attention from this drive the Italian Corps on the western Gazala front were ordered to demonstrate. The Africa Corps called in its outlying reconnaissance battalions and these formed a shield on the eastern flank. The number of 'kills' reported for the 28th – 241 tanks and armoured cars, 46 guns including anti-tank weapons – gave a hope that there would be a successful outcome to the battle. The destruction of so many 8th Army's tanks was slowly reducing the numerical superiority which the British had enjoyed at the start of the fighting and these 'kills' were the result of the piecemeal and unsupported charges which the British tanks still made against the gun and panzer lines.

At 02.00hrs on 29 May Africa Corps cancelled the order to advance upon Acroma and instead directed that the divisions were to take up a defensive posture. The 21st Panzer was to consolidate on Point 209, the 15th Panzer was to protect the northern flank against the thrusts of 7th Armoured Division, while 90th Light was to stand on the defensive south-east of Bir el Harmat. But on the western flank a small ray of hope was visible: Trieste Division had gapped the mine-field in two places – at about the level of the Trigh Capuzzo and the Trigh el Abd. Rommel had, meanwhile, led a convoy along the route he had found and brought it forward to where the vehicles of 15th Panzer lay stranded. His arrival was timely for 2nd Armoured Brigade advancing from Knightsbridge was seeking to drive a wedge between the panzer divisions to the north of and the Ariete Division south of the Trigh Capuzzo. Rommel called up a battle group from 21st Panzer to strengthen the 15th Panzer and then Ariete Division came up. The British advance then came up against the three Axis armoured divisions and from wireless intercepts it was clear that the British brigade had suffered heavily. A second armoured brigade, the 22nd, moved up to stiffen the attack by 2nd Armoured Brigade, and then a third Brigade, 4th Armoured, was drawn into the battle. The 7th Royal Tank Regiment fell victim to the lure of weak panzer forces and was enticed into range of a gun line hidden in the dust of the *khamsin*.

Then 15th Panzer Division moved forward to the Trigh Capuzzo where it gained touch with Ariete and had thereby cut off large numbers of 8th Army troops. Many of these made desperate efforts to escape under cover of the sandstorm and one group of 40 tanks and 200 lorries made repeated attempts to smash the encircling ring and escape to the east. Artillery fire drove back the British convoy. Although there had been a slight improvement in the supply situation it was still critical and seemed likely to remain so. Accordingly, Africa Corps commander proposed that the troops east of the British mine-fields should move westward through the newly created gaps and thus regain their start line area. Rommel proposed another alternative; he would reverse his front, giving ground as he moved slowly back towards the gaps through which the convoys of lorries would come. Once refuelled and re-armed he would then regroup and renew the attack.

At 02.00hrs the Africa Corps began its westward withdrawal protected by rear guards against a possible British move. Despite some losses in the mine-fields, Corps reached Bir Sidi Muftah at 06.00hrs where they surprised and were surprised by British troops. Corps had run head on into a 'box', held in strength by 150th Brigade from 50th Division, positioned between, and thus dominating, the two mine-field gaps. The first attack by the panzer division was halted at the edge of the mine-field and then driven back by anti-tank guns. The order was issued that the box must be taken quickly for by 11.30hrs the situation had deteriorated alarmingly and fresh crises were at hand. The 90th Light was being pressed by 1st Tank Brigade at Bir Harmat, there was heavy fighting along the Trigh Capuzzo where 22nd Armoured Brigade was trying to outflank Corps; 21st Panzer was wincing under a bombardment of unusual ferocity coming out of Gazala and the Royal Air Force was attacking every enemy column.

Victory now seemed certain for 8th Army; Rommel's forces, constricted within a small area bounded by the Trigh Bir Hachim, Trigh Capuzzo, and Trigh el Abd, were being pressed on to the British mine-fields. The two gaps which the Axis engineers had managed to create were so narrow that movement was slow; they were dominated by British artillery and movement only by night was possible. The whole determination of Africa Corps was centred upon holding off the British in the east while consolidating in the west, but this was impossible so long as the 150th Brigade box remained.

But if Rommel had his hours of anxiety the British, too, had had their moments of concern. The attacks by 2nd and 22nd Armoured Brigades had been crushed by the anti-tank gun screen and Guards Brigade had been hit while making a sortie from the Knightsbridge box and had been driven back with heavy loss.

Rommel's luck did not, however, desert him for during the night of 30/31st supply trucks reached Corps concentration area and, when in the morning both panzer divisions reported themselves ready for action, army head-quarters ordered them to expand their fronts and to take out the box at Got el Ualeb – the 150th Brigade position. The first unprepared and hastily organised assaults were driven back by the determined defenders supported by the remnants of a tank regiment.

The 8th Army, unaware that Rommel's supply position had been eased still optimistically believed that the Panzer Army was withdrawing from battle through the mine-field gaps and considered that the German loss of 371 tanks represented a more damaging blow to the Africa Corps than its own loss of 384 vehicles meant to it.

German attacks against the 150th Brigade box at Got el Ualeb came in during the day and one which captured Point 174 enabled the panzer division's artillery observation post (OP) to direct the fire of his guns with devastating effect. The concentration of the whole effort of Africa Corps to take out the box dominated 1 June. At 07.30hrs, 30 panzer from 15th Division and a battalion of 104th Regiment, together with the Corps battle group struck down from the north, while from the south came 90th Light and then from the south-east elements from Trieste Division. Within the perimeter of the box the last five tanks of 44th Royal Tank Regiment formed line and went out to fight an unequal duel. In the great silence which, for a few minutes, hung over the stricken field the only noise was the creaking of the tracks as the armoured fighting vehicles moved towards the anti-tank gun line. Only one returned. Still resistance was being offered and Rommel led an abortive attack by 5th Panzer Regiment thrusting westwards through the northern lane intending to swing this assault through the mine-field and to attack 150th Brigade from the west. Uncleared mines destroyed 12 of his tanks and the assault was called off. Under cover of almost continuous Stuka dive-bomber assaults the German infantry supported by tanks beat their way through the British opposition until they had linked with the spearhead of the Italian division. Other German units on the eastern flank held off the weak and unco-ordinated attacks aimed at relieving the trapped brigade but by midday it was all over.

With the central box destroyed the German supply route was secure but the real significance was that the Axis armies held a firm bridgehead out of which they could advance. Rommel now directed his attention away from the dying battle and decided to clear the southern wing before reverting to his original plan of striking northwards. Thus, for 2 June, he ordered that 90th Light Division together with Trieste Division were to capture the Bir Hachim box under cover of a mock attack launched by the remainder of Africa Corps.

During the days from 2 to 10 June a battle of attrition was fought in the Knightsbridge and Bir Hachim areas. The 21st Panzer Division was at first ordered northwards while 15th Panzer was held to await developments in the southern sector. This order to split the armoured force was queried by the staff officers at army headquarters for the secret of the great success won by Africa Corps was that it had always struck as a single, invincible block. The officers realised that to follow the commander's order would spread the power of the Corps thinly across an area from Bir Hachim to the Via Balbia and this against a British Army which still retained freedom of manoeuvre together with a great number of tanks which it could commit to battle. As if to confirm the fears of the army staff, 8th Army launched a series of attacks under cover of the *khamsin*. The first drove in against 15th Panzer, then against Ariete, and finally against 21st Panzer. Rommel cancelled the original order and led 90th Light and Trieste Divisions southwards intending to capture the box at Bir Hachim.

There was little alteration in the battle scene on 3 June for both sides were regrouping, rearming, and preparing for the next round. Ritchie, 8th Army commander, was determined to gain the initiative and wireless intercepts were able to supply the intelligence to Panzer Army headquarters that 2nd and 4th Armoured Brigades, a total of about 400 tanks, were forming south of Bir Harmat. Other British armoured and infantry forces had formed along the southern front of Ariete Division. Rommel ordered that Bir Hachim was to be taken, that the two Axis mobile Corps were to remain on the defensive, and the Crüwell Group was to continue its attacks on the northern and western flank. The 15th Panzer was instructed to drive by night, together with 114th Rifle Regiment, along the Trigh el Abd north of Sidi Belafarid and then in a general south-easterly direction to pass through the mine-field, to gain and to enlarge a bridgehead from which an encircling attack would be made at some later date.

During the early morning of 5 June British artillery opened a barrage upon the forward elements of Ariete Division and forced that division to give ground. The barrage then switched to 21st Panzer's sector and behind the shells came the armour striking towards the gaps in the mine-fields. The 8th Army was making a pincer movement to destroy the German bridgehead. Aware that, if the British controlled the exits to the mine-field gaps, the Panzer Army would again face supply difficulties the German counter-attacks were frequent and furious. Within the small desert area between the Trigh Bir Hachim, Capuzzo, and El Abd there was then fought the hard and bitter tank battles which have passed into British military history as the Battles of the Cauldron.

The assaults by Indian infantry and by the 22nd Armoured Brigade struck Ariete Division and forced its troops back past Bir el Aslagh and to Bir el Tamar but then 8th Panzer Regiment swept forward and the 22nd Armoured Brigade, already halted and baffled by the German gun line, was flung back by 8th Panzer Regiment with considerable loss. The 15th Panzer Division, too, had had successes and claimed no less than 50 'kills'. In the afternoon of 5 June, the tanks of 15th Panzer were moved from the bridgehead position to Bir el Harmat but 21st Panzer, which should have collaborated in the counter-attack, had been held by the British tank force which realised that it was now fighting for its life. With the tanks in front of 15th Panzer driven back in confusion the British and Imperial infantry bore the full brunt of the German counter-attack and were overrun.

Late in the morning the assaults of the British had been driven back on both the northern and the southern sectors and the pincers of the panzer divisions storming forward in pursuit of the withdrawing armour had met and thus had cast a ring around 8th Army's tank force. During the various thrusts and advances not only had the Bir el Harmat box been overrun but the headquarters of both 5th Indian and 7th Armoured Divisions had been dispersed while among the British units in the Trigh Bir Hachim and in the Knightsbridge area havoc had been created. Only at Bir Hachim itself was there still the iron resolve to hold out, and to reduce this troublesome box

Rommel ordered that an especially strong battle group be formed and that the French were to be destroyed.

During the night of 5/6 June the British and Indian forces on the Aslagh ridge had been destroyed and the losses reported to 8th Army headquarters included not only two brigades of infantry but four regiments of artillery and more than a hundred tanks. Losses on this scale could not be accepted and it was clear that the initiative was once more in German hands. This was demonstrated by the move which 15th Panzer Division made during the afternoon of 7 June when it captured the high ground north of Knightsbridge against the determined, but unco-ordinated, attacks by 22nd and by 4th Armoured Brigades. The fierce fighting of the past days had consumed a higher than normal amount of tank and artillery ammunition and the supply columns were victims of the aggressive British armoured car patrols. To combat these patrols and to ensure the safe arrival of the supply columns, Rommel detatched some of his panzer force as escort, a move which he could afford for now it was clear that the British effort was weakening. The 8th Army's attacks were becoming less strong in intensity, less frequent, and of shorter duration and among the Panzer Army staff there grew the impression that it was the British intention to draw back upon Tobruk and to commit its armour west of that town.

Upon the defenders of Bir Hachim the full force of the German attack was now concentrated. Stuka bombers attacked with monotonous regularity and the French, who had been fighting since the offensive opened, faced with bombardment from the air and from the ground, attacked by tank and infantry without cessation, had been compressed into a small perimeter. When armoured infantry from 15th Panzer Division captured a dominant feature the defence became impossible to maintain and during the night of 10/11 June the French withdrew. The evacuation of the Bir Hachim box opened the final chapter of the defeat for with its fall collapsed the British defence system. The central and southern sectors had been cleared of the British forces; only those in the Gazala sector needed to be attacked and Rommel's plan would have succeeded although its execution had not followed his time-table or sequence.

The 8th Army then pivoted back on the untouched boxes of 1st South African Division and 50th Division and formed a new line from Gazala to Knightsbridge. Once again these newly organised positions were garrisoned by infantry.

Rommel then varied his original plan by moving the area of the main thrust from west to east of Knightsbridge to intercept and catch the greatest number of the two British divisions on the northern sector. The advance began at 15.00hrs on 11 June and while 21st Panzer hemmed the battle area of the Cauldron in from the north an encircling group swung towards El Adem. This armoured fist had Trieste Division on the left wing, then 15th Panzer with the two reconnaissance battalions on its right flank, and then the motorised element of 90th Light Division. By 18.00hrs the panzer wave had reached the first objective of Naduret el Gheseauso having encountered only weak British opposition and there Rommel waited for 8th Army's counter-attack. But there was no reaction and the advance was then renewed. The 21st Panzer had, meanwhile, driven south of the box at Knightsbridge intending to attack the British armour from the rear. The battle on 12 June did not unfold with dramatic suddenness for both sides were waiting for the other to make a move. Characteristically, Rommel ordered his anti-tank gun line to close towards the British armour daring it to charge and while attention was being held there he sent the right wing of 15th Panzer Division swinging like a scythe blade towards Bir Lefa and the high ground north-west of that place. As the German tanks advanced they were opposed by tanks from 2nd and 4th Brigade and heavy fighting then ensued. At 11.00hrs, three hours after the battle opened, the 90th Light reported that it had reached El Adem and the 21st Panzer, which then came in, struck 7th Armoured Division in the flank. The whole British force was now trapped between the jaws of 15th Panzer closing in from the front and the 21st Division striking from the back. At 14.00hrs the 15th Panzer Division reported that the British front was withdrawing and two hours later announced that Bir Lefa had been taken. By last light the division had reached Point 174 on the Hagiag el Raml by which time 90th Light had attained the high ground north of El Adem. The 21st Panzer Division was given the task of covering the northern flank.

The turning point in the battle came on 12 June; the British armoured fragments had been smashed and 120 armoured fighting vehicles had been lost. The Africa Corps strength return for 11 June had given the number of runners as 124 with 60 more serving with the Italians.

Wireless intercepts indicated that the British armour had been ordered to be offensive west of the remaining boxes and in the dawn light of 13 June the 8th Army's tank regiments attacked southwards but they were seduced into the range of 8.8cm guns and destroyed. The 15th Panzer then went into a counter-attack upon Knightsbridge at 05.30hrs on 13 June but came up short against two belts of mines and remained halted while 21st Panzer, on its left flank, swung along the Rigel escarpment to the north-east of Knightsbridge. Holding position on the ridge were men of the Scots guards supported by South African field and anti-tank artillery. British armour was committed to halt the victorious advance of 21st Division's panzers but they would not be gainsaid and by 17.56hrs could report that the box on Rigel ridge had been captured.

The capture of that high ground made the defence of Knightsbridge box an impossible task and the guards brigade, or rather the remnants of it for its battle had lasted for nearly a fortnight, broke out to join the main body of 8th Army. Ritchie, the Army commander, realised that the victory which he could sense at the end of May had turned to bitter defeat. The Gazala Line would be abandoned and the Army would withdraw and rally before coming on again.

Rommel now had a clear field and flung his forces northward again to trap, within the northern sector, the South African and British divisions at Gazala. The battlefield was tidied *en route* by the destruction of the box at Eleut el Tamar, taken only after the most bitter fighting. Intercepts reported that the British were moving large bodies of troops from the boxes around Gazala eastwards.

Immediately Rommel ordered that 21st Panzer Division gain the high ground dominating the Via Balbia while 15th Panzer cut the road and held back the attempts to escape. But the opposition put up by British tank forces during the panzer advance northwards had delayed their arrival for long enough to allow the South Africans to begin their withdrawal. The 50th Division faced with blocks on the road east carved their way through the Italian 10th Corps and journeying via Bir Hachim reached the main of 8th Army. Two British boxes, those at El Adem and Acroma, were still resisting the most determined assaults of the Axis troops.

Reports reached Army headquarters at 05.00hrs that South African forces were still moving down the Via Balbia. It was clear that the night drive by the panzer divisions had been in vain. The 21st Division, which had been now cast in the role of pursuing force in the next stage of the Gazala battle, was pulled out of the line and directed upon El Adem where 90th Light and Trieste Divisions were still engaged with the British garrison. The 15th Panzer Division which took over the tasks of 21st Panzer made only slow progress against attacks from both east and west and not until evening was the coast reached. Rommel's plan had been fulfilled.

The tons of stores gathered at points throughout the desert, the half a million mines laid in the Gazala positions, and numerical superiority had proved of no avail against a commander of a force in which armour was used *en masse*. The British cavalry charges, for that is all they had been, however gallant and however destructive of the German panzers, had failed and now there was only the bitter road eastwards back to the Egyptian frontier.

Spirits in the Axis Army were jubilant. The British had been beaten in the field, their armour dispersed or destroyed, and panzer spearheads were already at El Adem, thrusting deeper and deeper past Tobruk hoping to intercept and catch the 8th Army before it could halt and regroup. German diaries and letters of that time are exultant in tone *'Angriffsziel Tobruk'* ('the target is Tobruk') or 'now it is Tobruk's turn', were recurrent themes.

Rommel's plan to capture the town was based upon the experiences which he had gathered during the unsuccessful attacks of the previous year and upon a new idea. He would bluff the British into believing that he was pursuing them into Egypt with his mobile forces and then, suddenly he would swing back and attack Tobruk from the south-east with one group, while 90th

Light Division carried the attack forward to Bardia. With only a day for re-grouping, the Axis forces were ready to continue the battle and an advance was ordered for 17 June upon Gambut. The two German and one Italian panzer divisions moved out against minimal British tank opposition and then fanned out in a race eastwards. The German commentaries on the battle describe how both Rommel and the Africa Corps commander drove the advance forward and how, for as far as one could see, the surface of the desert was covered with tanks and lorries all moving eastwards towards Egypt.

At 18.00hrs at Sidi Maftah the direction of the march changed as the armada swung northwards and Rommel ordered the pursuit to be carried out during the night to reach the sea so that the Via Balbia would be blocked by 18 June. The whole Axis panzer force was spread out, each unit making the best progress it could, while to the west the remainder of the panzer army had invested Tobruk.

It was not until 16.00hrs on 19 June that the panzer regiments of the Africa Corps moved forward and the hours of waiting had been put to good use by the workshops to carry out the maintenance necessary to keep the vehicles running. Their efforts brought the total of runners with each regiment to between 70 and 75. During the night heavy artillery had come forward into position around the town and the engineer battalion had constructed bridges across which the panzers could pass as they navigated through the anti-tank ditches and defences. The preparations to assault Tobruk had been completed and now only the hours needed to pass until zero at 05.20hrs on the morning of 20 June 1942.

Punctually to the minute the Stukas made their entrance and the crash of the explosions of their bombs was hidden by the noise of the artillery barrage. All fire, whether from land or air, was directed upon the south-eastern corner of the town. Under cover of the barrage engineers began to work on lifting mines and then the Africa Corps armour moved forward with the Italian XX Corps on its left both Corps with the same battle order 'Forward to the sea'. By 06.35hrs the barbed wire around one defensive position had been cut away by a unit from 21st Panzer Division and an hour later the 15th Panzer was able to report that they had captured a strong point on their sector of the narrow attacking front. Then, against increasingly heavy British artillery fire, two more positions fell and at 08.30hrs the 15th Panzer Division sent in the first vehicles across a bridge brought forward to span an anti-tank ditch. On 21st Panzer Division's sector German infantry swarmed across the ditches and by 08.50hrs the first tanks of that division had crossed. A break-in had been made, now the situation had to be exploited. British artillery fire and mine-fields reduced the pace of the advance but could never halt it, and, despite the use of heavy artillery and then of tanks, the Africa Corps forced its way through the British defences; for although Tobruk had a very strong garrison the defences had been run down and it was in no state to stand a new siege.

The Italian Corps had failed in its intent and was still outside the Tobruk perimeter, a situation which resulted in severe flanking fire being poured down upon the German attackers as they moved steadily forward through the maze of defensive positions. The Brescia Division was then brought forward to consolidate the battlefield behind the advancing spearheads. By midday 21st Panzer had reached an important defence point and having sent out groups to clear the ground to the east of the captured box then advanced upon Tobruk harbour. The 15th Panzer, too, had reached the Via Balbia and had turned its guns upon the town and harbour. The Italian Corps still held up outside the perimeter was then brought in behind Africa Corps and ordered to begin to roll up the British front from east to west. The pace of the advance quickened as the perimeter in which the British were imprisoned grew smaller in extent and the defensive positions were no longer able to bring cross-fire to bear upon the attacking Germans. By 17.00hrs 21st Panzer Division had begun to attack the town – by 18.30hrs the 15th Panzer Division had captured another box against a defence that held out to the last, and by 19.00hrs Fort Pilastrino had fallen. Then the harbour and town was seized together with the town's water supply.

The onset of darkness did not halt the fighting and shortly before midnight 21st Panzer had captured the El Auda area and the pumping station. All through the night detonations rocked the town as the British supply dumps were blown up and thick clouds of black smoke rolled slowly across the desert. The next morning was spent in consolidating the gains made, clearing out the last areas of resistance, and pursuing the British rearguards. No less than 33,000 prisoners were taken and sufficient supplies to nourish the next stage of the Africa Corps' advance. A fortress with a massive garrison, and large masses of supplies, and which had held out for eight months, had fallen within 40 hours. Now the way forward into Egypt was free and Tobruk, the essential harbour was in Axis hands. But then came the blow from Commando Supremo; the advance was to halt so that the forces for Malta might be assembled, and the Corps was not to pass the line Sidi Omar-Halfaya-Sollum. The 90th Light and an infantry battalion had already pushed the advance that far, had reached Bardia, and had halted at Capuzzo which was held by units of 8th Army.

A small comedy of errors was then played out in Tobruk. The British officer, who went to offer the surrender of Tobruk, was directed in error to the headquarters of the Italian Corps commander who then passed him on to the German commander. But this error was enough for Mussolini to proclaim to the Italian people that the offer had been made to the Italians, by implication that the Army had borne the greatest burden in the capture of Tobruk. To trump this Hitler promoted Rommel to the rank of field marshal whereupon Mussolini trumped his partner's ace and first Cavallero and later Bastico both received their marshal's staff.

The battle for the Gazala position had ended with the capture of Tobruk and the balance sheet showed that no less than 45,000 British soldiers had been taken prisoner, five of them generals. Nearly 1000 British tanks had been either destroyed or captured, and more than 400 guns had been taken. But this was not the end as Rommel pointed out in an 'Army Order of the Day' 'Now we have the chance to destroy the enemy absolutely. In the coming days I shall make fresh demands upon you in order that we reach our objective.'

8. The Axis tide ebbs, November 1942

'We have Tobruk, we do not need Malta'
The Chief of Armed Forces Planning Staff, June 1942

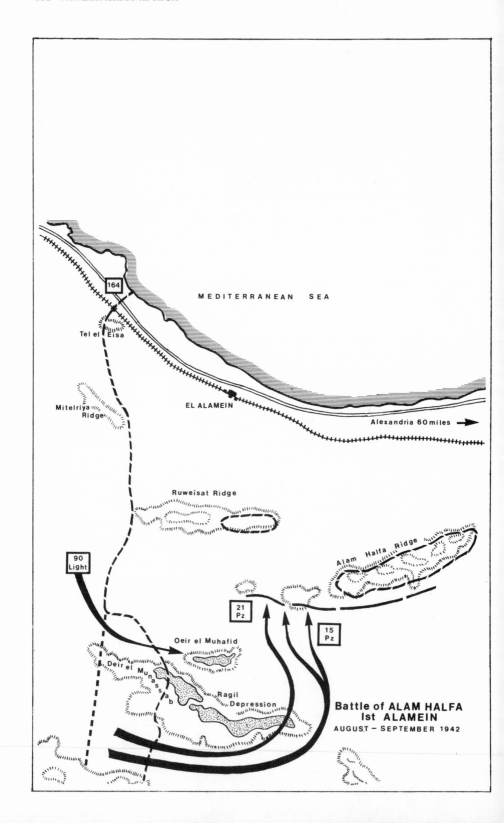

MEDITERRANEAN   SEA

164

Tel el Eisa

Mitelriya
Ridge

EL ALAMEIN

Alexandria 60 miles ➡

Ruweisat Ridge

Alam Halfa Ridge

90
Light

21
Pz

15
Pz

Oeir el Muhafid

Deir el Munassab

Ragil
Depression

**Battle of ALAM HALFA
Ist ALAMEIN**
AUGUST — SEPTEMBER 1942

The battle for Marmarica was over and on 22 June Rommel, Bastico, and Kesselring discussed the idea of a continued advance. Bastico demanded a halt in accordance with orders but Rommel, pointing to the materials which had been taken in Tobruk, said that the 8th Army was on the run and that with these supplies the pursuit could be continued. The agreement of the Axis leaders was obtained; the attack could proceed. One group thrust forward to capture Sollum and the Halfaya areas while 15th and 21st Panzer Divisions swept eastwards towards Egypt, with the Italian Motorised Corps left far behind in the tempo of their advance. The pace was exhilarating for all ranks knew that speed was of the essence and despite the weeks that they had spent in battle without rest or respite, it was with high hopes that the battle-hardened warriors of Africa Corps drove towards the wire. They crossed it at 20.30hrs but the advance was not halted and the pursuit was maintained throughout the hours of darkness.

Shortly after first light on 24 June the report was received that the British were withdrawing and the speed was increased to cut them off. The pace of the pursuit had been so furious and the columns so widespread that the supply trucks were again having difficulty in locating the columns. Water began to run short for the ration had been cut so that the vehicles could carry more petrol to bring the advance forward. Even so 21st Panzer Division's tank regiment ran out of fuel and to prevent loss of contact with the 8th Army rearguard, petrol was siphoned from other vehicles to keep the point unit mobile. The speed of the advance, the long periods without servicing, the high temperatures, and the appalling going had so affected the panzers that the drop-out rate was high and the strength of the Africa Corps dropped to 60 runners. The Italians were in little better shape: Ariete had been reduced to 10 tanks, 15 guns, and 600 Bersaglieri. The Trieste had 4 tanks, 24 guns, and 1500 Infantry.

The 8th Army was withdrawing with all speed to its prepared positions at Alamein and relied heavily upon the Royal Air Force to impede by bombing the Panzer drive. On 26th the fierce and unrelenting air attacks prevented the panzers from refuelling and neither division was able to resume the advance until 09.00hrs; four hours of daylight and campaigning time had been lost. During the following day the British rearguard near Mersa Matruh, attempting to hold back the panzer drive, was broken and in the ensuing scrimmage 90th Light cut the Via Balbia. Auchinleck took over command of 8th Army and Mussolini wired from Rome orders which included the naming of Suez as the first objective of Panzer Army. In a bid to hold the Germans west of Matruh the 1st Armoured flung in a series of attacks but these were beaten back and the British forces lost another 18 of their armoured fighting vehicles. Fighting continued all through the night of 27/28th as groups of British units, by-passed during the advance of the day, tried to fight their way out of encirclement. During the afternoon of 28th, the 21st Panzer Division had captured the high ground south-west of Fuka and then went on to seize the aerodrome and to cut the road. The advance was putting a strain on the Axis armour and the evening vehicle state showed that the Africa Corps had been reduced to only 41 runners.

Mersa Matruh fell on 29th to a thrust by 90th Light and more than 6000 prisoners were taken. With Matruh fallen the advance swept forward towards El Daba and XX Corps followed closely behind the armoured spearhead now approaching close to the Suez Canal.

Less than 2 hours drive from the point unit's position at midnight on 29 June, lay the British fleet base of Alexandria. Only 60 miles separated the African Panzer Army from the objectives for which it had been fighting for over a year but already the ground conditions were deteriorating. East of Mersa Matruh the Libyan plateau is cut by numerous steep-sided and deep wadis and the passable country begins to narrow until at El Alamein it is only 40 or so miles wide. This was a natural barrier for one flank rests on the sea and the other on the impassable sand seas of the Quattara Depression. The only route to Alexandria was across this cut-up, stony desert whose narrow width had been set with strong fortifications and extensive mine-fields. As at Gazala these fortifications were a line of mutually supporting boxes and at Alamein they pivoted around the principal box bearing that name. Into these defences streamed the remnants of 8th Army and, passing through the lines of boxes, held by fresh and untried troops the formations which had been shattered at Gazala and at Knightsbridge halted for breath and within a short time had turned, once again, at bay.

The strengths of both armies was about equal at that time, but the morale of the Panzer Army was decidedly higher than that of 8th Army for the Germans could see before them the successful end to the campaign. Leaving little time for proper planning Rommel decided to make a quick thrust in the hope of penetrating the Alamein line and planned that the heaviest blow would fall in the north while the Italian Motorised Corps carried out a feint attack in the south. A British spoiling attack came in during the afternoon of 30 June under cover of a sand-storm but 21st Panzer struck back and the British armour withdrew.

On 1 July after an all-night drive the Africa Corps was ordered into the attack at first light. Three-quarters of an hour after that time at 06.46hrs, the assault rolled with troops who were desperately tired. Rommel could see before his eyes the glittering prizes of the Middle East and drove his men on. But the British, too, realised that this was the preparation for the final battle and fought with a bitterness that was born of desperation. All through the long July day the fighting swung back and forth; the box at Bir el Schine was taken but 90th Light Division lost all its artillery without making any impression upon the British defenders. Throughout 2 and 3 July the battle continued and into the fight the British flung the Royal Air Force to carry out an intensive, almost continuous, bombardment of the Axis troops. British counter-attacks against the lost box were beaten off with a loss of 30 tanks and in 90th Light Division's sector the advance inched forward against fanatical opposition right to the edge of the British prepared defences. There the attack collapsed through sheer exhaustion and weakness; the strength of 90th Light had been reduced to only 58 officers, 247 non-commissioned officers, and 1023 men.

Rommel swung the emphasis to the central sector dominated by the Ruweisat ridge but in the south the New Zealanders had attacked the Ariete Division which broke and ran, leaving the flank open, and only a vigorous counter-attack by the panzers held the New Zealanders back. The loss of Ariete in the line reduced the strength of the Axis forces to a level at which it was no longer possible for Rommel to continue with the offensive and the assault against the Ruweisat ridge was called off on 4 July. The ensuing pause was used to regroup and to bring forward ammunition, particularly artillery shells and this piece of husbandry proved itself when a British tank force broke through the positions held by 21st Panzer, rolled over an infantry battalion, and had practically thrust through the gun line when it was brought under fire by an army artillery group and driven back with loss. An ammunition column reached the forward positions and these new supplies were able to ensure that for the immediate future the German artillery would be able to reply to British barrages, although on a much more modest scale.

The Littorio and the Ariete Divisions each had 5 tanks, 2 and 1 gun respectively, while the Africa Corps' panzer divisions had a combined total of 50 vehicles. There were only 1500 men in 90th Light's infantry component, the reconnaissance battalions had only 15 machines between them, 20 armoured trucks, and 2 batteries of guns. The Italian X Corps had 11, partly motorised battalions each of 200 men, 30 light, and 5 heavy batteries of guns. Thus, the position at the end of the first week of July was that neither side had the reserves whose commitment would have broken the deadlock. An exhausted British Army which had lost 80,000 men had halted an equally exhausted Axis army along a defensive position, which had been selected by one former commander and prepared by another.

After the necessary regrouping the Panzer Army was ready for action again and the first attacks on 9 July, against the Alamein position, went in from the south. The mine-fields were crossed, the field defences taken by storm, and a penetration of the main defensive area looked possible when a British counter-attack against the Italians on the northern sector tore Sabratha Division apart. A battle group from 15th Panzer Division closed the gap but then, on 11th, the 8th Army struck at another Italian division and destroyed two battalions of infantry. There were no reserves to commit and Rommel was forced to send in his batteries of 8.8cm guns to hold the gap until he could mount an assault upon the Australians. This counter-attack drove them back and on the central sector the Ruweisat ridge was, once again, the scene of desperate struggles to gain the high ground. During the following days the battle roared around this narrow strip of desert with the 8th Army selecting weak Italian units and destroying them one by one. On 15 July Brescia was rubbed out; two days later Trento followed Trieste and the British began the first move to roll up the German front from the south. A small sector around the Bir el Schine became the focus of the fighting as the 8th Army strove to capture the place and thus divide the Axis forces. A desperate counter-attack restored the situation but this battle of attrition could only end in German defeat unless the supply position was eased.

The appearance of both Kesselring and Cavallero upon the field of battle allowed Rommel the rare opportunity of asking them directly for supplies. Both the senior officers brought promises but no certain information. Berlin had proposed and promised so many things but high seas, strong winds, and any number of excellent reasons were given for the non-arrival of the ships. Rommel was sick at heart and his bitterness was increased at the news of the latest losses, for at the reported rate the time would soon come when the Africa Corps would no longer exist. As well as this fear of impotence was the added worry that Italian units were becoming less and less able to stand the lightest stress. There was no alternative; Rommel called off the attacks and, realising that the British commander would capitalise upon this weakness, made a point of organising personally the defence of the captured sectors. So effective were his efforts that the British probing assaults made on 23 June were flung back with a loss to the 8th Army of 146 of its tanks and 1400 of its men. Both sides now began to prepare for the trials ahead.

A heavy sense of destiny hung over the battlefield during those months of late summer and early autumn 1942. Instinctively, it seemed both sides knew that the clash for which they were preparing would be the one to decide the fate of Africa. If Rommel could revivify his exhausted soldiers and their dilapitated machines, if the magic of his personality could bring them forward once again and this time with sufficient impetus to smash through the Alamein defences, then the prizes for which he had fought lay within the grasp of his veteran warriors. But if he failed, then he and his armies were condemned to watch, with a full knowledge of its grim and awful consequences, the 8th Army increase day by day in strength and confidence until one moon-filled night a roar of guns would beat the drum roll of defeat of Axis hopes in the southern Mediterranean.

Slowly the supplies and reinforcements came into the line and by 1 August 15th Panzer Division numbered 6407 men, 65 panzers, and 36 field guns. The strength of 21st Panzer Division was a little higher with 8996 men, 68 armoured fighting vehicles, and 47 guns. To these two veteran divisions and to that of 90th Light was added a new formation, 164th Division, which had been garrisoning Crete and which had been sent across in such haste that its

6903 officers and men were without trucks of any sort.

The Italian Corps, too, were gaining strength but slowly, and X Corps had one infantry battalion on establishment for which there were no weapons available. In XX Corps only 4 of the 9 battalions of infantry were motorised and XXI Corps presented an equally depressing picture. Only the Folgore Division, the Italian parachute unit, had a satisfactory establishment of anti-tank battalions – two on establishment and both up to strength.

The losses to the Axis armies from the end of May had been average: 2908 Germans and 1338 Italians were killed or died of wounds; 9260 Germans and 11,457 Italians were wounded, and 4000 Germans went missing against 6000 Italians. The German establishment was short by 484 officers and 11,500 men. It was a depleted army which faced the growing might of Britain and her Empire.

From the German and the Italian High Commands came promises of fuel and supplies to nourish the offensive for, having accepted the need for the attack, they were now demanding action from Panzer Army Africa. Rommel stressed that the 6000 tons of fuel promised by Cavallero must arrive within two days of the promised date, otherwise the offensive would have to be postponed for a month and within that time the British would have grown too strong. The Axis armies were ready for the assault and, given the petrol, the break-through could be accomplished and the battle fought to a successful conclusion. The tanker bringing petrol was torpedoed and as an interim measure Kesselring offered to fly in fuel. A second tanker came in on 30 August and at 22.00hrs on that day the battle opened but with an alteration to Rommel's original plan and one which had more modest objectives. Rommel intended that the main effort of his new assault would be in the south and it was there that he massed the Africa Corps and two Italian divisions. Once the breakthrough had been achieved then the whole southern wing would pivot and drive northwards with the intention of trapping 8th Army in the field and there destroying it. The original plan had foreseen a wider and deeper southern drive.

The keys to the battle were two ridges and it is the more important one, whose name, Alam Halfa, records this battle in British military history. Along the central part of the front was Ruweisat ridge and this dominated the whole of the middle sector. Alam Halfa was about 10 miles to the east of Ruweisat and observation from its summit allowed its occupants to control the course of the fighting. The six Axis divisions struck at the British forces holding the southern end of the line whose farthest extremity was marked by the Himeimat ridge, a small pimple of ground but one of local tactical importance. Throughout the night of 30 August German mine-clearing teams had gapped the fields and by first light there was a space through which the armour and the infantry might pass. The tanks of the 8th Army, with the Rifle Brigade in support, flung back the first assaults but the army commander's orders were that the British Army was not to allow itself to be pinned down but was to give ground, leading the enemy on to where the armoured might of 8th Army waited on a ground of its own choosing. The pace of the Axis advance slowed against the British holding assaults but the thrust was carried to within 20 miles of Alamein. The Italian XX Corps was still stuck in the mine-fields and could give no help to the German spearhead, while on the central sector 90th Light had struck and forced back the 5th Indian Division's garrison on the Ruweisat ridge. As the armoured wedge of 15th and 21st Panzer Divisions drove northwards the tanks of 4th Armoured and 7th Motor Brigades struck at the flanks from the east while from the west came the flank assaults of 7th Armoured Division. Directly south of Alam Halfa ridge Montgomery had positioned 22nd Armoured Brigade and to support this unit there was the 10th Armoured Division. The British intention was that every step of the German advance would be contested and to help delay the panzer thrust the Royal Air Force bombed the columns by night and by day.

The fierce fighting knew no break and, indeed, grew in intensity. Generals striving to carry out Rommel's intentions died at the head of their men as they brought them forward for one more charge: Bismarck of 21st Panzer fell and Nehring, commanding Africa Corps, was wounded. Losing men and tanks but slowly gaining ground the Germans beat their way forward and in the moonlit night of 31 August the point units, having reached the 40-kilometre point east of the start line, were ordered to swing out in a wide scything movement. As the panzers were refuelled the Littorio and other Italian divisions came up slowly on to the left flank and 90th Light Division dug in to consolidate the ground which it had won. But the fuel situation was once again desperate for the ships promised by Commando Supremo had been sunk *en route*. There was no immediate prospect of another ship, the Luftwaffe could not air-transport the amounts of fuel required, and the supplies still available could not reach the battlefield in time. For the last time Rommel regrouped his depleted and exhausted troops in one, final desperate panzer assault but it died and with it died the German hopes in Africa.

The last panzer assault upon the Alam Halfa ridge had failed and now nothing remained but to withdraw the troops back behind the mine-fields and there to establish some sort of bridgehead. In the afternoon of 3 September British reconnaissance patrols reported that three large Axis columns were moving westwards. The New Zealanders, who had borne the brunt of the panzer drive moved forward to cut the mine-field gaps through which the Axis armour would have to pass and thus cut the Africa Corps off. Fierce fighting marked this final stage of the battle but the Germans held the corridors open long enough and completed the withdrawal by 5 September.

Now with the knowledge that each succeeding day would see the British growing stronger, and certain of the fact that the promised supplies would never arrive, Rommel organised *his* positions to defeat the British thrust when it came, for if Alamein was a good defensive position for the 8th Army then it was a sufficiently good position for him. It was now his task to hold out for as long as possible for there was only the road back.

The medical officer of 21st Panzer Division, writing his report on conditions in the field, remarked that cases of lice infection were being found among the troops and that rodents were making their appearance behind the lines. A later report noted an increase in dysentry cases and, as a result of the men sleeping in the open without cover or rest, there was an increase in other illnesses and diet deficiencies were responsible for the great increase in hepatitis. In order to conserve his thinning ranks Rommel ordered that the strictest camouflage measures be undertaken to hide his precious panzers from air attack. The commander-in-chief threatened to fly over divisional positions to check that his orders were being carried out and this warning was sufficient.

This enforced rest was the first break from battle that the German troops had had since Gazala four months before and not only was the opportunity taken to carry out maintenance on the vehicles and to care for the artillery but refresher courses were run and the army settled down. They would not have been soldiers if they had not grumbled and their complaints were very much those of front line soldiers everywhere. The German troops in Africa felt that they were being neglected by the artistes of the front-line theatres in favour of rear echelon units and the Luftwaffe, who had more comfortable quarters and better food. It was a well-known secret that Luftwaffe planes flew between Africa and Europe bringing back fresh vegetables and delicacies unobtainable in the southern Mediterranean.

In order to pass the time more pleasantly, regimental officers tried to obtain sports gear but found that this would have to be indented for from Italy. Entertainments at regimental level and from regimental sources were organised and the group of comedians from 104th Panzer Grenadier Regiment were very popular. Army reported that there were 12 speakers available who could talk amusingly on many subjects and issued 1200 sets of games among the troops. The 21st Panzer received musical encouragement in the shape of 8 piano accordians and among the visits received by division were the bands of 5th Panzer Regiment and 104th Panzer Grenadier Regiment. Copies of the soldiers' newspapers printed in the Mediterranean theatre of operations – *Die Oase*, *Adler von Hellas*, and *Kolonie und Heimat* – were distributed as well as guides to historic Africa and various books written by divisional officers.

During this period there were certain ceremonies for which there had been no time while on active service. The 5th Panzer Regiment received a certificate for its 500th 'kill', the Panzer Artillery Regiment No 155 for its 80,000th round fired, and the divisional bakery company for its four millionth loaf baked.

Naturally there had been planning at high level and alternatives were drawn up to the main defence plan in the event of a British breakthrough at the south or the north. The growing realisation that Italian troops were now completely unreliable produced the scheme under which the Axis forces were inter-mingled so that each major Italian formation had a stiffener of German troops either with or near it. For all the fact that they were an unreliable element the amount of shipping space taken by the Italians was out of all proportion for no less than 77,000 men of that army's total strength of 146,000 was engaged in security or in administrative duties and the allocation of space in the convoys was computed upon Italian requirements and not upon the demands of the front line. Thus the ridiculous situation arose in which Italian rear units were up to establishment in trucks while German lorries for fighting units were waiting for space on docks in Italian harbours. Not once during the first seven months of 1942 did the amount of supplies received by the Africa Corps come up to the indent figures and less than 50 per cent of the minimum requirements of 30,000 tons of fuel was received. By adopting the most draconian measures, including cutting the bread ration, the Africa Corps was able to find shipping space to bring in the battle equipment it so desperately needed. One indent for 2400 tons of fuel produced a supply – 100 tons. But not all these shortages were attributable to Italian selfishness. The Royal Navy and the Royal Air Force, had combined to strangle the armies in Africa by cutting off supplies and had had such success in sinkings that the total number of ships available to the Axis forces was 4 fast and 7 slow steamers. Even the fast ships could only make one journey each month and the slow ships had to wait for a convoy.

The despair of the senior officers of Panzer Army was best summed up in the words of Stumme who commanded while Rommel was in Germany, 'We stop one hole only to tear another hole open. Freedom of manoeuvre is for the Army an absolute necessity.' As if to underline the complete misunder-standing of the situation facing Panzer Army which was held by OKH, an order was sent that all men who had served in Africa for longer than a year were to be returned to Germany. Then, the Malta operation having been can-celled, the Ramcke Parachute Brigade, all of them specialists in parachute operations, were put into the line as ordinary infantry.

Throughout the long weeks of waiting British air supremacy kept the Germans in ignorance of the tremendous build-up of 8th Army strength but then came the first night of Alamein. A British force of 177,000 men, 2180 guns, 1110 tanks, and 700 aircraft faced an Axis force of 93,000 men, 1400 guns, 500 tanks, and 700 aircraft. The Panzer Army's 15th Panzer Division had only 3840 men, the 164th Division only 6343, 21st Panzer only 3972, and the 90th Light Division 2827 men. There were 24,173 men in the forward zone, including artillery and the flak division. Also in the front line sectors were 230 panzers with the Africa Corps and 300 with the Italians. There was

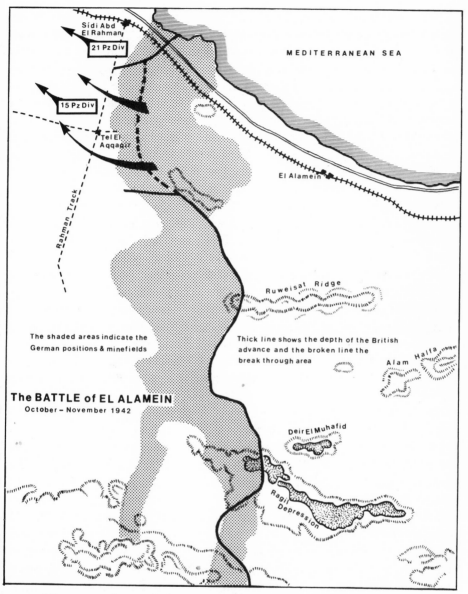

The shaded areas indicate the
German positions & minefields

Thick line shows the depth of the British
advance and the broken line the
break through area

The BATTLE of EL ALAMEIN
October – November 1942

no mobile reserve because there were neither troops, tanks, nor fuel to provide one.

The area of the 8th Army's assault and its power surprised Stumme and Rommel, who flew back from Germany immediately news came through, realised that it was too late to alter the situation. By the fourth day of battle the southern sector had to be robbed of men to fill out the northern flank and by 26 October the number of tanks with 15th Panzer had shrunk to 39 and to 98 with the 21st Panzer Division. Being less involved in the fighting the Italian tank losses had been correspondingly lighter. These figures were further reduced and on 27 October the Africa Corps had only 114 runners and the Italians 206. The losses in armour to 8th Army had been 215 machines.

The crisis in supplies was renewed and in desperation Rommel signalled to Hitler that the Army after 10 days of hard fighting against an over-whelmingly numerically superior enemy was exhausted. Shortage of petrol would condemn the non-motorised units to annihilation and even the mobile units had insufficient fuel to take them any great distance. Rommel's message concluded with the bitter forecast that Hitler must be prepared for the total destruction of the Army in Africa. The German commander had telegraphed no less than the truth for the artillery had no fuel to tow the guns and the panzer strength of the Corps had sunk to 30 machines.

Hitler's reply was characteristic: 'The German people follow with me . . . the men of the Italian and German units in their heroic battles . . . Not one step back. Victory or death.' This sort of armchair strategy did not suit Rommel who needed freedom of action. With Hitler's reluctant permission to move back to the Fuka pass came the usual promises of future supplies, including the improved 7.5cm anti-tank gun and the new 8.8cm weapon; but no immediate help could be given and in the retreat to take up the Fuka positions there were more serious losses when Montgomery's tank regiments, impatient for revenge, overhauled and smashed the less speedy Pavia, Brescia, and Folgore Divisions, wreaking such havoc that XX Corps was reduced to one weak battalion without tanks and Ariete was completely destroyed as a fighting force.

On 1 November a new and temporary front was built at Sollum and the panzer divisions held, as usual, the open desert flank against 8th Army's thrusts out of the sand seas. At every defensive line along which the Axis armies tried to halt the British advance certain situations repeated themselves. Firstly, the mobile troops would restrain for as long as possible 8th Army's assaults and appeals would be made by Rommel for permission to evacuate the non-motorised units of the Italian Army. From Hitler or from Mussolini would then come the order to hold the stated line to the last, but then they would finally give the authority to ferry back the Italian infantry to a new line. Lastly, in this series of frustrations the panzers would cover this with-drawal and conduct another fighting retreat to the next position, at which the same sequence of events would be repeated.

Rommel knew, as OKW and Commando Supremo must have known, that if the Panzer Army was to survive it must avoid a war of attrition and stay a potent force, for now there was a new menace.

On 8 November Anglo-American divisions had landed in Algeria and were racing for Tunisia aiming to cut off the Axis armies in the desert. If their drive succeeded then Panzer Army Africa and its Italian allies would be trapped, although Axis forces had been rushed to the Tunisian bridgeheads and the situation though desperate did not seem to be quite hopeless.

But in the desert it was clear that the whole of Cyrenaica would have to be abandoned and Rommel put forward a plan to dig in and to hold what line he could while the main of the Army was evacuated back to the mainland. Hitler rejected this plan and proposed to reinforce the army in Africa, supplying it with every requirement, but on the condition that the line of the Marsa el Brega position be held as a base for future operations.

The movement into these new positions was carried out in heavy rain which halted Montgomery's advance. The new defence line was a disaster. The so-called strong points were often 5 miles apart and not mutually supporting. The whole front covered 110 miles, that is a greater depth than at Alamein, with only 30,000 mines to form a barrier and with the open flank guarded by one unreliable, native battalion. Thus, with a weaker line, with fewer troops, and his losses not made good, Rommel was expected to delay the British advance indefinitely. Panzer Army was weak in numbers. From an establishment of 264 anti-tank guns there were only 12 with the troops, and only 35 of the establishment strength of 371 tanks, 16 armoured cars from a total of 60, and 12 howitzers instead of 60. The Italian divisions which had been rushed across from the mainland to replace that army's losses were without front line experience and were, therefore, nothing but a dead weight of useless mouths to feed. There was no ammunition reserve, only three days supply of fuel and the army had had no bread for a week.

In view of his weakness and so that 8th Army's blow which would come in during the middle of December would strike into a vacuum, Rommel withdrew from El Agheila back to Marsa el Brega and the point from which the Africa Corps had set out with such high hopes 18 months previously. The whole of Marmarica and Cyrenaica had been given up and there was neither a geographical obstacle nor the forces available to hold back the British advance for any great period of time. The Gabes line in Tunisia was the next and best possible natural barrier and in view of the Allied and Axis landings in that country, a withdrawal of the Panzer Army into that region could be made without infringeing French sensibilities.

Rommel demanded a withdrawal to Buerat as an interim measure only, presaging the anticipated move back to Gabes and pointed out that there would be no fuel for the portering of the Italian infantry at the height of the battle and that in such a retreat as he was proposing the speed of the slowest unit determined the pace of the whole. His force must remain mobile; there could be no question of being tied down to fight an attritive battle. It was imperative that the non-mobile infantry divisions be sent back to Buerat before the battle opened. A lost battle would mean not only the destruction of the army but that Tripolitania would be lost and the Axis' new bridgehead in Tunisia would be smashed.

Commando Supremo and OKW ordered that the Marsa el Brega position be held to the last and Kesselring who flew to Libya asserted that any with-

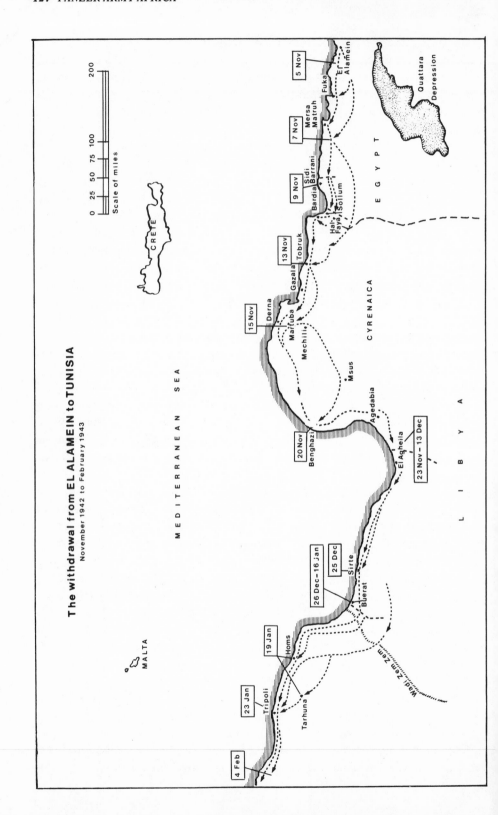

The withdrawal from EL ALAMEIN to TUNISIA
November 1942 to February 1943

drawal to Buerat would encourage an Allied attack. To this Rommel bitterly replied that, whether his army was rolled over and destroyed in the Marsa el Brega or in the Buerat position was irrelevant, unless he had freedom of action he could do nothing to stop the Allies winning the war in Africa within the shortest possible time. The strength of the Africa Corps was reduced to 54 panzers, 18 armoured cars, and 66 anti-tank guns, his men were sleeping in the open in pouring rain in mid-winter, and the rations had been cut and cut again. German losses alone during the month of November had been 1122 killed and 3885 wounded. If the Panzer Army was to hold the positions demanded by OKW and the Commando Supremo then each German battalion would be holding a front of two miles and there would be no reserve. Rommel demanded the supplies which Hitler had said he would send and the Führer promised them all again but demanded as his price that Tripoli would be held. Political necessity as well as military requirement demanded the maintenance of the largest possible bridgehead on the African coast.

It was clear that Hitler still saw the African theatre of operations as two separate battles whereas Rommel considered that his Panzer Army and 5th Panzer Army in Tunisia formed a single combat zone. In a conference with the Führer Rommel repeated the advantages which a withdrawal to the Gabes line inside Tunisia would bring, whereas the only advantage of the Buerat line was that it gained time to allow the Gabes feature to be properly manned. Rommel's arguments were coldly logical and their conclusions inescapable. The withdrawal began even as 8th Army's carefully prepared advance began its forward movement. First the Italian infantry was evacuated and then in the bitter winter weather of 13 December the remaining panzers moved westward again. But once again the critical shortage of fuel held the panzers prisoner and they were threatened with encirclement by the swift-moving 7th Armoured Division. In the nick of time supply columns reached the armour and enabled the panzer regiments to fight their way through the British ring, battling now with the despair of a forlorn hope and with the bitter knowledge that their Supreme Commander Hitler had dismissed their efforts and had ignored their urgent needs.

Without fuel and lacking the supplies which the Führer had promised, Rommel could not hope to hold the Buerat position and once that line had been abandoned then Tripolitania would have to be evacuated if the Army was to be saved. In desperation the German commander asked for permission to march back to Gabes and received Mussolini's bombastic reply 'Buerat will be held to the last'. With only 38 panzers in action, a further 12 in the Buerat line, and 10 without fuel in Tripoli, there was little that the Panzer Army could do to fight a defensive battle. On 29 December the 8th Army stood ready to assault the Axis positions. A crisis conference attended by the senior German and Italian commanders from the mainland demanded that Mussolini's orders be respected but Rommel pointed out that the length of time that the Buerat position could be held depended less upon him and his Army than upon the British and theirs. There were 30,000 Italian troops who were a dead-weight and their transport from defence line to defence line used petrol which the panzers needed. Of the daily minimum requirement of 400 tons only an average of 152 tons arrived. The panzer arm was operating with only 20 per cent of its establishment and the infantry was 50 per cent below its requirements. There were two lines of defence along which minimal resistance could be offered: Homs–Misurata and the final perimeter around Tripoli. This was the last chance to save the army from destruction. The evacuation from Buerat began on 3 January; once again Rommel's logic had proved to be irrefutable.

In Tunisia the dangerous military situation compelled von Arnim, commanding 5th Panzer Army, to ask for one of Rommel's infantry divisions to be withdrawn from the line and sent to occupy Sfax against any Allied move from the Kasserine sector. Rommel appealed to Hitler against this demand and was ordered to send 21st Panzer but was instructed to withdraw the tanks from that unit and hand them over to 15th Panzer Division. That division withdrew and as the Axis forces pulled back from the Buerat position on 15 January they could see from the Tarhuna heights the fires which marked where 18 tanks of Centauro Division had been blown up to prevent them falling into British hands. Other pillars of smoke indicated where lorries for which there was no petrol had been destroyed. The German observers of that sad scene would also have seen spread before and below them a panorama of the whole of 8th Army's armoured might as it moved towards the Tarhuna pass. Against the full weight which Montgomery could commit to battle the Panzer Army Africa could send in only 23 panzers and 16 Italian tanks. Then, as this last remnant battled with the British, a telegram was received from Mussolini complaining that the Buerat position had been abandoned prematurely.

From the direction of Montgomery's thrust Rommel appreciated that the British intention was to bypass Tripoli and then to wheel inwards. Thus the Germans would be pinned with their backs to the sea. They would be cut off from Tunisia and the whole of the southern Tunisian flank would stand open to 8th Army's direct assault. He signed the order to evacuate Tripoli with a heavy heart for he realised that this meant to his Italian allies the end of the empire but Rommel knew that if he was to save the Panzer Army then there was no other decision he could make.

With the evacuation of Tripoli and the withdrawal into Tunisia the desert campaign came to an end but in the northern bridgehead Rommel still hoped that there might be more hopeful prospects and that a position could be held from which, with the promised reinforcements and fresh supplies there might one day again burst forth from the confines of the Tunisian bridgehead a reborn Panzer Army Africa.

9. The Tunisian bridgehead, November–December 1942

'Send a staff officer. One with wide red stripes on his breeches'
Kesselring, November 1942

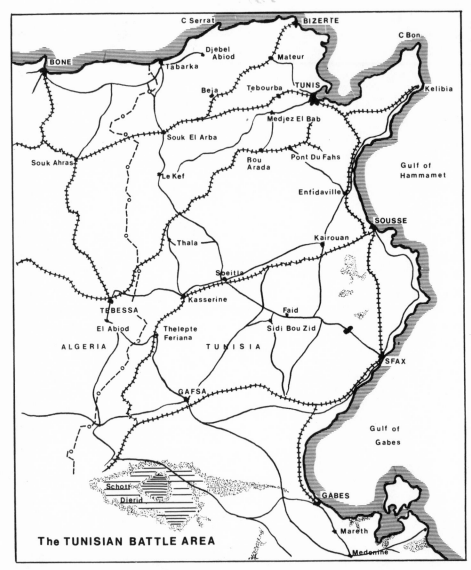

The TUNISIAN BATTLE AREA

TUNISIAN PRELUDE

During the late summer of 1942 the attention of the western Allies as well as that of the OKW was directed towards the western Mediterranean in general and upon the North African colonies of France in particular.

The Anglo-Saxons were concerned to relieve pressure upon the Russians by mounting a so-called Second Front but the British, aware that Allied forces were at that time too weak to undertake successfully a landing and a campaign in north-west Europe, suggested other alternatives. In a memorandum President Roosevelt offered his military chief of staff three options. The top priority was given to the idea of a landing in French North Africa and by a rapid advance eastwards to cut off the enemy armies in the desert. The second option was for the Americans to link up with the British 8th Army in Tripoli and by joint action defeat Rommel and his Italian allies. Finally there was the option of landing in France and then establishing in the southern part of that country a bridgehead out of which, at some future date, reinforced Allied armies would burst in a campaign of liberation. But whatever the choice Roosevelt's order was that an offensive operation on land, and in the European theatre of operations, had to be launched during 1942. As Commander-in-Chief he committed the United States to the first option. Reluctantly the American chiefs of staff agreed; French North Africa was to be invaded.

That this undertaking, code-named Operation Torch, would entail an armed assault upon the territory of a neutral nation was dismissed. The fact that the Axis powers had so completely respected French neutrality, that there was no German or Italian soldier stationed in any of the French possessions, was considered a positive advantage, for thus there would be no opposition to overcome on the road to Tunis. Further to smooth the path of the invaders secret service agents had contacted French officers and civilians loyal to the Allied cause and on the basis of their reports it was anticipated that resistance to the attack would be minimal. It was further expected that both the native population and the French colonial settlers would welcome the Allied forces as liberators, although as liberators from what or from whom was never made clear.

General Eisenhower was appointed to command this first offensive undertaking by the American Army in the western hemisphere and the choice of an American commander was intended to convey to the French in North Africa who may have had anti-British feelings, the totally false impression that Operation Torch was an entirely United States operation.

There were four strategic areas which the western Allies could have chosen as target areas but only two had the qualifications necessary for the success of a major naval and military operation. Of these two we can ignore the landings in western Algeria. We are concerned only with the assault upon eastern Algeria, and upon the Allied formations which debarked upon the shores of that region. The troops of that Anglo-American force were directed to thrust towards Tunisia and to seize the principal towns of Tunis and Bizerta. The capture of these major ports as well as that of less important harbours would bring an Allied army into position behind the Axis troops, at that time fighting in Tripoli, and thus between those troops and the ports from which they might make their escape to the mainland of Europe. The success of Operation Torch would make the question of whether the Axis or the Allies won the war in Africa academic. All that was needed, so it seemed to the Allied planners, was to race for Tunis sweeping aside any weak resistance from the Germans or Italians who might be encountered on the way.

Adolf Hitler, reviewing the strategical situation from his headquarters, came to the conclusion that if there was to be an Allied landing then this would take place either on the islands of Sardinia or Corsica, or possibly in southern France. The Führer excluded North Africa completely from the possible targets for a sea-borne assault. German naval headquarters in the Mediterranean was not so confident, and, anticipating Allied landings, had drawn up plans for U-boat action against these. By a coincidence the Axis planners, as early as July 1942, chose as the most likely debarkation points those areas along the French North African shore which the Allied strategists themselves had selected. As U-boat strength in Italian waters was not enough to mount a whole series of widespread assaults against the ships of the Allied armada and was too weak to cover all possible target areas, a pair of intercept patrol lines was charted in the waters of the western half of the Mediterranean sea across which the Allied ships would have to sail to their landing areas and along which they could be attacked.

Reports reaching German naval headquarters which spoke of a concentration of shipping in Gibraltar were misinterpreted by Axis supreme commands, as was later intelligence of this build-up as a major convoy to Malta. But then reports reaching Rome brought graver and reliable news so that by 4 November it was clear that the naval preparations which the Allies were making presaged an invasion of North Africa. The evidence convinced both Mussolini and Kesselring, the German Supreme Commander South, but Hitler still clung to his beliefs of a landing upon Corsica or Sardinia, although on 6 November he did send a signal to the senior German naval officer in the Italian waters telling him that the fate of the army in Africa depended upon the destruction of the Gibraltar convoy and demanding from the U-boat crews relentless and victorious action.

During the night of 6/7 November every submarine which could be pressed into service headed westwards to the patrol lines, on an intercept course with the Allied convoy of 190 ships which was now sailing, completely blacked out, through the waters of the Mediterranean.

At 04.00hrs on the morning of 8 November the Allied assault opened at selected points along the Algerian coast and continued throughout the day. In some areas there was little or no opposition but in others there were French naval forays of such ferocity that the intervention of American heavy naval units was required to overcome them. By the morning of the following day an Allied army was ashore and was streaming along the roads towards Tunisia.

Hitler received the news of the invasion while at a wayside railway station *en route* to Munich and his immediate decision was to hold Tunisia. There would be no retreat. As a first reaction he offered air support to help Vichy France (the French under Pétain) in its defence of the North African possession and under cover of this offer Luftwaffe units began to move into Tunisia during the night of 9 November. Meanwhile a telephone conversation between Hitler and Kesselring had taken place.

To answer the question on the number and type of troops which could be rushed without delay to bar the Allied advance, Kesselring could reply that only two battalions of Lieutenant-Colonel Koch's 5th Parachute Regiment and his own headquarters defence battalion were immediately available. 'Fling in everything you can', was the Führer's dramatic command. The orders for their despatch went out to the units on standby and then Kesselring's staff officers swung into a long-planned routine; the transport of a complete division from the strategic reserve in Sicily. But the German Supreme Command did not have the same view of Mediterranean strategy as Kesselring and, determined not to infringe French neutrality, refused to allow this stand-by division to be deployed to Tunisia. Not until 24 hours after the first Allied landings had taken place did Kesselring receive from Hitler the powers he needed, but even then the French authorities were handled with extreme delicacy. Permission was sought and obtained from Marshal Pétain allowing the German troops to move into Tunisia.

Then began what has been described by some German military commentators as 'the poor man's war'; for with only a small force of troops, one wing of fighter aircraft, and a general without a staff, the German forces which had begun to land in Tunisia were ordered to stop the advance of the onrushing Allied troops by forming a bridgehead with a short, defensible perimeter and situated at an adequate distance from the main ports of Tunis and Bizerta.

Either as a bluff or as a piece of absolute cynicism Kesselring commented that a general should be sent to Tunisia – one with the wide red stripes of the general staff on his breeches – for his presence would be reported back to Eisenhower via the intelligence network, and who on the Allied side would believe that a German general could be sent into the field without the necessary troops for him to command. On the evening of 8 November, General Nehring was recalled from convalescence and ordered back to Africa. But not to his old command, for in Rome fresh orders awaited him. He was to take charge of operations in the Tunisian area and was quickly briefed on the task he had been given.

The terrain over which the battles of the next six months were to be fought was hilly, almost mountainous, particularly in the west and in the north-western frontier area where it bordered Algeria. To the east and to the south the ground became more flat, leading to a plain, and in some areas there was marsh. In the valleys between the western hills and on the plain there was extensive cultivation but the hills themselves were bleak and covered with scrub. The lie of the land favoured the defence for the high ground ran in a general north-easterly direction and the defenders would withdraw from peak to peak while denying the valley roads to an Allied advance. This was particularly the case on the eastern side of the country where the Mediterranean formed one flank which could not be turned. On this coastal side of

Tunisia the mountains reached, at some places, almost to the sea and thus formed narrow gaps across which the Axis armies formed defensive lines.

The Tunisian road network was poor both in number and durability and only the few macadamised highways could be used in the rainy period which extended through the winter and into spring, by unhappy coincidence, the two seasons of the campaign. In the winter the principals were torrential rain creating mud and destroying the secondary roads, and low cloud, which curtailed combat flying, and bitter cold which could not be escaped by the infantry since the hills in which they had to live were generally devoid of man-made or even natural cover. By the middle of March the returning warm weather dried out the ground allowing wheeled movement off roads. There was much horticulture, with orchards of olive trees, cork forests, wheat and fruit growing. The cactus bush was everywhere and was used widely to form hedges, particularly around the larger, French-owned farms. When the Germans took over these buildings and prepared them for defence the cactus formed a natural type of barbed wire entanglement and helped to turn these farms into fortresses, almost unassailable by infantry and armour.

The few strategic and all-weather roads extended from the capital or from the principal port of Bizerta westwards towards Algeria, south-westwards to Kairouan, or southwards to Tripolitania. The junctions of roads were of strategic importance and whoever controlled these and the towns which had grown up around them dictated the course of the fighting. As this narrative of the events which took place in Tunisia between November 1942 and May 1943 unfolds then the names of those towns and villages which were important to the campaign will become familiar: Beja, Mateur, Tebourba, Kasserine, Enfidaville, and Medjez el Bab. It is this last named place which was the key to the whole campaign and its capture by the British opened the great offensive which finally brought the war in Africa to a close.

Roads, then, and particularly road junctions were strategically important but it was not necessary to have troops on the highway itself; possession of high ground overlooking the road produced the same result. Thus each side fought to attain or to eject the other side from the mountains or the valley road.

The population of Tunisia was predominantly Arab with a large number of French inhabitants, both military and civilian, and a lesser but still sizeable Italian contingent. These latter hoped for an Axis victory and many were called up to serve in locally raised Italian regiments. The French were divided into those who supported the western Allies and those whose sympathies lay with the Government of Marshal Pétain. The Arabs had no strong feelings and were capable of betraying British soldiers to the Germans and German positions to the British with complete impartiality.

The Tunisian campaign can be seen to fall into three distinctive phases. In the first of these, lasting from the Allied landings to the end of December, there

Top: The crew of an Italian 11/39
Ansaldo tank, the principal armoured
fighting vehicle in service with the
Italian Army

Left: The artillery forward observation
officer watching the fall of shot from
his sangar in Tunisia—1943

Above: A Panzer III in action against
British armour in the Gazala battle

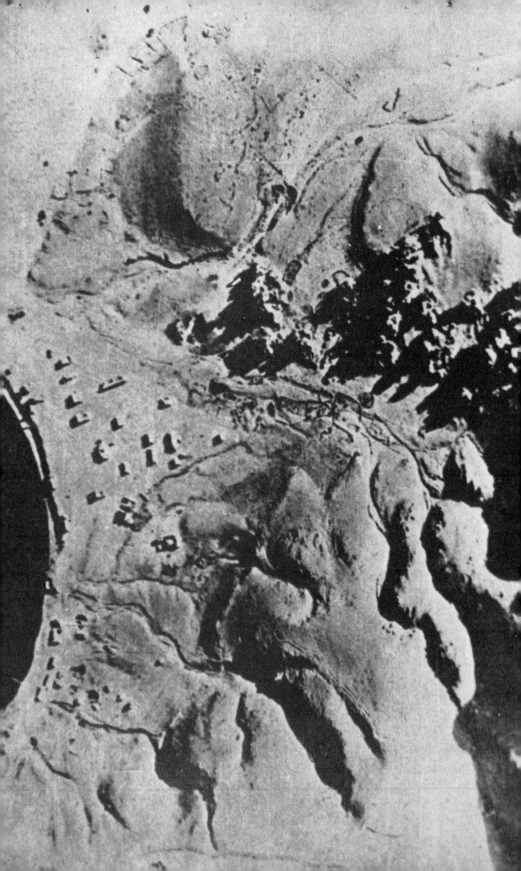

Left: An aerial view of Halfaya Pass under bombardment by Axis aircraft

Above: Burying the dead —men of a 17cm gun crew holding a funeral service for one of their fallen comrades

Right: An SdKfz 251 armoured personnel carrier and an MG 34 mounted in an anti-aircraft role

Top left: A heavy field howitzer 15cm sFH 18 taking up position

Bottom left: Rommel and his staff visiting the battle area—1941

Above: Field artillery in action—a 10.5cm lFH 18—1941

Right: A 15cm heavy howitzer sFH 13 mounted on a French Lorraine chassis, and used as a self-propelled gun, moving forward at Alamein

Above: An 8.8cm gun in a well constructed defensive position near Alamein

Left: An Italian gun crew manning a German 15cm field howitzer near Tobruk

Right: Light field artillery supporting an infantry attack—1941

Following page: The grave of a German corporal killed on 2 July 1942

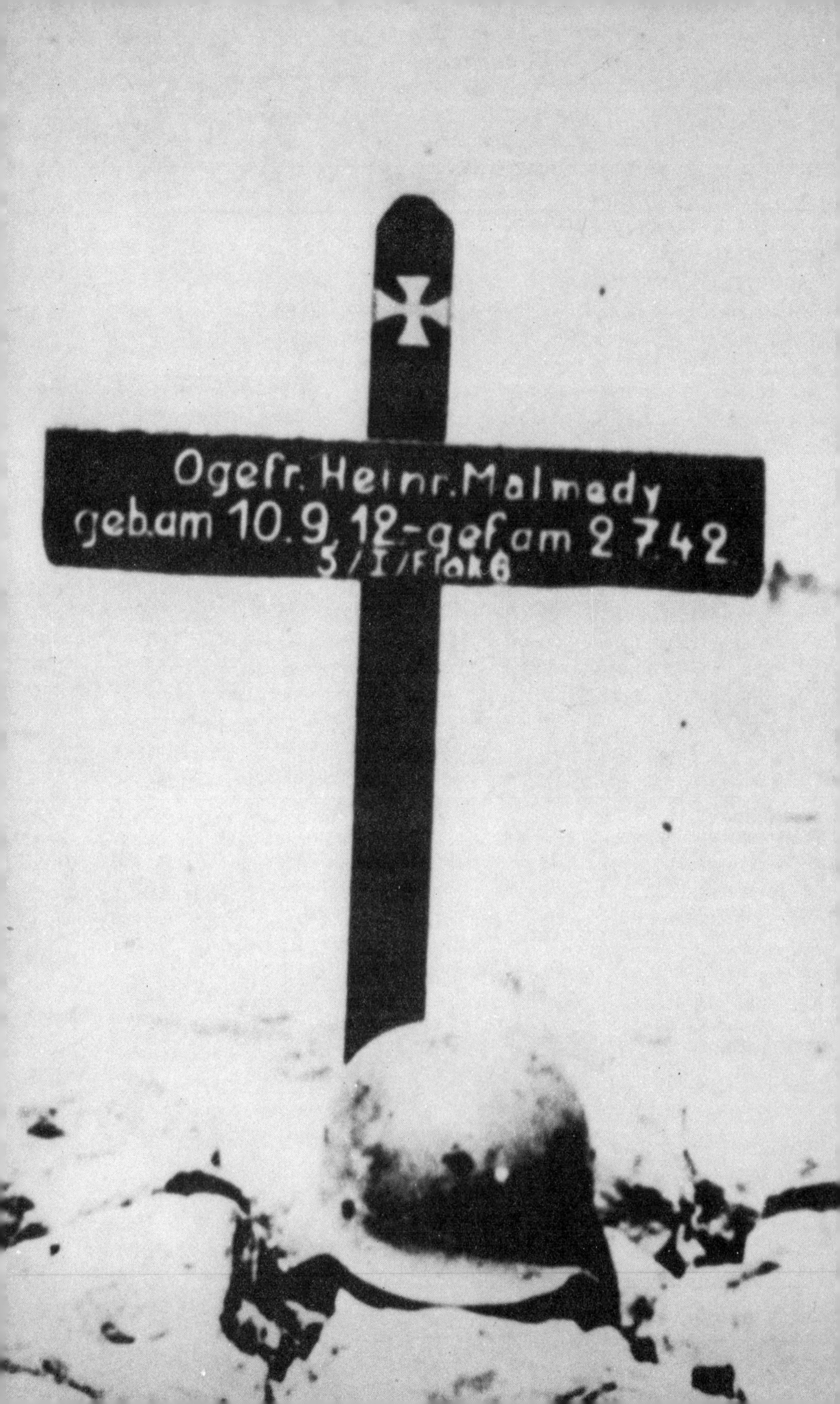
Ogefr. Heinr. Malmedy
geb.am 10.9.12 - gef.am 2.7.42
5/I/Flak6

was a race to obtain tactically and strategically important positions. During this first period the descents upon Tunisia by both sides were followed by a thrust made by a force, mainly British in content, and aimed at the capture of Tunis and Bizerta. A German counter-attack drove back the weak Allied force and a line was formed along which there was for some time a stalemate.

The second phase began with a resumption of the German offensive aiming to expand the bridgehead area. These attacks lasted until April and within this period there was the major assault upon the American forces forming the right flank of the Allied army in Tunisia. When the United States' forces drove back Rommel's panzer thrust they joined hands with the British 8th Army which had entered Tunisia from the south and thus formed a noose around the Axis armies.

The third phase saw the build-up of strong Allied forces, the tightening of the noose, the switching of some 8th Army Divisions to the 1st Army, and the final thrust from Medjez el Bab which smashed the Germans and their Italian allies.

When compared to the battles of the Titans which were being fought in Russia the events in Tunisia seem of small proportion. The whole Axis force which fought there was not even half the size of any one of the army groups fighting on the eastern front, but it was a campaign that was significant for it showed that the Anglo-Saxon Allies had the capability and the knowledge successfully to mount a major sea-borne invasion. This fact was not lost upon the German High Command who as early as February 1943 telexed an *Abwehr* appreciation that further sea-borne landings could be expected to take place during March in the Mediterranean area and aimed either at Sicily, Crete, Sardinia, or Corsica.

The Tunisian campaign also 'blooded' the green Americans enabling both the leaders and the led to learn the business of war at combat and at command levels. These lessons they then applied to the fighting which was carried out in Sicily and in Italy where the terrain was much the same as Tunisia. As a military parallel the war in Tunisia was, by accident, to the Allies the same sort of testing ground that Spain had been for the Axis forces.

If the Allies learned much to their future advantage as a result of the fighting in Tunisia then the German and Italian troops were to learn the bitter lesson of their vulnerability to Allied air power. By early spring this superiority had driven the Luftwaffe from the skies which it had dominated from the earliest days of the fighting and left, naked to the American and British air attacks, the transport aircraft lumbering slowly through the skies above the Mediterranean and the Axis merchant ships steaming their way through its waters. Both ran an Allied gauntlet and suffered terrible losses. It has been calculated that at the bottom of the sea lie more than twice as many tanks as the desert and Tunisian armies ever received.

Other than the experience of the loss of air cover the fighting in Tunisia provided no new experience for the Germans. Their flexibility in the matter of battle groups, their ability to improvise, the exploitation of time and means to overcome shortages and difficulties were no new phenomena. Only at highest command level was there hesitation and lack of direction. At medium and junior level, as well as at that of the ordinary soldier there was a determination to do the job well, and in this they succeeded.

In a campaign which lasted six months it would not be possible to describe in so few words as this book contains each or every major action. Some are more important or interesting than others and it is these which have been selected to represent the whole. The period covering the landings, the thrust and the riposte leading up to the battle of Longstop Hill in December 1942, is the first to be described. Then follows an account of the fighting in which the Axis forces tried to expand their bridgehead during which period there occurred the action by 10th Panzer Division at Sidi Bou Zid which led to the battle of Kasserine Pass.

THE PRELIMINARY ENCOUNTERS

By this time the desert army of Erwin Rommel and the panzer army of von Arnim had combined in a prickly partnership with each leader having different ideas of how to conduct operations. British pressure by 8th Army on the southern Tunisian front led to the evacuation of successive defensive positions and illustrating these actions is the account of the fighting by 164th Infantry Division in the Schott and the Enfindaville lines.

The final phase of the war in Africa is covered in a description of the engagements in which 999th (Africa) Division took part on the western front of Tunisia. This division was made up of men convicted for military crimes; desertion, insubordination, striking a superior, and neglect of duty. Only through battle could these men win back their military honour and, although their unit never reached full strength but was made up of individual battle groups, the men served loyally and bravely winning back not only their own self-respect but more important still the respect of their military comrades.

To the desert veterans of both sides the war in Tunisia was completely different to that which they had fought in Egypt and Cyrenaica. The rocky mountains of Tunisia limited the horizons of the men who had come up out of Egypt. For the men of the old Africa Corps there would be no longer the exhilarating hundred-mile advances; no more the battlefield restricted to a 50-mile wide strip of desert south of the Via Balbia; no more the goals of Alexandria and the Suez canal to spur them on. Instead there were the eternal bare hills or djebels, the ever-vigilant OPs, and an awareness to every soldier of the Axis armies that with defeat Tunis would become the first of a series of stepping stones leading on to Sicily, from thence to the mainland of Italy and, finally, to Germany and to the defeat of the German–Italian Axis.

On 8 November, the day of the Allied landings, an *ad hoc* collection of remnants from Ramcke's Para Brigade was formed into Battle Group Sauer and flown to Tunisia to secure the airfields at La Marsa and at El Aouina. Fighter aircraft of 53rd Geschwader touched down on 9 November and these first 27 machines were followed by 24 JU 87 Stuka dive-bombers. On successive days JU 52 and ME 323 machines came in bringing supplies, light anti-aircraft guns, and the two battalions of Koch's 5th Para Regiment. These landings met with no resistance from the French for diplomatic negotiations had ensured that the Germans would not be met as enemies.

Colonel Harlinghausen of the Luftwaffe was given overall command of the Tunis lodgement area and Colonel Lederer assumed the same powers in the perimeter around Bizerta. Once these bridgeheads had been consolidated then began the build-up of the forces and, to effect this, all available means of sea and air transport were switched from supplying Rommel's army to the reinforcement of the Tunisian front. So efficient was this organisation that by 12 November, two Italian ships had docked at Bizerta and within three weeks nearly 2000 men, 160 armoured vehicles, 127 pieces of artillery, and over 1000 soft-skinned vehicles, in addition to other military supplies, had been brought in by sea alone. Germany was fortunate in having a pool of transport aircraft and these were used to air-land reinforcements at a rate of nearly 1000 each day. By the end of November more than 15,000 troops had been air-lifted into the two perimeters.

As these new troops arrived they were fitted into gaps in the bridgehead, irrespective of regimental or national allegiance. Two infantry battalions from the Italian Superga Division were among the first to arrive and came under command of Battle Group Sauer. By such draconian methods, and as early as 14 November, the sector Tunis South had been secured. With a firm base line the German commanders could fling out battle groups westwards to gain ground and to seize important tactical positions. Koch's paratroops moved out in an advance to contact and hoped that this would not take place until they had established bridgeheads across the Medjerda river at Jedeida, Tebourba, and Medjez el Bab. Between the Allies and the Axis there was to be a race to see who could bring the stronger force to the decisive point in the fastest time and, although the Axis powers had reacted quickly, the western Allies had not been inactive nor unimaginative.

A British paratroop attack had captured Souk el Arba and the British force went on towards the important road centre of Beja. A British sea-borne landing had captured the ports of Bougie and Bone and had brought two brigades of the British 78th Division to within 140 miles of Bizerta. The next obvious objective for both sides was the town of Medjez el Bab, the gateway to Tunis. In the several sectors at which they were disposed during the night of 16 November the Axis and the Allied soldiers prepared themselves for battle. With the next day possibly, within the next two days certainly, contact would be made with the enemy and the battle for Tunisia would begin.

General Nehring's return to Africa on 14 November was dramatic in that his aircraft crashed on landing and was totally wrecked. Determined not to let this accident upset his plans he called conferences in Tunis and Bizerta and, before returning to Rome to make his own assessment of the situation to Kesselring, he ordered that the troops in the Bizerta area be pushed westwards from Mateur to Tabarka to frustrate the British drive from Bone.

Nehring's opinion of the general situation was that the Allies had landed between 5 to 6 divisions in the initial assault and that this number had increased by a regular flow of reinforcements to a strength of between 9 and 13 divisions. On the German side there was no complete formation, excepting only the two paratroop battalions. There were so few troops that there was no real continuous line but a chain of outposts defending the two main towns of Tunis and Bizerta. Behind this outpost chain there were two strategic areas – Mateur and Tebourba – around which there was grouped a small reserve whose task it would be, should the Allies break through, to delay their advance and to protect the disembarkation of the Axis reinforcements. The only real mobile reserve available to Nehring was a panzer company in Tunis and in Bizerta and these belonged to a panzer battalion which had been on its way to reinforce Rommel.

With such forces General Nehring realised that he could never halt but only delay any strong Allied assault and indeed, if we may anticipate the course of events, we shall see that the Allied thrusts which began on 21 November caused such alarm that the Germans were preparing to burn their secret files. It seemed to the German commanders at that time that their forces would be in occupation of Tunisia for only a few days and that the length of their stay would depend upon the speed and power of the Allied advance and the defensive ability of the Axis forces. But Nehring was too old a soldier not to realise that even with massive reinforcement a German victory was no longer possible and that the most his troops could do was to delay the inevitable Allied victory.

The problems facing Nehring were daunting in the extreme. He had no staff of officers to help him run his embryo Corps and he asked for the senior staff of 10th Panzer Division to be sent to Tunis to command the splinter groups which he nominally led and to establish a military system. There was neither radio nor signals equipment for HQ Nehring, as his command was called, and no transport. Strategically the situation was even more desperate. Nehring saw that the Allies' successful landings had given them the military initiative and that he must prepare for Eisenhower's forces to make the next move. This could be either a direct thrust for the principal objectives of Tunis and Bizerta thereby strangling the supply line to Rommel. Alternatively, part of the Allied armies could strike for the Gabes Gap, and thus contain Rommel while the main striking force of the Allied army attacked Sicily. Alternatively, the main thrust could drive from Gabes to the sea and thus separate the forces in Tunisia from those in Tripolitania while a smaller force contained the Axis armies in northern Tunisia. Thereafter, the 8th Army in the desert and the Allied armies in Tunisia could destroy the Italian-German armies piecemeal.

Nehring saw that his only counter lay in converting Tunisia into a strong area into which Rommel could withdraw his African army. This then, linked with the forces which he had been promised would arrive from Europe, would enable him to convert Tunisia into a wound in the Allied side. By switching his forces he could counter any assault in the north or south by threatening the flank of the attackers. But even more important was the supply route to Rommel's army and, with the expected loss of the port of Tripolitania, only the Tunisian harbours remained open and they were the nearest to Sicily and to Italy. But the political situation had to be regularised. Permission to enter and to transit through Tunisia was not sufficient; militarily he must occupy the country. For his part Kesselring aided the movement and on 16 November, in the interests of military administration, formed out of HQ Nehring the XC Corps with Nehring as General Officer Commanding and having power over German and Italian military forces in the Tunisian area.

Although the naval and air forces of Germany and Italy were not under Nehring's control the paratroop battalions – technically on Luftwaffe establishment – and two battalions of Italian San Marco Marines were assigned to him. The composition of the small force which had been dignified with the title of XC Corps was part of 5th Para Regiment, the Barenthin Para Regiment, of which at that time only Witzig's Para-Engineer Battalion was available, a battery of four 8.8cm flak guns, a reconnaissance squadron of six-wheeled armoured vehicles each armed with a 7.5cm cannon, and an infantry replacement battalion. The Italian component, in addition to the two battalions of marines already mentioned, was two battalions of infantry from Superga Division which had been rushed across from the mainland of Europe. Everything else was formed on an *ad hoc* basis. In the absence of signals equipment the Axis forces were forced to rely upon the French Post Office to maintain communication with their forward units. Until military vehicles arrived from Europe civilian lorries had to be hired to maintain the supply system and there was no military medical organisation; for the first months the sick and lightly wounded were treated in civilian hospitals. Even Nehring's driver was not German but a captain of Italian extraction serving on the French Army reserve. With this insufficient and un-coordinated force Nehring's orders were to strike for the Algerian–Tunisian border and to establish good defensive positions on the western side of the hills there. At all costs the Allies must be prevented from gaining observation points from which they could dominate eastern Tunisia. High ground was to be the key to success in the forthcoming battles.

The attitude of the French in Tunisia was dichotomatic. The senior officers of the services were either wholly or partially loyal to the Vichy French Government of Marshal Pétain which had concluded an armistice with the Axis in 1940. Many of these officers and their civilian counterparts were prepared to tolerate and, in some cases, support actively an Axis occupation of the French North African territories. Other officers, particularly in the lower echelons of the military hierarchy, were pro-Allied and hoped to prevent an Axis occupation by delaying the Germans and the Italians and by allowing unhindered passage to the Allied armies.

Certainly the troops of Koch's paratroop spearhead had found the delaying tactics of the French quite exasperating. It was important for the German commander to know the French intention; whether General Barre was intending to remain neutral and passive or whether he was determined to go over to the Allies and deny to the Germans access to the bridgeheads across the Medjerda river. The area which his division was holding was of strategic importance and delay in clarifying the situation was of benefit to the Allies and a disadvantage to the Germans. French senior military officers deferred conversations between the paratroop officer delegation and the commanding general until leading elements of British troops, men of 6th Battalion the Queen's Own Royal West Kent Regiment, had entered and occupied Beja. The British 78th Infantry Division at that time comprised almost the whole of the Allied fighting strength in northern Tunisia and one of its Brigades, the 36th, was advancing as a left-hand column upon Bizerta, spreading a thin film of troops across the countryside.

The head of the column, the striking point, was aiming at Djebel Abiod and the important road junctions, in that place, of the Bone–Beja, and Bone–Bizerta highways. A second brigade of 78th Division, the 11th Infantry Brigade, was advancing along the Beja road towards Medjez el Bab with the ultimate intention of thrusting towards Tunis. Supporting the two British infantry brigades was an Anglo-American motorised and armoured unit called Blade Force. The Allied fist with two fingers thrusting towards the enemy's vitals was preparing to strike.

The first major clash between the British and the Germans in Tunisia happened during the early afternoon of 17 November, when Major Witzig's battle group advanced upon Abiod from Mateur, aiming to reach Tabarka. His column was made up of two paratroop companies from the Para-Engineer Regiment's 11th Battalion, a squadron of 15 Panzer IVs, two Italian SP guns, a troop of 2cm flak guns, and a battery of 10.5cm cannon.

At Abiod three rifle companies of the West Kents, supported by a troop of 25-pounder guns and elements from 5th Battalion The Northamptonshire Regiment, were in position and dug in around the houses on the eastern side of the small town. The British infantry held fire even as the vehicles of the German battle group rolled past the houses and not until the 25-pounders opened up at almost point-blank range did the battle open. With the first shots some of Witzig's tanks were destroyed and the column was brought to a halt. The lorry-borne paratroops debussed and formed a firing line in front of the town while others raced for high ground and the artillery began a bombardment of the British positions. Under this barrage the soft-skinned vehicles were withdrawn. Witzig flung out a small infantry group to probe the British defences while the 2cm flak gun, which had halted and taken up position on the road, opened fire and poured a barrage into and upon the West Kent positions until a direct hit from a 25-pounder shell smashed the weapon and killed the crew.

Towards evening the firing died away and both sides took stock of the situation. Witzig had lost eight of his tanks and had failed to take the road junction but his infantry was on the important high ground and he was, therefore, in a superior tactical position. He could feel content; his small force may not have reached its given objectives but it had halted the eastward advance of a British column. A reshuffle of German forces during that evening brought the Witzig Group under the command of the newly formed von Broich Division. To build up the striking power of this division all Witzig's heavy weapons were withdrawn from him and handed over to Broich.

For the next two days barrage and counter-barrage succeeded each other in the Abiod sector while both sides sent out patrols to probe for weaknesses in the enemy's front. One German fighting patrol made up of No 1 Company of the Para Engineer Battalion set out on the night of 21/22 November just after midnight and had, by 03.00hrs, reached the road outside and to the north of Abiod. A challenge rang out from the British sentries, the para-engineers rushed the houses firing their machine pistols and hefting explosive charges into the buildings destroying British opposition. They returned to their own lines with minimal casualties.

The Luftwaffe was much in evidence during this period bombing and strafing the forward British positions and thereby aiding the efforts of the German ground forces. During the latter half of November Witzig's battle group, shrunken in number by casualties, received an Italian paratroop battalion as reinforcement. This crack unit was immediately committed to battle and launched an attack upon the 36th Brigade positions around Abiod. The assault collapsed in the fire of the British infantry and was beaten into the ground. Shattered by its losses the Italian unit was withdrawn and Witzig's men took over their former positions.

Vehicles of the only German armoured car reconnaissance unit in Tunisia were caught and destroyed in an ambush set by a British paratroop company in the area of Sidi Nsir during 18 November. Both sides were testing each other. This process continued on 20 November, when part of British 11th Brigade thrust a column along the valley of the Djournina towards Mateur with the intention of outflanking Witzig's group. The German commander relying upon the support of some Italian SP artillery switched the guns from flank to flank — at Abiod halting an infantry drive at Sidi Nsir stopping the advance of part of a British paratroop battalion. During this period a British armoured force was assembled to drive back the Axis forces from their positions on the Djebel Abiod and under this armoured pressure Witzig's men made a methodical, step-by-step withdrawal until they reached prepared defensive positions at Jefna.

Allied pressure during 18 November served to convince the Germans that the time of crisis was at hand and that an all-out Allied offensive could be wholly expected. This anticipated advance, as the Germans saw it, would be facilitated by the attitude of the French *vis-à-vis* the Allies, for the Anglo-Saxons would be allowed to move with best speed towards the German bridgeheads. Nehring at that time had only four 8.8cm guns in Tunisia and he personally selected the sites on which they were placed. One was on the Pont du Fahs road and two others were set up to act as the last artillery defence for the capital. But, as the hours passed without the decisive thrust being made, Nehring grew more confident and flung out more and more battle groups to seize and to hold key points and vital heights. There could be no question of forming a battle line, just pockets of battle hardened men utilising every minute and every feature and turning both to their advantage. As new units were formed or arrived in the airports they were rushed to the front and injected piecemeal into any sector where the need was greatest.

Kesselring, meanwhile, had promised that with 10th Panzer, the Hermann Goering and the 334th Infantry Divisions, together with two infantry divisions which the Italians had promised to supply, a new Army would be created.

Thus, on 19 November and from the German command point of view, the situation was that the northern area around Djebel Abiod was secure. In the centre, around Medjez el Bab, the position was still uncertain. In the south the western Allies had, as yet, made no appearance. The time had come for Nehring to seize quickly and to hold open the southern gateway, the Gabes area, and thus permit the safe withdrawal of Rommel's forces. But from where were the men to come to carry out this operation? An immediate solution presented itself in a small group of para-engineers who had been serving with Rommel in the desert and who were now in the Gabes region. Many of this handful of men were sick or convalescent and all were due to go on leave to Germany. But at the call of duty they took up battle positions, occupying key points in the region and determined to hold them until reinforcements reached them from the bridgehead area.

Back in the northern sector a company of 5th Para was assembled and together with No 3 Company of Kesselring's headquarters defence battalion was embarked into 12 JU 52s with the intention of landing upon and holding the aerodromes at Gabes as well, the Gabes Gap itself. The arrival of the

German machines on the runway at Gabes was the signal for the French troops holding the area to open fire with machine guns and artillery. The Junkers aeroplanes and their paratroop load were driven off and headed north-wards again back to the aerodrome from which they had taken off. *En route* to Tunis a hurried conference between the leaders of the enterprise produced a new plan and it was decided to make an emergency landing on a suitable piece of flat land some 30 miles from Gabes. The machines landed, the paratroops disembarked, and sent out a reconnaissance patrol to Gabes. A second patrol went out to capture the airport to prepare for the landing of follow-up troops. The remainder of the small command then took up all round defensive positions. A third patrol went out – seven men under command of a lance corporal – and these, having been taken prisoner by the French, were brought back to Gabes aerodrome for interrogation. By bluff they convinced the French commander that unless he surrendered the place by the following morning it would be laid flat by a Stuka attack. On the morning of 18th the sound of aircraft was heard and a stream of JU 52s was seen roaring towards the aerodrome with the intention of air landing the troops who were to occupy the Gabes Gap. The French, convinced that they were to be bombed from the air, abandoned the airfield and the JUs landed.

One of the vital positions for the passage of the desert army had been taken almost without bloodshed. As early as 19 November small detachments of German and Italian troops in southern Tunisia had been active on recon-naissance patrols. Based on Zarhouan and Pont du Fahs they had ranged across the Goubellat plain, had reached Tebourba, El Bathan, and the whole area to the south-west of Tunis without meeting any serious opposition. Axis troops occupied Ksar Tyr on 20 November and El Aroussa three days later. The towns of Sousse and Sfax were taken over and a force of Germans and Italians hastily assembled and moved westwards to hold the hills around Kairouan against an expected Allied thrust in that area. On other sectors demolition teams went out to mine roads and to destroy bridges in areas which the Germans were too weak in number to hold. The whole region was sealed by the second day and the paratroops prepared defensive positions from which they first held, and then threw back, the initial thrusts made against them by American forces striking towards Gabes.

Back on the line of the Medjerda river, at Medjez el Bab, the spearheads of British 36th Brigade were posing a threat to 3rd Battalion of Koch's regiment. Worried at the approach of the British and angered by the prevarication of the French, the German commander ordered an advance to the river to secure the vital crossings. As the German advanced guard moved towards the first houses on the eastern bank of the river they were met with fire from French troops in a bridgehead which they still held on the eastern side. To destroy this bridgehead and to attack the Allied armoured and motorised units which had now been identified and which had mixed with the French vehicles, a Stuka assault was ordered for 19 November. Under cover of this an attempt would be made to seize Medjez el Bab by *coup de main* and should this fail then the paratroops were to occupy and to hold the high ground, thereby preventing the British and the Americans from advancing eastwards towards Tunis.

Meanwhile another company of paratroops had taken over the aerodrome at Djedeida and had begun to prepare it for use as a forward air base by the Luftwaffe's fighters. With the small forces at their disposal the German commanders were achieving a great deal.

At 04.00hrs on the morning of 19th, along the line of the Medjerda river, German infantry and paratroops were in position, hidden in olive groves, ready to attack and to seize the crossroads behind the west bank. To secure the southern flank of the attack an anti-tank gun was positioned on the road going down to Goubellat, with orders to halt any Allied move northward. Contingency plans in the event of a pre-emptive move by the French were drawn up and any advance by them would lead to the bridge being blocked while a secondary move would thrust into the flank of their assault.

The dawn bombardment to open the attack did not materialise and not until 11.30hrs in the light of a bright, fine day did four ME 109s appear escorting a Stuka squadron; these machines swept down upon the French positions with sirens screaming. Under the noise of the bombardment, the crash of bombs, and the howling sirens, the ground assault began with fire from every available weapon. The sudden vicious attack broke the French and many rushed for shelter in the nearby houses. Those who remained were smashed aside by the German infantry, who fought their way into the houses on the eastern bank while the paratroops stormed towards the bridge. But there the advance halted for none could cross the structure in the face of the curtain of fire which the French artillery had laid around it. The German thrust was then moved to a flank and a storm troop detachment was sent across the river at a point to the left of the bridge and ordered to carry the attack forward by indirect assault. The small detachment waded through the icy waters firing their rifles and machine pistols as fast as they could reload them. They attained the western bank, took out a French defensive position, worked their way towards the bridge from which they drove the French defenders, and established a bridgehead. But losses had reduced, and were continuing to diminish, the group. When, finally, the numbers were down to four men the survivors withdrew to their own units on the eastern bank.

THE ALLIED DRIVE FOR TUNIS

During the evening of 19 November Koch formed 10 assault groups, armed them with explosives, and set them tasks of destroying given targets inside Medjez el Bab: either a French defensive position, an artillery post, a depot, or some other installation. The first group melted into the November darkness at midnight and others followed at intervals. By 01.00hrs the first explosions were destroying the targets and as the detonations continued and fires began to rage in the town a panic arose among the French and their troops fired wildly about them. Some of the assault detachments were engaged in street fighting when just before dawn the sound of tank tracks announced the arrival of Allied armour. A group of paratroops rushed the tanks, fixed hollow-charge grenades to their exteriors and blew them up. The remainder of the column withdrew towards Oued Zarga. Medjez el Bab, the gateway to Tunis and the lynch pin of the defence, was in German hands.

Without halting, the paratroops took the advance westward gaining ground up to Oued Zarga and meeting only medium opposition until they struck British paratroop columns ranging in the area. In the afternoon of 20th, Koch was forced to halt the advance, for his front was over-extended and his point unit was in danger of being cut off. Back in Medjez the Germans consolidated their gains and occupied a farm at Smidia to form the right flank of their thinly held perimeter. French counter-attacks came in during the night of 21st – Spahi horsemen mounted on Arab stallions – but these were driven off by machine gun and mortar fire. The area then entered upon a period of calm. The central region of the front, like the northern and the southern flanks, was sealed and behind the thin line of paratroops Nehring could form the army which would be able, given the supplies it needed, to hold the Tunisian bridgehead for some time.

The German commanding general was still deeply concerned with the weakness of his lodgement area and, to strengthen the Tunis bridgehead, divided it into a northern and a southern zone. An Italian force, under Lorenzelli, took over the southern part and Colonel Stolz, withdrawn from the Bizerta bridgehead, took over Tunis north. His command on the Bizerta front passed to Colonel Barenthin. Djedeida had by this time been established as the advanced air base and Mateur as the sector from which German motorised patrols either probed the Allied front or guarded their own exposed and weak southern flank.

Although the machines of the Luftwaffe's transport command were still ferrying men and supplies across the Mediterranean, the slow-flying JU 52s had become the prey of Allied fighters. But sufficient men were arriving to thicken the perimeters and in Koch's regiment the supply of reinforcements brought the strength of 3rd Battalion to nearly 2000 men. By this time the 1st Battalion of the regiment had begun to arrive in the bridgehead and was posted southwards to take up positions near Pont du Fahs. During the night of 21st the advance parties of 10th Panzer arrived from southern France and took over paratroop positions in the Tebourba area and at Djedeida, leaving the paras free to reinforce their comrades in position around Medjez and at El Aroussa. The first thrust by American tank units in the El Aroussa sector came in during the afternoon of 21st and, although they seized the little village, their advance further eastwards ran into a strong defence manned by men of a motorised company from 104th Infantry, a flak detachment, and paratroops. The United States thrust was beaten back with heavy loss.

The first major, Allied offensive which was intended to capture the objectives of Tunis and Bizerta and thus fulfil the terms of reference for Operation Torch began on 25 November. The first target was Tunis, considered by the Allies to be the less important of the two perimeters. With the fall of that city the whole weight of Allied power could be directed to the capture of Bizerta.

The British plan foresaw that the main thrusts would be an advance to the line Mateur–Tebourba by the two infantry brigades of 78th Division supported by the mobile and mainly armoured Blade Force. To divert German attention from these main thrusts there were to be diversionary operations; the one a commando assault from the sea and the other an air drop on the southern flank.

The 36th Brigade of 78th Division was to advance from Djebel Abiod towards Mateur and then press onwards to seize a junction on the Mateur–Bizerta road. Possession of this would cut the route between those towns and would form a base line for the final advance northwards to Bizerta. The 11th Brigade assault was to move upon and through Medjez el Bab and then strike north-eastwards towards Tebourba. Blade Force would be the mobile centre column protecting the left flank of 11th Brigade and be advancing upon Sidi Nsir. At that place it would turn due east, seize the Chouigui pass, debouch on to the plain at El Bathan and the aerodrome at Djedeida. Once Mateur and Tebourba had been taken the advance upon Tunis could begin.

The assault by 11th Brigade opened disastrously. Defending Medjez el Bab were three companies of Koch's 3rd Battalion, an Italian anti-tank gun detachment, a pair of 8.8cm guns, and some armoured fighting vehicles belonging to 190th Panzer Battalion. Signs of the impending British offensive had not been lacking and the Axis defenders stood ready for battle. The British pincer which struck from the north was made up of the 2nd Battalion The Lancashire Fusiliers and this unit made a night assault upon the town. In the bright moonlight Koch's men saw the extended line of British Fusiliers moving across the open plain and opened fire with terrible effect. The German paratroops had a higher than usual establishment of mortars and light machine guns which, when mounted on tripods, were converted into medium machine guns with a greater range. These weapons were also being handled by men who had years of training and combat experience and in the short days of preparation had calculated the distances of objectives to a foot. The first mortar bombs of the barrage struck the Fusilier's battalion headquarters as it moved, with the rifle companies, across the plain to the west of Medjez and in the minutes which followed and under a storm of bullets and shrapnel, the Fusiliers were driven to ground.

The British advance was halted. There could be neither a going forward nor a going back and Koch's paratroopers made the British battalion suffer all through the night. A German barrage at dawn brought more casualities, but then the Fusiliers moved forward to the Medjerda river, determined to force a victory. The machine guns sited to fire along and across the shallow river caught the British infantry as they struggled to climb the crumbling banks and blasted them back across the Medjerda. The German paratroop commander seeing that the initiative now lay with him put in a sudden, determined counter-attack, which caught the Lancashire Fusiliers as they were preparing to withdraw to the start line from which they had begun the advance, and caused a certain amount of confusion. Later in the afternoon the German paras showed their potency when they attacked a British force at Djebel Bou Mouss, known to the British as Grenadier Hill, and located to the south-west of Medjez.

The threat of being outflanked by United States armoured forces nearing Goubellat forced Koch to evacuate Medjez el Bab and, covered by a rear-guard furnished from men of No 10 Company, the Germans left the town after blowing the bridge. The British moved forward and occupied the deserted town. The paras then took up positions on both sides of the main highway to the west of Massicault. Near Bou Arada the 1st Battalion of Koch's regiment had been fighting against an Allied tank thrust and in short but bitter engagements had destroyed three armoured vehicles. The Allied attack was deflected and the armoured column turned back.

An American tank battalion, part of Blade Force, and numbering more than a hundred tanks in addition to other vehicles, moved out to reconnoitre the ground across which 11th Brigade would progress after its capture of Medjez el Bab. The armoured battalion's line of advance lay through the Chouigui pass and to the west of that feature, just after noon, the United States armoured unit struck No 3 Company of Witzig's battalion. This group, which had formed the reserve for Brioch's division, had been re-inforced with a troop of Italian SP anti-tank guns and sent up the line to hold the Allied assault.

In the face of superior numbers Witzig's men withdrew into the shelter of a walled farm which they defended tenaciously and held at bay the repeated assaults of the American tank men. With bursts of machine gun fire and sorties armed with explosive charges the German para-engineers obstructed the American advance and, having then fulfilled their purpose, slipped away in the hours of darkness.

During the morning of 26th a virile thrust by the American tank battalion brought a new crisis for Nehring for during their advance 'C' Company of the United States tank battalion caught the aerodrome at Djedeida unguarded and in a short fierce fire-fight destroyed 17 of the aircraft drawn up there. The news that the Allied armoured spearheads were only 10 miles from the capital alarmed Nehring. He had viewed with concern over the period of the past few weeks the struggle of his men to hold back the furious assaults of the Allies and this new alarm confirmed in his mind the intention he already had; he would withdraw the perimeter line back towards Tunis and Bizerta. By shortening the line thus, he could perhaps have a chance to regroup his forces, to form a more solid line and maybe even build a proper reserve. All along the line of the German bridgeheads the orders to disengage went out and small, silent groups of men left the positions which they had fought for and defended with such tenacity and moved eastwards back towards the principal cities.

The German defensive line, if it can be called that, extended at that time from a point north of Djebel Abiod to the area of Mateur, along the Mateur–Djedeida road to St Cyprien and from thence to a point south of Hamman Lif. To the south of the perimeter there were detachments either guarding or extensively patrolling along the open southern flank.

It was imperative that the United States tank thrust around Djedeida be halted and the Luftwaffe was called upon to support the ground forces by air attacks upon the Allied spearhead. Nine separate attacks went in, and destroyed some vehicles but the others continued their advance. It seemed as if Allied boldness might yet win the race for Tunis, but as the American armoured fighting vehicles thundered along the western road they came into the defence sector which had been specially created to guard the approaches to the city. The backbone of this was the two 8.8cm guns which Nehring had himself sited.

The Luftwaffe gun crews held their fire as the American column came closer and still closer. At almost point blank range the gunners opened fire and the crack of the first shot was barely heard in a greater detonation as the lead tank blew up, then a second burst into flames, a third slewed round with its track destroyed, another and then another; the gunners firing as fast as they could load until six machines had been put out of action. In the face of such a weapon as the 8.8 with its high rate of fire and its great powers of penetration, the American tank unit could make no further advance. The American column turned and withdrew upon Djedeida.

During the early morning of 26th, Witzig's Group, which had received reinforcements of No 3 Company of the Tunis Field Battalion and a squadron of tanks from 190th Panzer Battalion, resumed its march upon Tebourba. To carry out this advance it had to cross ground in which American tank columns were ranging. Then followed the first battle between German and American armoured forces.

The German Panzer IVs were fitted with the long 7.5cm high velocity gun and the Panzer IIIs with the 5cm weapon. The United States tanks had smaller cannon but their force was not only numerically stronger but was in a better tactical position. The Panzer IVs advanced in a shallow wedge formation with the lighter armed Panzer IIIs in the intervals. Firing rapidly the panzer squadron advanced towards a company of American self-propelled guns but it had fallen into a trap and was taken in flank and from the rear by US tank groups hidden in hull-down positions. The United States tank crews fired at close range and to such good effect that all the Panzer IVs and several of the Panzer IIIs were knocked out within minutes. The remnants of the armoured elements of Witzig's command pulled back to the farmhouse which his para-engineers had defended so tenaciously.

Now that Medjez el Bab was in British hands Tebourba had become the next most important stepping stone in the advance by 11th Brigade and it fell to 1st Battalion the East Surrey Regiment at dawn on 27 November. The concentration of Blade Force armour in and around Tebourba and the Chouigui pass, some 4 miles north of the village, convinced Nehring that this was the area and the direction from which the decisive Allied assault would be made. The possession of Tebourba would determine whether Tunis would fall or would be held. Nehring sent in a series of armoured probing attacks to ascertain the Allied strength in the area. Two columns of infantry and tanks attacked; one from the north-east and the second from the east. Small, bitter battles were fought in the olive groves which are laid out all around the town.

Early in the morning of 27 November the East Surreys in the perimeter around Tebourba were attacked by a German tank column, Battle Group Lüder. Leading the assault were two of the giant Panzer VI Tigers, which had been rushed over to Tunisia. A dozen or so other tanks completed the armoured group. The first wave of panzers rolled over the forward British infantry positions but then came under fire from a battery of British 25-pounder guns positioned behind the East Surreys. The tank gun versus field gun duel was short and predictable: all 8 guns of the British battery were knocked out and lay smashed and silent. But dotting the rolling countryside were 10 tanks of Battle Group Lüder, completely destroyed. At last light the German panzer column drew off down the road to Djedeida taking a further four damaged vehicles with it.

During the night of 27/28 November both sides improved their tactical positions or regrouped their forces. The British commander intended to capture Djedeida and then to move 11th Brigade in a north-westerly direction to cover the flank of the Allied force which would then thrust for Tunis. The elaborate plan for 36th Brigade to attack Djebel Abiod was not required for Witzig and his men had slipped away in the night and had moved back upon Bizerta. They had dug positions in the area of Jefna on the road to Mateur and stood there waiting.

On the morning of 28 November the 36th Brigade column led by the carrier platoon of 8th Battalion the Argyll and Sutherland Highlanders advanced into the valley between the Djebel el Azag, known to the British as Green Hill, and the Djebel el Ajred, known as Bald Hill. Hidden in position on the slopes above the valley lay the men of Witzig's para-engineers and a pair of Italian SP guns. The German fire discipline was excellent and no shot was fired as the rifle companies of the Argylls moved into the valley. The Scots opened fire at 13.45hrs with machine guns and mortars upon suspected German positions but still no fire was returned. Emboldened by this lack of opposition the Argylls moved into the valley and Witzig gave the command to his men to open fire. A single shot from an anti-aircraft gun opened what became a hurricane of fire upon the Scots. The Italian SPs' first round smashed the last carrier on the track and the ground on either side of the track was mined. There could be no advance in the face of the fire which was being poured down upon the British nor could they withdraw. Within minutes eight carriers were smashed and blazing as they were picked off one after the other.

Nor did the screen of riflemen forming the Argyll's advanced guard escape the fury of the German fire which smashed into the killing ground, and only six men of the leading company reached the British lines. Further assaults on succeeding days by 6th Royal West Kents and No 6 Commando were also beaten back with heavy loss to the attackers. Exhausted by their fruitless efforts the men of 36th Brigade could make no further effort and fighting died down on this sector.

THE GERMAN RIPOSTE

To divert Nehring's attention from the main thrust, to compel him to split his force and thus to ease the British assault, General Evelegh ordered a para drop by 2nd Battalion upon Depienne on the southern flank of the advance. The British drop would capture the Luftwaffe's advanced air base at Oudna after which it was to join up with Blade Force. Meanwhile 1st Commando on the sea flank would make an assault landing near Sidi el Moudjad, behind the back of the German force which was opposing the advance of 36th Brigade.

The sea-borne assault was betrayed to the Germans by local Arabs and Nehring, with his forces committed to holding 78th Division's thrust, had no reserve upon which he could immediately draw. The German troops were so thin on the ground that only 30 men garrisoned Tunis town. Nehring's only solution was to use the men who were arriving by air. As the aircraft landed the soldiers were hastily embussed and taken to Cap Serrat, the area in which the commandoes had debarked. In the densely wooded hills, which are a feature of that coastal sector, the newly arrived German troops and the British élite troops fought desperate hide-and-seek battles in the darkness of the trees. Commando pressure pushed towards the Sidi Salah crossroads only 18 miles west of Bizerta, but fresh German troops were flung into the battle and the commandoes were compelled to re-embark.

The British para drop was also unlucky. The airfield objective was found to be abandoned and, in the absence of a relief force, the British paras prepared to make their way back to the Allied lines. But their move was intercepted by

men of Koch's 1st Battalion as well as by the German armoured car reconnaissance company. Although they were harried, the British were not beaten
and when the German paratroops, supported by tanks and armoured cars,
made a frontal assault upon them, the British parachute troops destroyed the
lead panzer. The Germans, riding into battle on the outside of the armoured
vehicles, leaped off and formed action groups, moving forward under the
protection of the armoured cars. In hand-to-hand fighting the British 'red
devils' and the German 'green devils' of Koch's regiment fought a running
battle which lasted until 2 December. When the British battalion reached the
safety of its own lines a count showed that it had sustained over 200
casualties.

As neither the paratroop drop nor the assault from the sea had achieved
any reduction in the German opposition, General Evelegh ordered a temporary halt to allow his offensive to regain breath before making the final
attack. But his hope of a pause was to be thwarted by the German offensive
which was launched by the aggressive commander of 10th Panzer Division,
General Fischer.

Although the British and the Americans had been carrying out plans to
finish the campaign, it must not be assumed that the initiative had been only
with the Allies. The Germans, too, had been very active. The greatest number
of troops in their bridgeheads, particularly in the early weeks of the fighting,
had been paratroops. These men were among the élite of the German forces
and were capable, aggressive, and skilled. On the northern sector their idea of
aggressive defence took the form of deep penetration into the Allied rear
areas. Witzig's men had the task of delaying the advance of 36th Brigade and
had decided that raids behind the British front and demolitions on the supply
routes to the forward positions would have a greater effect than a straightforward blocking action. Night after night, often in pouring rain, the patrols
went out slipping into the darkness to mine roads, to demolish bridges, and to
intercept convoys of lorries, or even single vehicles well behind the British
front line. But this was not enough for Witzig. Deep penetration to halt the
convoys of supplies and reinforcements coming to Algeria would help to
strangle the Allied supply routes and he increased the radius of his
commando-type operations by para drops. In a short series of night jumps the
German para-engineers landed far in the hinterland of the Allied armies
demolishing and mining, causing confusion and alarm to the men on the
ground and to their commanders alike.

The men of the para-engineers were all-round specialists and professionals.
To cover the weakness in men and further to delay the Allied advance, they
laid mine-fields covering every sensitive area, particularly the approaches to
those defiles in the hills through which assaults must come. Because of the
shortage of real mines many of the fields were sewn, either wholly or in part,
with dummies and further to increase the difficulty of lifting them, sophisticated

anti-handling devices were fitted.

It can now be appreciated that as a result of the build-up of troops, Nehring had been able to form a small infantry and panzer reserve. No longer was the military situation so desperate that it was the case of having to plug gaps with newly debarked troops. Now their placement and replacement could be carried out in a more regular manner than had been possible heretofore. With no real divisional organisation, for as yet no complete division had arrived in Tunisia, there was still a need for battle groups, those *ad hoc* formations, in the construction of use of which the Germans were masters. With this reserve of men and armour in hand, Nehring could make plans and he found himself faced with the choice of two very risky alternatives. Either he could use his new panzer force defensively, that is wait until the Allies were strong enough to beat him, or he could act aggressively and throw it against the Allied force around Tebourba, and risk losing it at the first throw.

His mind was made up for him by an order from Kesselring to carry out an attack. The Supreme Commander South was convinced that the Allies were still too weak to make their final thrust and was also critical of Nehring's precipitate retreat. An offensive was ordered to regain the ground which had been lost.

To command the troops in the forthcoming offensive Nehring chose Fischer, commander of 10th Panzer Division, whose unit's advanced party had arrived in Tunisia and who had taken over the responsibility for the defence of Tunis West. Due to Allied air raids the unloading of 10th Panzer's vehicles took three days but by 30 November two panzer companies together with other troops, were in position around Protville ready to deal with any Allied thrust aimed at Tunis or Bizerta. The units which had arrived in Africa included 80 Panzer IIIs from 7th Regiment and these were formed into two companies. In addition, two companies of a motor cycle battalion had arrived, followed by elements of an anti-tank battalion, one company of which had its 7.62cm guns mounted as SP. Among the essential vehicles which had not arrived were those of the divisional command. Fischer had to be content with a scout car without wireless as his command vehicle. The rest of his head-quarters' group was mounted in motor cycle combinations.

Nehring's order to Fischer was simple and brief. 'You will attack and destroy the enemy troops in and around Tebourba', and in accordance with his instructions Fischer moved his command during the night of 30th to a point north-east of that small town and made ready for battle. Nehring then withdrew 5th Para from the line and posted it to El Bathan, south of Tebourba and gave Fischer units from other battle groups as well as four infantry replacement battalions. The 10th panzer commander realised that as he was weaker than his enemy he would have to defeat the Allies by cutting their retreat and stopping reinforcements from reaching them. These re-inforcements and supplies had to come through two passes. The road from

Medjez to Tebourba ran through one, the second pass being the Chougui, through which ran the road from Beja to Sidi Nsir.

If the Germans could capture these passes – and the lie of the land favoured them in this enterprise – they could block any attempt by the Allies to break the German ring and could then go on to defeat the enemy forces one by one.

Fischer's plan proposed an encirclement attack from three sides to pin the Allies against the river and the hills. The Allied positions were roughly triangular in shape with a mainly infantry force to the east and to the southeast. The armour belonging to Blade Force held the apex of the triangle at the Chouigui pass.

Battle Group Lüder was located some 3 miles north of the pass and Fischer armed it with a company of 20 tanks, 3 field guns, and a company of infantry. The task of this group was to block the road from the Chouigui pass. On the left flank of Battle Group Lüder, was Battle Group Hudel, the strongest of the four battle groups. This had two companies of tanks under command, numbering perhaps 40 vehicles, two companies of anti-tank guns, and a company of infantry. The task of this force would be to destroy the Allied armour by enticing the tanks on to an anti-tank gun screen or by ambushing them. This group would move from the position it held about 5 miles to the north-east of the pass and would converge to form a wedge with the Lüder Group. Together their task would be to attack Tebourba from the west or else to block the Gap at that place. The seven companies of Battle Group Koch's paratroops, together with three companies of infantry, a German and an Italian anti-tank gun company, and two field guns, as well as a bicycle platoon of para-engineers had a holding role and were to advance north-westwards towards the Gap cutting off the Allied forces from their escape route. The fourth and final battle group, Djedeida, was to act as a reserve for the first part of the attack. Once the Chouigui pass had been penetrated this group would press westwards, driving the British infantry from their positions on the ridges west of the village.

To carry out its part in the attack, the Battle Group had under command a company of paratroops, two companies of infantry, two anti-tank companies, 18 guns of 2cm calibre, a motor cycle engineer platoon, a battery of 3 5.5cm SP guns, 2 Panzer IIIs, 2 Panzer VIs, and several 8.8cm guns.

There was little time for adequate planning or accurate reconnaissance to be undertaken and to overcome the problems raised by the lack of signals equipment Fischer arranged for motor cycle couriers to bear messages. The Tiger tanks, too, presented difficulties for they had been sent only for testing under active service conditions and had, therefore, to be given to the battle group with the least difficult task – Medjeida Group. D-Day for the operation was 1 December and General Fischer expressed his intention of leading the attack in person.

Allied observers on the hills around the Chouigui pass would have seen in the bright light of a December morning, two columns of tanks heading towards them. As the panzer columns came within range they took up battle formation – in each case a shallow wedge, a tactic which allowed each gunner a good field of fire. The wide but shallow wave swept down upon the Allied tank forces at the mouth of the pass. At long range the panzer cannon opened fire and smoothly, efficiently, and destructively the German armour smashed at Blade Force overrunning some part of it and dispersing the remainder towards the Tebourba Gap.

A British counter-attack was certain to come in and in anticipation of this a troop of Panzer IIIs was concealed under olive trees in one of the extensive orchards which dotted the area. From another olive grove the tanks of 17/21st Lancers broke cover moving forward in a counter-thrust but as these passed the hidden Panzer IIIs they were taken in flank. Within minutes five of the Lancers' tanks had been destroyed. The others withdrew. The German infantry component was brought in personnel carriers more than halfway up one djebel – marked on the maps as Hill 104 – were quickly debussed, and then raced for the summit of the feature from which they fired upon the columns of Allied soft-skinned vehicles which were already being withdrawn through the Gap. The German tank wedge was thrusting strongly for the main road when it came under Allied artillery fire skilfully directed by British and American gunner observers. The Allied fire halted the Lüder and Hudel Groups north of the road. The attack on that sector was stopped.

Fischer then changed the direction of his offensive and brought up the Djedeida Group, leading this into the assault in person. Shortly after 14.00hrs the giant Panzer VIs led the German armoured column westwards along the road to Tebourba. In the leading Tiger, Captain von Nolde searched the area ahead of his column for the American tanks which had been reported. There they were, some distance ahead heading down the road towards his group. The 16-foot long, 8.8cm gun on Nolde's tank swung, aimed, and fired. High velocity shells struck and destroyed the American vehicles blowing off turrets and tracks and 'brewing up' others. Nolde swung his Tiger off the road and entered one side of an olive orchard, through which he passed to emerge on the other side ready to intercept and to cut off the American tanks as they withdrew down the road towards Tebourba. The American armour had been engaged and defeated but there was still the British infantry holding the high ground – the ridge above Djedeida. It must be stated at this point that the German replacement battalions were of very low calibre and, in fact, their poor showing was the subject of bitter comment in Fischer's report of the battle. The German Grenadiers' attacks, although heavy, were not pushed home with vigour and determination and were driven off with heavy losses. It is, however, fair to record that Colonel Buerker, in his report on the battle, stated that the infantry had had no previous experience of collaborating with tanks in an assault.

Now was the time for the troops of the southern pincer to come into action and small parties of Koch's men began to filter through the Allied defences making for high ground from which they would be able, at a later date, to fire with effect upon the retreating Allied columns. The short December day ended with a stalemate. To the north the early success against Blade Force armour had ended with the main thrust baulked and unable to move forward. To the east the important high ground was still in British hands but a tactical victory had been gained through the destruction of the American armour. To the south and south-west Koch's men were slipping their noose round the Allies, but the end was not yet in sight.

Both sides took the opportunity, during the night of 1/2 December, to improve their positions and to re-organise. New and fresh American armoured forces arrived in the area and relieved the shattered remnants of Blade Force. A small battle group from the Lüder Group made a direct and vicious drive towards the Tebourba Gap but the attack faltered and died away in the Allied defensive fire. Then the German tactics changed; Fischer had decided upon a change of plan. He really had no need to move forward at all. If he could bleed the Allied tank strength then this would reduce its potency to a point where it would no longer be able to attain the objective of Tunis. All his battle groups needed to do were to weaken the Allies by continual assault and to confuse them by infiltration. Already there were signs that the Allied forces were becoming nervous as a result of the penetration of their lines by Koch's paratroops for these had, by now, almost completed the southern investment of Tebourba.

The situation on the Allied side was not as serious as the local commanders believed it to be. The Allied tank force was now grouped in and around the Tebourba area gathered into one compact mass, and, given the right leadership, might have driven the Germans back, for Fischer's men were not in a sound tactical situation. They were confined in a narrow area between Tebourba and the Gap and, therefore, subject to fire from all directions. Whichever way they turned to attack they could be fired at. But the Allied tank commanders, and particularly those on the American side, had still not learned the basic lesson of armoured warfare – the use of mass and the need to conserve their machines by not wasting them in tank versus tank combats. The Allied tactic was still to engage in what were, in essence, cavalry charges and the first of a series of such assaults – isolated and unsupported – was launched against the Djedeida Group.

The United States tanks rolled eastwards towards the waiting panzers and at 11.00hrs battle was joined. The American light tanks drove forward, thirty of them seeking to destroy the panzers and quite unaware that during the night a battery of 8.8cm guns had been sited on the flank of their advance. As the tanks poured through the orchards advancing towards the German positions, they met not only the fire from 7.5cm tank cannon but also a battering from the fast-firing 8.8s. Within 15 minutes, eight American tanks lay smashed or burning on the battlefield. Other American squadrons went in in futile assaults and their efforts, too, were smashed by the fire of the 8.8s and that of six Panzer IVs. The Allied armoured weapon was shattered against the steely panzer defence.

Slowly Battle Groups Lüder and Hudel fought their way towards the Medjerda river suffering casualties from the well directed Allied artillery fire, but with every yard gained, threatening to cut the main road. At dusk the protagonists broke off the tank fighting and left the battle to aggressive and violent infantry patrol clashes. Slightly, very slightly, but very certainly the Germans had gained the upper hand and were beginning to win the battle.

During the night of 2/3 December Panzer Grenadier reinforcements arrived for Battle Group Djedeida. The infantry component of this battle group had been too weak to drive the British from their positions on the ridge above the village and, with no reserve immediately to hand and upon which he could draw, Fischer had airshipped to him from Europe two of the Grenadier Companies of 10th Panzer Division. These had barely arrived upon the battlefield when they were put into action and into an attack upon the British infantry. The Djedeida Group had been promised Stuka support for their new drive but this had not materialised by 10.00hrs and so the infantry was committed to the assault without it. The German Grenadiers mounted a two-pronged thrust against Djebel Maiana and had captured this by midday. During the afternoon British counter-attacks came in but these were beaten off and, having regrouped, the German attack was resumed, this time with tanks. The armoured punch smashed through the position held by the Hampshire and cut off part of that battalion. The East Surreys were sent in to restore the situation and carried out a determined assault upon Djebel Maiana but even their *élan* failed in the storm of defensive fire which the Panzer Grenadiers poured down upon them. Lüder Group reached the Djedeida thereby cutting the road to the Tebourba Gap while Battle Group Hudel, which had co-operated in the thrust to the river, closed and held tight shut the escape routes to the north and north-west.

The situation for the Allied force in the Tebourba area and, particularly for the infantry battalions of 11th Brigade, had become more and more precarious. A withdrawal through the Gap was authorised. The Allied retreat from the village began after dark but was soon caught in the storm of artillery fire which the Germans brought down upon the columns. Lorries, tanks, guns – all were abandoned on the western road upon which the machine guns of Koch's paratroops were also now pouring a rain of bullets and mortar shells in an effort to destroy the Allied convoys. By 3 December there was no doubt that the advantage lay with the Germans and they crowned their success with the capture of Tebourba on 4 December. Just after noon of that day Koch's men met up with the Lüder and Hudel Battle Groups and jointly they pursued the Allies westwards and back along the road to Medjez el Bab.

That it was a German victory there could be no doubt for the Allies had voided the field and had abandoned 55 tanks, 29 pieces of artillery, 300 vehicles, and had lost over 1000 men as prisoners of war. The immediate threat to Tunis was over; now the Germans could begin the extension of their perimeters.

QUIET ON THE NORTH-WESTERN FRONT

The Allied withdrawal continued until a point was reached some 8 miles east of Medjez. In position there was another force of Allied soldiers and the officers of 10th Panzer Division were surprised that this force had made no attempt to resume the advance to Tunis and it was supposed that, either, the Allied group was intended to hold the bridgeheads across the Medjerda river or, alternatively, that the Allies had suffered a more serious setback than had been at first believed. If this latter were the case, then the weakness of the Allies must be exploited and the Axis perimeter enlarged by aggressive action.

The panzer commanders laid their appreciation of the situation and their plans for the resumption of the attack before the Corps commander but on the same evening changes in administration raised the command structure to that of an army and the new Army commander, von Arnim, took up post. The complicated chain of command which had been responsible for so many of the disappointments that Rommel had suffered was reproduced here. Although von Arnim and his 5th Panzer Army would be subordinate to the Commando Supremo, in practice he would have direct dealings with Supreme Commander South. His position *vis-à-vis* Rommel was never made quite clear and was later to lead to difficulties and to complications. Nehring left his command on 8 December, three days after the arrival of von Arnim.

The leaders of 10th Panzer Division realised that in view of the new administrative changes no decision would be forthcoming that evening and acted on their own initiative and, as they believed in accord, with the principle of General Nehring.

A three-pronged attack was made during the morning of 6 December. One prong made a reconnaissance in force towards Medjez el Bab with the intention of uncovering Allied weaknesses, of testing strengths, and of gaining time to build up the 5th Panzer Army's numbers. A second prong struck at American tanks at El Guessa and such was the pressure that the British Commander-in-Chief, General Anderson, withdrew the American armour to Djebel Bou Aoukaz, and the British 11th Brigade to Longstop Gap. The attack was showing every sign of being another success for 10th Panzer Division with the Americans abandoning equipment and vehicles but then the advance was halted on the command of von Arnim. The intelligence officers of 5th Panzer Army had interpreted the slowness of the Allied advance as difficulties in supply and had forecast a resumption of the assault to coincide with one which was likely to go in against Rommel. Von Arnim thereupon gave orders that all operations were to be defensive in character to conserve strength. To meet the anticipated assault a re-organisation was undertaken and boundaries changed. Command of the right flank went to von Broich, of the centre to Fischer's 10th Panzer, and of the southern flank to the Italian Superga Division.

In anticipation of the new attack and with movements halted by the heavy rain which fell between 6 and 9 December, the central Tunisian front entered upon a period of quiet which was only broken by a British offensive to capture Djebel el Ahmera, known as Longstop Hill. This feature remained in German hands until Easter 1943.

The intention of the offensive, to dominate the gap between the Djebel Lanserine and the Medjerda river, had been achieved by 10th Panzer Division's armour while other units from that formation had gone on to seize Bou Djebel Toum. The 334th Division had captured the pass area to the west of Chouigui and the important high ground was then in German hands. To the south of the Tunis bridgehead, Koch's regiment and Superga Division had advanced their positions on both sides of Pont du Fahs.

Thus by the end of the year the Germans had gained their objectives. There was a bridgehead of such depth that it could not be destroyed by a surprise attack. A firm link existed between the forces in the southern half of Tunisia and Rommel's desert army and the military initiative had been seized from the Allies.

This sudden transition from defence to attack was an example of the flexibility of the German military mind as well as a demonstration of the ability of the infantry and the panzer men. But the role of the Luftwaffe during those tense and difficult days and weeks must not be overlooked for it was crucial to the success of the Axis defence and counter-offensive. Indeed it is true to say that the Germans could not have survived the first days of the campaign without the active and vigorous support of the Luftwaffe in attacking, obstructing, and, in some cases, destroying the Allied spearheads. As an example of its activity, during the period from 20 November to 12 December, a daily average of 18 dive-bombing attacks and 25 missions by fighter and fighter-bomber was carried out. During the three days of the 10th Panzer Division counter-attack the number of missions flown was 54 and 108 respectively.

This short-lived superiority in the air enjoyed by the Germans was due in part to the fact that their bases at Tunis and Bizerta were all-weather airports and aircraft could and did operate from them when the Allied airfields were unusable. This all-weather facility and the close proximity of the aerodromes to the combat zone enabled the Luftwaffe to give complete cover and almost immediate support to the troops in the field as well as protection to the machines of transport command which were airlifting men and materials from Sicily. The achievement of that command was that it brought into the bridge-head areas during those first months no less than 7 battalions of infantry, whole batteries of field guns, 2 armoured reconnaissance companies, and at least 19 tanks, of which 4 were the giant Tiger Panzer VI.

German impressions on how the campaign was progressing are interesting for they show how clearly the men in the field anticipated the future turn of events. All ranks from Rommel and von Arnim down to subaltern officers realised that the Allies would seek to separate 5th Panzer Army from 1st German/Italian Panzer Army by an attack from one of the western passes through the mountains, and that the decisive blow would be delivered from the area of Medjez el Bab. It was apparent to all German commanders that Medjez el Bab held the key to the whole campaign and in order both to protect their own bridgehead as well as to deny this key point to the Allies, 5th Panzer Army proposed to seize the town in a pincer operation code-named *Olivenernte*. The time set for the opening of this offensive was the second half of January and the plan was that 334th Division would strike from the north and meet the pincer of 10th Panzer ascending from the south. To divert Allied attention and to gain important features, other German battalions would capture Djebel Mansour while Superga Division secured the Pichon heights.

To hide from the Allies the fact that 334th Division had left the line to prepare for the forthcoming assault, 'Chinese' attacks were launched in Djebel Chirich area and at other points along the Medjez sector. The Allies however were not inactive and an attack which was launched at Jefna on 6 January involved the German garrison in battles which swayed to and fro for nearly a week until 5th Para were sent in and restored the situation. Down in the deep southern half of the bridgehead the Superga Division, in position east of Djebel Chirich and west of Sbikha, was attacked by a French Corps which was now fighting alongside the Americans. The poor showing of the Italian soldiers in this sensitive area renewed the fear that they could no longer be trusted to defend themselves or their positions and that they could no longer be stationed in an area from which an Allied assault might strike to the sea. German counter-attacks recovered the ground which the Italians had lost but it was clear that given the shortage of infantry from which both Panzer armies were suffering, there could be no forces to undertake *Olivenernte*. Von Arnim therefore decided to strike at the weakest of the Allied armies and organised an offensive against the French Corps with the code-name *Eilbote*.

The 334th Division which had by now left the line was selected as the most suitable unit. It was moved by night drives in commandeered and requi-sitioned vehicles to a sector south-east of Pont du Fahs. The gap, which had been created by the removal of this division from the battle line, could only be plugged by shortening the line and a number of tactical withdrawals from mountain crests was undertaken and had been completed by 17 January.

Eilbote began on the following day and achieved immediate and important successes. The 334th Division captured the pass east of Djebel Mansour and the heights at Djebel Chirich while the motor cycle battalion of 10th Panzer Division seized Djebel bou Daboussa. The Allies moved back under this pressure and the whole Axis line moved forward to occupy the ground. British counter-attacks around Bou Arada began on 21st and for days there was bitter fighting for high ground but then the northern arm of the German assault, coming through the Chirich pass, linked with a mixed German/Italian group on Djebel bou Daboussa. This sector was now dominated by the Axis troops holding the high ground and the Allies withdrew from it on 24 January. But the strain of battle in the mountains and in the terrible weather began to tell upon the Axis troops who had fought for six days without rest or reinforcement, and they no longer had the determination or the strength to achieve new objectives. *Eilbote* was called off but the results were satisfactory: the high ground between Pichon and Pont du Fahs was in Axis hands, the immediate threat to the southern half of the Tunis bridgehead had been averted, and the French Corps had been badly hit.

Successful French counter-attacks against the Italians revived the fears that these would not stand their ground. When one particularly severe counter-attack around Djebel Chirich forced a German unit to fall back east of the gap the 5th Panzer Army commanders saw a chance to counter-attack, to outflank, and then to roll up the French line. They mounted a second *Eilbote* operation on 1 February. Tiger tanks of 501 Panzer Detachment, extra infantry, and increased artillery were posted to the assaulting units and, with this added strength, advances were made along the Pont du Fahs–Rebaa ad Yahia road. The French had by this time been reinforced with American equipment and men so that heavy fighting developed but the German forces went on to capture high ground on the right flank of the attack. There was less success on the inner left wing south of Djebel Chirich where the advance had to be made across open country dominated by American and French artillery of all calibres. Under the barrage of defensive fire the German attack in this area faltered and then halted. On the extreme left flank, however, Pichon fell to 47th Infantry Regiment and Ousseltia was captured by a storm troop detachment. Allied strength grew daily and the resistance which the Germans were meeting compelled them to break off the battle. The Axis wave receded as their troops gave ground and withdrew to strong defensive positions on the heights to the east of the Ousseltia valley.

The far southern extent of 5th Panzer Army's territory was an area in which there had been little fighting, for neither side had been strong enough to force a decision there, but in the second half of January, von Arnim at last had the opportunity to carry out an operation which would secure his links with Rommel's force. German positions to the east of the Faid pass, which had been lost in December, could be outflanked by any French debouchment aimed towards Sfax. Were this to happen then the rupture of the Axis front would have been brought about. As the other sectors of 5th Panzer Army front were relatively dormant there was an opportunity to carry out an operation against and to seize the Faid pass and to hold it as a barrier against the Allies.

To carry out this operation the 21st Panzer Division which was refitting at Mahares was placed under command of 5th Panzer Army and despatched to Faid. The battle plan was simple. Four battle groups would take part. One, with a holding role would attack from the east and under cover of this assault a second group would scale the height of Djebel Kralif. A third force would hold the Rebaou pass while a fourth column cut through the Maizila pass to block any flow of reinforcements to the Faid garrison and also to attack those troops from the west. On 30 January the battle groups struck and the storm troops on the heights of Djebel Kralif descended upon the northern flank of the French positions.

By nightfall it was over and the pass had been seized, but the Americans were not content to let so tactically important a feature be lost so lightly and 1st Armoured Division sent forward two armoured columns to attack the Rebaou and the Faid passes. The group which struck at the Rebaou pass penetrated some distance inside it but was then repelled. A column of infantry, artillery, and tanks commanded by Colonel Stark which charged into the Faid pass struck against experienced panzer men who had had time to prepare their defences.

An artillery barrage halted the American advance and then the Stukas went in to break up the cohesion. One company of 1st Armoured Regiment was drawn to within range of an anti-tank gun line and lost 9 tanks. The United States forces withdrew but came in again on 2 February against the Rebaou pass and this time using infantry ahead of the armour. But this assault, too, failed and the combat command went over to the defence in that sector. On other sectors, too, the American advance had halted and the troops of 1st Armoured Division began to move back upon Gafsa.

Plans had been made to attack Pichon and these were quite far advanced when intelligence reports indicated a strong build-up of American forces in the Sheitla–Tebessa–Sidi bou Zid sectors. This could only mean that an attack would be launched against the German troops in those sectors and that this would probably be made in conjunction with an expected British offensive at Mareth.

Arnim then decided to attack the American force in the Sbeitla sector before it had grown too large and if this move met with success then to exploit it by rolling up the Allied front from south to north. If he could compel the Allies to evacuate Medjez el Bab then the strategic aims for which the Germans had been striving since November and of which operation *Olivenernte* had been the most recent plan, might yet be achieved.

There were certain temporary difficulties. Fischer, an experienced and forceful tank commander, was killed in action while on a reconnaissance and his death resulted in a general reshuffle of senior posts. The loss of Fischer meant that the new commander would have to 'work' himself into the post and in view of the shortage of time von Arnim called off that attack and concentrated instead upon the objective of Sidi bou Zid.

Fischer's death and the difficulties which this caused can serve to illustrate at this point one weakness of the German command structure in Tunisia. From the first days there had been no adequate staff organisation and no staff officers at all. Most divisions reaching Africa were not complete formations but usually individual regiments, and, of course, were without divisional hierarchy. It can be appreciated that staff officers, even of quite junior rank were seized upon to fill empty staff appointments at fairly senior levels. Thus there was no Corps structure because there were insufficient numbers of efficiently trained officers and 5th Panzer Army formed *ad hoc* groupings and then called these Corps, although they seldom had the strength of even a division on the continental mainland. Only the length of front which such units had to hold, the tasks given them to perform, and the requirements of command structure led to these groupings being called Corps.

10. The attempts to expand the bridgehead, February 1943

'Africa? I have already written Africa off'
The Chief of the German General Staff, February 1943

In the last days of January to the accompaniment of icy winds and in bitter cold the advanced guards and then the main of Panzer Army Africa crossed the frontier into Tunisia and by 12 February, the second anniversary of the German arrival in the African theatre of operations, those Axis positions still on the soil of Tripolitania were also withdrawn into the bridgehead area. Here in this fertile country the desert veterans of the years of 1941 and 1942 returned to a European-type warfare in which the infantry arm carried the main burden of battle.

The 1st German/Italian Panzer Army was ordered to stand on a position at Mareth which had first been constructed and then destroyed by the French. At the high echelons of command in Rome and Berlin it was perhaps believed that the Mareth line was strong and well fortified; but this was not the case. The whole position was badly sited and quite weak. Immediately in front of the main defensive position a ridge dominated the Axis positions and to garrison this took men from the battle line. In the south the flank was wide open and the gap between Djebel Ksour and the coast required a strong garrison to protect the over-long western-flank against an outflanking movement. Then too, the Allied presence in Gafsa required that intensive and heavy patrols be maintained in the area of the Djerid Schott.The French had constructed this weak line against the Italians in Tripoli and had left the western flank open for it would have been from Algeria and Tunisia that their reserves would have come. But to the Axis commanders the passes leading from the interior of Tunisia and debouching on to the coastal plains were a constant source of worry because it would be out of these passes that the attack might come which would sever 5th Panzer Army from 1st German/Italian Army. Every one of these passes lay behind the troops who were defending the Mareth position, and they would be a threat until the Enfidaville line was taken up. But that is to anticipate because the Mareth Line was ordered to be held to the last.

The whole line was a geographical and not a military position and certainly not one which any soldier would have chosen to defend nor risked men trying to hold.

Rommel was disappointed but not surprised to find that the arms and fuel had not arrived as Hitler had promised they would. So little had been received that there was no barbed wire and only a small number of anti-tank mines. Once again his army would have to make do: the men, turning to obsolete and, in some cases, obsolescent weapons, and depending upon the fighting spirit of those whose time spent in the front line was now being measured in weeks and not in days.

Rommel deployed the Italian XX Corps and 90th Light Division to hold the main battle line and placed in reserve the 15th Panzer and 90th (Africa) Divisions. The east–west passes at Kieddache and Halouf were blocked by 164th Division. In support of the thin infantry and panzer line there were 65

German and 340 Italian field guns. There were also 36 batteries of Italian anti-aircraft guns; 18 light and 18 heavy, while among the 12 batteries of German 8.8cm flak were 2 batteries fitted out with guns of the new, improved 1941 pattern. Another defensive grouping was made up from 10 batteries from 19th Flak Division.

There were, however, grave and serious shortages of infantry. The 90th Light Division had had such losses that regiments had been reduced to an average strength of 350 bayonets and the whole division was almost completely defenceless against armoured attack for most of its anti-tank guns had been lost and not replaced. The total artillery fire-power of 164th Infantry Division was a single battery of field guns, for it was anticipated that the German infantry would be able to sustain a defence in the mountains with only minimum support. The most dangerous military risks were being taken and there were sectors which were covered only by patrols.

On 28 January, Commando Supremo, fearful of an attack to the sea by American forces which were being assembled in the Tebessa area and conscious of a similar threat posed in the Gafsa area, ordered that an offensive be launched to seize and to hold the western passes,

Kesselring's orders to Rommel were to attack and destroy the American forward line and once the United States forces had been driven back on Sbeitla and Feriana, then Sidi bou Zid could be taken and the Gafsa and Touzeur sectors could be seized. To carry out his part of the plan von Arnim's army, with two panzer divisions under command, would strike for Sidi bou Zid in an operation code-named *Frühlingswind*, while 1st German/Italian Panzer Army, in its operation *Morgenluft*, would drive to secure the west and the north-westerly flanks and then return its armoured units back to the Mareth front. The Luftwaffe Brigade would be used to garrison the captured areas.

There were deep and fundamental differences between Rommel and von Arnim as to their respective strategies for the forthcoming operations. Von Arnim, with his cautious approach considered that his task was to hold the bridgehead for the longest possible time and, not wishing to risk his forces, intended to launch only large-scale spoiling attacks. Rommel, with his greater flair for far-flung battles grasped the opportunities which such an operation presented.

By combining the Axis forces the western passes could be captured and then in a massive punch the Allied front could be smashed open. Through the breach would flood the armoured divisions aiming for Tebessa and then for Souk el Arba, deep behind the front of the Allies' 1st Army. Faced with this thrust in the back the Allies would have to give ground and withdraw to Algeria. The Axis bridgehead in Tunisia would, therefore, have been enlarged.

Von Arnim could not agree to Rommel's bold plan and both commanders appealed for Kesselring's decision. Mussolini's order, transmitted through

Kesselring as Supreme Commander South, was a dilution of Rommel's plan for the objective was not to be towards Tebessa and Souk el Arba but towards Le Kef, a road junction immediately behind the Americans. Rommel argued that it would be at Le Kef that the Allied commander would have his strong reserve forces, and that, in any case, a successful advance upon Le Kef would achieve only a tactical and not a strategic victory, nor would it lead to a collapse of the Allied front in Tunisia, nor to the withdrawal of Allied forces which Rommel had planned.

Thus the die was cast. The two independent operations had as their intention the seizure of the western passes with Faid as the first objective and with this in Axis hands then the drive towards the Kasserine pass. Then would follow the attack against Gafsa and if this were successful then the sensitive south-western flank of the Tunisian bridgehead would have been secured, and the threat to the desert army holding the Mareth line would have been annulled.

The 10th Panzer, one of the two armoured divisions which von Arnim was to use in operation *Frühlingswind,* moved through the streets of Tunis in the dark and cold days of early February and arrived in positions south-west of Kairouan. By now the men of the German panzer divisions had learned the need for correct camouflage and had dispersed their vehicles under nets among the cacti which grew profusely in the area. The infantry was dug in for better concealment in the sides of wadis which crossed the region and the division prepared itself for action. Ration and supply points were built for armoured actions, for particularly when these were fought at night, easily locatable dumps were required at which the tanks could refuel and rearm before returning to battle. It had become standard practice for extra drums of fuel to be carried on the outside of the tanks, despite the fire risk, to increase the length of time that the vehicle could stay in action. So that the tanks did not have to return for extra ammunition it had become usual for an additional box of armour piercing shells to be carried inside the tank.

In the workshops of each panzer company fitters carried out the final adjustments and minor repairs. Sand and dust which had clogged the air filters were cleared out. The dust which penetrated into every crack of the machinery reduced the life of the engine and the standard filters, originally fitted to the outside of the tank, had proved ineffective. These had, therefore, been enlarged and placed inside the vehicle. The increased life of the motor, which this refitting produced, was offset by the disadvantage that the interior of the machine was quickly covered with sand which affected the gun and its ammunition. Even the gun muzzle had to be fitted with a cloth to protect the inside of the barrel from the scouring effect of the sand.

During the night of 10 February the division moved southwards to an area 25 miles east of Faid and the vehicles went, as matter of routine, into the olive groves which bordered the road. These orchards were ideal ambush positions for the trees were tall enough to hide a tank from the gaze of an enemy commander standing in his tank turret.

Reconnaissance on 11th showed that there was no organised American opposition in the area around Faid. In the evening of 13 February the assault troops of 10th Panzer moved forward to the forming-up area, an olive grove eight miles east of Faid, where the attack orders were given out.

Ziegler, the commander of this operation and whose task it was to co-ordinate the assaults of the two panzer divisions, had already carried out his own personal reconnaissance and had drawn up his battle plan. The 10th Panzer was to form three battle groups and was to send two of these armoured forces through the Faid pass while the third remained in reserve. The non-motorised units of 21st Panzer which had been in position near Faid since the end of January would attack from the village under an artillery barrage and exit from the Rebaou pass to strike towards Sidi bou Zid. Meanwhile armoured elements of 21st Panzer would penetrate the Maizila pass and upon exiting would divide into two battle groups. The Schuette Group would advance northward to approach Sidi bou Zid from the south-west, while Stenkhoff Battle Group would move on Sidi bou Zid via the Bir el Hafey Road.

Shortly after 10th Panzer Division had arrived in its forming-up area, the General Officer Commanding issued his orders and laid down the composition of the forces which would fight the battle. Reiman Battle Group would attack along the Faid–Sbeitla road and capture the Poste de Lessouda and for the assault it would have under command 2nd Battalion 86th Panzer Grenadier Regiment, 5 Tiger tanks of 501st Tank Battalion, a platoon of the Panzer Engineer Battalion, an assault battery of 4 10.5cm guns, and 2 platoons of SP anti-tank guns.

Battle Group Gerhardt was to thrust through the pass and then swing northwards to pass completely round the Djebel Lessouda and then to cut the Faid–Sbeitla road. The forces for this attack were 1st Battalion 7th Panzer Regiment, 2nd Battalion 69th Panzer Grenadier Regiment, 2 platoons of the Panzer Engineer Battalion, 1 platoon of SP anti-tank guns, and a battery of 10.5cm guns. Battle Group Lang was in reserve.

During the night divisional engineers went in under the protection of the Italian troops, who held the high ground at the mouth of the pass, and cleared the mine-field just before zero hour. Shortly before 04.00hrs, just as the panzers were about to move forward into the attack, a sudden sandstorm swept the area and reduced vision forcing the engineers to hand-guide the tanks through the pass with lamps and hand torches. Despite the darkness which the sandstorm had intensified, the two assault groups from 10th Panzer made good speed.

St Valentine's day 1943 dawned and with it began the battle for Sidi bou Zid. The advance by Battle Group Gerhardt made good time in its swing round the Djebel Lessouda but as the light became stronger, heavy and accurate artillery fire was directed upon it from OPs positioned on the crest of the djebel. Immediately the tempo of the panzer drive was raised to pass behind the mountain and to attack the troublesome American guns. Quickly the panzer formation opened into attack grouping and formed a series of echelons. Behind the lead company came battalion headquarters with the lighter vehicles and the whole unit was so deployed that an attack on either flank could be met by the whole battalion pivoting to form a broad front. The panzer attack flowed forward, despite the United States artillery barrage, while behind the armoured spearhead the carriers of the Panzer Grenadier Battalion roared up the slopes of the djebel bringing the infantry to the nearest point from which the American positions could be assaulted.

As Battle Group Gerhardt swung south-westwards it intercepted a United States self-propelled artillery unit which was trying to escape from the advance of Battle Group Reiman. Desperately the United States column tried to make good its escape but the panzer point unit increased speed and began first to overhaul and then to outflank the Americans. In a panic some of the American vehicles were driven headlong into swampy ground and were cut off. The Gerhardt Group, having reached its first objective, the Faid–Sbeitla road, halted and took up all round positions ready to face the inevitable counter-attack.

Meanwhile Reimann Battle Group had emerged from the pass and had thrust towards the Poste de Lessouda engaging a vedette of two Stuart tanks which were hit and destroyed by the longer ranged 8.8cm guns of the Tiger tanks. Other United States tanks belonging to an artillery SP unit began to withdraw but were intercepted by Battle Group Gerhardt as described above. As the panzers reached the Poste de Lessouda, a radio report from a Luftwaffe aeroplane indicated that a strong force of American tanks was moving down upon the Poste in a counter-attack. Reimann Group went into 'hull down' position and as the Allied machines came into range they were picked off one after the other. Both battle groups then waited for the thrust by 21st Panzer to capture Sidi bou Zid but then received intelligence that bad going had delayed the unit's advance. In any case the success of 10th Panzer Division had made the thrusts by the battle groups of 21st Panzer redundant, but eventually Stenkhoff Battle Group, struggling through loose sand, reached the battlefield. Here it was able to intercept the United States tanks which had survived the assaults of 10th Panzer's battle groups and were advancing southwards. Stenkhoff Group blocked the road, the only firm surface in that region, thereby forcing the American vehicles to struggle through the sand. It was an unequal contest. The German group with 2nd Battalion 5th Panzer Regiment, 2 battalions of Panzer Grenadiers, and heavy artillery under command was not only numerically superior to the Americans, but the panzer guns had a longer range, and the whole force was under a central direction. Combat Command

A of 1st United States Armoured Division lost that day 40 tanks and other material including 15 SPs and 2 personnel carriers.

By the afternoon of 14th, the situation was that the Americans had been driven from the battlefield. Reconnaissance detachments belonging to 10th Panzer Division had entered Sidi bou Zid and the main of the division was in position north-east of the village. Panzer Grenadiers were combing the area for American stragglers and combat engineers were destroying the American vehicles. Ziegler, confident of victory, began to arrange for the move of 21st Panzer Division, but the aggressive action of the American troops, cut off and isolated on the djebels but still full of fight, coupled with the certainty of a counter-attack by United States tank forces, delayed the transfer.

During the night the vehicles were serviced, refuelled, and re-armed and as more panzers from Africa Corps arrived in the area they, too, were put into position south of Sidi bou Zid. At first light a panzer company with grenadier support put in a dawn attack to clear the American infantry from the djebels while other detachments strengthened the defences of the village. By the time that the Americans began their counter-attack the whole area had been prepared for defence with field artillery supporting the anti-tank line. Positions were occupied both inside and outside the village and other panzer units took post on the flanks. The area across which the Americans would have to advance was a flat and open plain cut across with wadis. These steep-sided, deep, dried-up water courses were impassable to tanks except at certain points where the wadi walls were lower and the Germans sited their artillery to cover these crossing points.

It was nearing midday when the panzer reconnaissance detachment raised the alarm that dust clouds were to be seen and that an American tank column was advancing from the direction of Sbeitla. This was one battalion of Combat Command C whose intention was to destroy the German forces and to release the isolated United States troops. The German defence plan went into operation and panzers from both divisions moved into ambush positions, thrusting two encircling arms along the flanks of the American advance. Soon the Allied tank force had crossed the first of the wadis and, assembling on the far side of this, took up battle formation again and headed for the second water course. But, as the tanks began to break formation to look for crossing points, the battery of 8.8cm guns which had been waiting opened up and smashed the cohesion of the assault with accurately aimed barrages of armour piercing shot.

On the flanks of the American advance the panzers were also ready and waiting. At a command the whole German column turned inwards and to the barrage from the village was added the cannonade of the vehicles on the flanks. The American charge advancing as a deep formation of column of companies was struck and hurled back. Caught in a pocket of fire the survivors were struck again as they tried to carry out their orders. And even when at last the American attack recoiled there was still a gauntlet of shells to be run before they could reach the safety of their own lines. By twilight the battle had ended.

On 16 February a unit from 10th Panzer reconnoitred to a road junction some 14 miles north-west of Sidi bou Zid and joined forces with a second force of panzers on the Faid–Sbeitla road. The mission for 10th Panzer ended and in accord with the orders of 5th Panzer Army it swung northwards. The 21st Panzer continued the drive to Sbeitla, a key point in the defence of the Kasserine pass, for it was through this pass that Rommel intended to drive in his ambitious attack upon the rear of the 1st Army.

In the face of German pressure the Allied line swung back to positions along a mountain range, the western Dorsal, in the area of Pont du Fahs, and then evacuated Gafsa.

According to Liebenstein Rommel's plan to attack Gafsa had been turned down by Commando Supremo who wanted to maintain the boundaries between the two panzer armies along the 34th parallel, but when Liebenstein entered the town upon Rommel's order he found the place evacuated. The Allies had withdrawn so quickly that contact with them was lost and a reconnaissance unit had to be sent out to regain this. This armoured recce unit moved towards Feriano which was then captured by 17th. Rommel was now convinced that his original plan, with its deep thrusting blow into the Allied back, could succeed and he proposed to move upon Tebessa, but von Arnim did not agree for he considered that such an advance through the mountainous country in that region would consume too much of the little infantry strength which the armies had, to say nothing of the supply difficulties which an extension of the supply line would involve.

With the end of the Sidi bou Zid operation, Ziegler returned to 5th Panzer Army and Rommel ordered the advance upon Tebessa to continue. The American troops around Sbeitla were struck by 21st Panzer who then went on to capture the village thus allowing Rommel to bring forward 10th Panzer and to direct this unit upon Kasserine, the vital pass.

Rommel's southern drive from Gafsa was also pressing forward and by 18th Thelepte had been captured. On 19 February the Axis forces in this area were nearing the Kasserine pass, and reconnaissance units pressed forward via Bou Chepka towards Tebessa. Orders for the attack upon Kasserine pass stated that the offensive would open during the night of 19/20 February.

When the attack began Buelowius Battle Group attacked the high ground on either side of the pass and had captured it by dawn forcing the Americans to withdraw, during the morning of 20th, towards Tebessa. The 10th Panzer units then came up and Rommel pivoted these behind the Africa Corps and sent them storming towards Thala to outflank the second range of hills blocking Tebessa.

Meanwhile, the 21st Panzer Division had advanced from Sbeitla to Sbiba but the efforts of the past days had overstretched it and the advance slowed to a halt in the face of extensive mine-fields and strong opposition. The division then took up defensive positions from which it beat off strong American attacks on 21st. To draw off Allied strength from Rommel's attack the 5th Panzer Army made a number of excursions and attacks in the Oued Zagra, Djebel Abiod, Beja, and Siliana areas. On 17th, its 47th Regiment and the Buhse Battle Group captured Pichon and advanced twenty miles past that place by 21st. On that day also 10th Panzer, pursuing the American forces, occupied Thala and Africa Corps gained to within five miles of Djebel el Hamra. The Americans poured more and more troops into the battle and these with British armour and infantry of the Guards Brigade recaptured Thala. The Buhse Battle Group tried and failed to capture Tebessa by *coup de main* on 22nd. The United States forces, occupying a semi-circle of high ground, beat back the Axis attacks and the whole valley to the north-west of Kasserine as well as the heights to the north and west of the pass were sealed by the Allied forces. A battlefield conference of senior officers which Kesselring attended, reluctantly accepted that the failure to take Tebessa, the tiredness of the troops, and the imminence of a British attack upon Mareth compelled a breaking-off of the offensive and a return to the start lines from which they had set out with such high hopes.

Threats to the flank of Africa Corps required this be the first unit to withdraw and then followed 10th Panzer on 23rd, while 21st Panzer, embroiled in a bitter fight to the south and south-east of Sbiba, guarded the flanks. German combat groups, acted aggressively in the Pichon sector, brought some relief by drawing off the American pressure but then the German withdrawal became so rapid that the Allied spearheads lost touch with the rearguards on 26 February and did not regain this until 6 March.

11. Army Group Africa fights in the north, west, and south, March–April 1943

'What is the role of the 5th Panzer Army?'
von Arnim to Kesselring

It had been clear since the first days of the fighting in Tunisia that the time would come when the desert Army and 5th Panzer Army would have to combine to form a single command. Thus it was obvious that the post of Army Group Commander would have to be created and that this post would be offered to Rommel. But his health deteriorated during the two years of his command and the strain of the successive withdrawals since October 1942 had brought him so low that his immediate replacement was essential. Von Arnim was selected to succeed him and the Italian general, Messe, was taken from the Russian front and appointed to command the German/Italian Panzer Army. Rommel formally took over command of Army Group Africa at 18.00hrs on 23 February, and very soon thereafter laid down the post and the fate of his soldiers passed into the hands of von Arnim.

But before he left Africa there was still much to be done and Rommel addressed a conference on the future situation in Tunisia. In the course of this discussion he stressed that without supplies no bridgehead could be held and said that even if the Axis forces took up their best defensive positions, the life of the Army Group could be reckoned in months and not years.

As if to underline the weakness of the Axis forces the limited attacks which von Arnim launched in support of Rommel's Kasserine thrust and to gain more tactically advantageous positions failed almost completely. *Olivenernte* – the operation to take out Medjez El Bab – was not able to be resurrected and a new plan code-named *Ochsenkopf* was designed to drive the Allies from their commanding positions along an arc of hills on the western and south-western front in the north to seize the port of Tabarka, in the centre to capture Beja, and in the south to gain such ground in the Medjerda sector that the British forces in Medjez el Bab would be cut off.

This plan can be described only as madly optimistic for no new major units had arrived in the bridgehead, excepting a rifle regiment of a Penal Division, the 999th (Africa) and, indeed, the only armoured element of 5th Panzer Army had been sent to support Rommel. By shuffling his forces Arnim managed to form a Lang Brigade made up of 47th Regiment, parts of 334th Division, and Captain Koenen's battalion of specialist troops from the Brandenburg Division.

Operation *Ochsenkopf* opened on 26th, and von Manteuffel's Division captured the station at Sedjenane. Witzig's parachute-engineer battalion made an encircling move to attack the Allied forces in Mateur from behind and to drive these towards the advancing Barenthin Regiment. A sea-borne landing by Koenen's Battalion, supported by 10th Bersaglieri Regiment on land, captured Cap Serrat. Sidi Nsir, the objective of 47th Regiment, could not be reached for torrential rain had washed away the roads, although the Alpine troops attached to 334th Division, which was attacking Oued Zarga, battled forward under the most appalling difficulties. The heavy Tiger tanks which were to support the attack could not be moved off the roads because of the state of the ground and without their help the situation at Sidi Nsir could not be exploited. On the right wing the intention to thrust through the Allied lines at Goubellat and around Djebel Mansour to attain the Siliana region could not make good progress because of incessant rain.

On the extreme northern front it seemed as if Tabarka might be captured and with this in mind Manteuffel asked Arnim for more troops to exploit the situation. There were no reserves and by the time that Manteuffel had re-organised his tired troops and could continue this thrust on Djebel Abiod the Allied defences had been built up.

At Oued Zarga the positions which had been captured allowed the Germans to dominate the Allied supply route with artillery fire by day and at night patrols went out to mine the roads. But no further advance was possible and the attack was halted on 4 March.

In the south Medjez sector the line was actually withdrawn to the position it held before the offensive opened, the Hermann Goering Jäger Battalion was driven back at Goubellat and the effort to cut Medjez from the south failed. But in the southern border at Tunisia preparations were in hand to launch a spoiling attack against the British Army's preparations on the Mareth front. The great weakness of the Mareth Line was that it could be outflanked by an Allied drive through the Foum Tatahouine pass and to disrupt the British time-table an attack was proposed to strike north of Medenine.

The situation at the beginning of March 1943 was that Rommel's Panzer Army Africa had only 34 German and 14 Italian battalions of infantry to hold the line. This means that each battalion had a front of 8 miles to cover and to back up this weak infantry force there were 49 batteries of artillery, 33 of which were light field guns. An additional five battalions of low-calibre troops held the seaward defences and these were supported by 15 batteries of fixed artillery.

With such weaknesses there could be no line in depth, indeed there was no line as such and it was not protected by a sufficient artillery force. Although the country into which the Panzer Army was withdrawing favoured the defence, the steep djebels reduced the effectiveness of Allied armour, there was no avoiding the issue that a concentrated infantry offensive would crumple the German front at Mareth like paper. Such reserves as could be scraped together once put into the line to restore a difficult situation would leave nothing to halt a further Allied penetration. The obvious solutions were either to withdraw to more favourable positions – in Rommel's opinion the Gabes area – or to carry out a series of spoiling attacks to delay the Allied build-up for the final blow.

The difficulties facing the armies in Africa were still not appreciated either at OKW or at Commando Supremo and neither Rommel's requests nor von Arnim's questions on supplies were granted or answered. Von Arnim indeed was to comment bitterly that one cannot fire from guns the shells which lie at the bottom of the Mediterranean.

For the German commanders the situation was nothing short of calamitous. The 5th Panzer Army had only 34 serviceable tanks and Rommel's Army a total of 89 German and 24 Italian vehicles. The amounts of material reaching Africa fell a long way short of the absolute minimum and of the average figure of 90,000 tons per month no less than 25 per cent would be sunk before it had reached Tunisia. Thus the amount which would actually arrive in the country would be barely sufficient for an army which was not engaged in active fighting. When Hitler was made aware of the African theatre's critical supply situation he immediately ordered the tonnage to be raised to 150,000 tons but gave no proposals on how this fantastic target could be achieved.

The only firm statement which Rommel received from Kesselring was Hitler's order that the Mareth Line was to be held to the last and that any British moves to outflank the defensive positions were to be met with offensive operations. Once again the Führer was either ignorant of the true facts or chose to ignore the facts that the Army had only 1.5 per cent of its battle requirements and only 0.5 per cent of its stated ammunition needs. In any case there was insufficient fuel to carry out Hitler's demand for aggressive operations.

With von Arnim, Kesselring fared even worse than with Rommel. Rommel had never had any of the promises fulfilled which OKW, or Hitler, or the Commando Supremo had made to him in respect of supplies and arms but this situation was a completely new one to von Arnim who expected promises and schedules to be kept. To Kesselring's criticisms of his conduct of the Army, von Arnim asked what his role was and received the reply that he was to halt any Allied advance by weakening this while 1st Panzer Army held Mareth to the last. Arnim then referred to the constant shortages in supplies, arms, and men but this was ignored and Kesselring asked instead the reasons for moving his panzer divisions. The simple answer, von Arnim replied, was that in the north there was a strong Allied army, in the south there was the strong 8th Army, and in the centre the growing power of an American Army whose strength he estimated as three divisions and against which he could throw only one regiment. He returned to the question of supplies but Kesselring refused to be drawn into stating actual tonnages or figures and then left to fly back to the unreal world of Commando Supremo and the OKW, where paper divisions had the strength of real ones, where ships and convoys were never sunk, and where armies, at least on paper, were always up to strength. He left behind him in Tunisia the men of the Axis armies, actors in a tragedy whose prologue began at Mareth at 20.30hrs on the evening of 16 March.

But before the British blow fell Rommel had planned and executed his pre-emptive blow at Mareth. His proposal for a pincer operation was rejected as unworkable by Messe and other officers for they considered that the advance by the northern pincer, in total darkness, and across areas in which the Germans had laid extensive mine-fields with sophisticated anti-handling devices, to be impossible. Gaps, they said, would have to be blown through the mine-fields and such activity would warn the 8th Army both of the time and the direction of the attack. Rommel allowed himself to be influenced and changed his plan to a direct and frontal assault upon the British concentration and artillery area.

The Panzer Army Africa attack opened at dawn on 6 March, two days later than planned, and this short period had been sufficient for Montgomery to reorganise his forces. The German plan was for 10th, 15th, and 21st Panzer Divisions to move down upon the British while 164th Division protected one flank of the thrust and Mannerini Group defended the area to the west. The 90th Light would make a diversionary attack southwards. The 10th Panzer emerged from the mountain passes and drove towards Metameur while the combined strength of 15th and 21st Panzer passed through the Pistoia Division and struck towards the hills north-east of Metameur around which the British artillery was grouped.

As the armoured might of the veteran panzer divisions poured out of the passes to attack, the British reaction showed that they were prepared and waiting so that instead of a drive round the flank and rear of 8th Army's artillery belt the panzers were being compelled to make a frontal assault against massed gun fire. Even before the panzer block had shaken out into attack formation the Royal Artillery had opened up and a quarter of the attack force lay smashed and broken. The panzers withdrew to come on again at 13.00hrs but this drive, too, collapsed in a hurricane of British fire. Cramer, the new commander of Africa Corps, saw himself faced with a string of disasters. His armoured thrusts had failed with a loss of 55 tanks and 10 times as many human casualties, the 10th Panzer had reached Medeinine but could carry the advance no further forward and there were reports of a British column of 400 vehicles advancing towards Medeinine from Ben Gardane. Finally the attack by 90th Light had been a blow into empty space for the British had simply moved back before the blow fell.

Cramer had no choice but to break off the attack and as the panzer columns withdrew during the night it was clear to the German commanders that they had shot their last bolt. The last major German offensive in Africa had opened and died on the same day and from this point on, with the exception of local and minor excursions with limited means and with strictly limited objectives, the Army Group Africa would play only a defensive role and that for a limited period. The life of the Axis forces in Africa could now be measured in weeks. The initiative had passed into Allied hands and was never to be recovered.

Rommel flew to Rome where Commando Supremo accepted that the Mareth Line should be evacuated and that new positions, the Schott Line, should be taken up. This new position would reduce the length of front and saving of men would allow these to form a thicker concentration of units at sensitive points. Rommel proposed an even more dramatic solution, nothing less than a reduction of the bridgehead to a compact defensive area manned by a battle hardened and tenacious garrison. All irreplaceable specialist troops would be flown back to the mainland together with the superfluous rear echelon troops.

These men represented a constant drain on the supplies of the Axis armies. At the beginning of March 1943, the strength of the Army Group was nearly one-third of a million men with a proportion of two Italians to one German. But not all these men were fighting troops and, indeed, there was a far higher proportion of non-combatants to be found in Africa than in other theatres of operation. The Italian administrative 'tail' had been organised for a massive colonial Army with a vast African empire and to this number was added the rear echelon units of divisions which had long since passed into British prisoner-of-war camps. Thus, by March 1943, there were three non-combatants to every fighting soldier and even General Messe's energetic combing out of men to form infantry battalions could not produce sufficient infantry to defend a battle line which ran for over 500 miles. The situation had deteriorated back to that which it had been in November 1942; that is no continuous line but a system of strong points between which patrols secured the ground against Allied assault.

Rommel's plan was rejected out of hand by Hitler and Mussolini who ordered that the Schott line be held to the last. In the Führer's eyes Tunisia had to be held at all costs for the Axis presence tied up Allied men and shipping which might be used elsewhere. Secondly, Tunisia commanded the Sicilian narrows and for as long as Tunisia held, the Allies could not use it as a springboard from which to invade the mainland of Europe.

Rommel then drew Hitler's attention to the situation regarding fuel, ammunition, and reinforcements and commented on how the supply situation had deteriorated. The Royal Navy dominated the sea routes and no ships had arrived in North African ports. Only individual German military ferries could now reach Africa and the amounts they brought in were insignificant. Crippling losses – 80 per cent was an accepted figure – to the sky trains of Junkers 52 transport machines had all but stopped supplies arriving by air. In short the situation was disastrous.

The losses in transport aircraft were unbelievably high and every unit could report numbers of men who had been killed in transit. Elements of the 999th Division were in one sky train from which 18 aircraft carrying men of the division were shot down in flames over the Mediterranean and, indeed, the divisional commander who had set off from Sicily with most of his staff perished *en route* to Tunisia.

Hitler, for reasons which he never made public, did not allow Rommel to return to Africa so that the Army Group passed under the command of von Arnim who began to prepare it for the final battles.

THE MARETH LINE

The British barrage which opened Montgomery's offensive at Mareth poured a flood of high explosives upon the Axis lines and in the fierce infantry fighting which followed the Young Fascist Division was driven from its position within a matter of hours. Determined to regain the lost ground the Italian troops went in at dawn with the bayonet and recaptured the heights. But this British assault was only a holding attack and from the area of Fort Tatahouine, to the south-west of the line, poured the forces for the main thrust. Farther to the north Patton's armoured division was thrusting towards the Gabes Gap. The under-gunned and under-manned units of the Axis desert army were under assault from the south, the south-west, and the west.

Despite this inferiority in everything but courage, the German and Italian infantry held out through the heaviest and longest bombardments which they had ever endured, backed by waves of Allied bombers who, arrogantly confident of superiority in the air, flew in rigid and close formation to cascade their bomb loads upon the front line troops and the rear areas alike. Not only did the Axis soldiers hold out – in some sectors they rose out of their positions to counter-attack and to recover the ground which they had had to void.

By 23 March, Montgomery had failed in his attempt to force a decision on the south-western front and regrouping his forces, thrust them in a long arc to outflank the Axis positions by driving in a north and then north-westerly direction south of Djebel Tebaga in the direction of El Hamma. In this sector 90th Light Division held the ground and took the full force of the violent British assault. German units were rolled over as 2nd Armoured Brigade struck deep into the German line. The 90th Light swung back, regrouped, and counter-attacked but the end result could not be gainsaid. Montgomery's left hook had torn open the German flank and withdrawal to the Schott position was the only solution. Then came the deadly thrust by the New Zealanders, whose night attack strode across pak-fronts and artillery belts into the area behind 90th Light, and threatened to drive to the sea. But then the advance was halted and before it could roll forward again von Liebenstein, the commander of Africa Corps, had formed an assault group and put it into action against 8th Army. A pincer operation by both panzer divisions then drove into the New Zealand flank and brought the British advance to a halt while the remainder of Africa Corps took up its positions along the Schott Line.

The end of March saw the beginning of the tightening of the noose around the Axis forces in Tunisia. From the probing attacks on the western and south-western sectors of the front the emphasis then fell upon the southern flank where 8th Army, having regrouped after the Mareth battles, was shepherding the desert veterans of 1st German/Italian Panzer Army into a killing ground towards a situation which would end the campaign.

THE SCHOTT POSITION

The position which the Germans called the Schott line blocked the 18-mile gap between the Schott el Fedjadj and the sea. The battle which was fought along this line is known to British military historians as the battle of Wadi Akarit. The Schott line ran from south of Djebel Heidoudi, via Djebel Tebaga Fatnassa and Djebel Roumana along the Wadi Akarit to the Mediterranean. The coastal plain north-west of Gabes is only five miles wide at its narrowest point and across the greatest part of this is the steep-sided, deep, anti-tank obstacle of the Wadi Akarit. The mountains of the Schott el Fadjadj were impassable to tanks coming from the west and the only danger lay on the western flank behind the Schott line for, from the direction of El Geuttar and Maknassy, strong United States tank forces might drive and overwhelm the 10th Panzer Division which held the position near those places.

The battles at Mareth had weakened the Axis forces and quoting the War Diary of 164th Division, it was calculated that at El Hamma manpower losses had amounted to 1100 men. The rifle strength of 164th Division was down to the equivalent of three understrength battalions although two companies from a replacement battalion belonging to 15th Panzer Division came on strength from 30 March. The usual divisional components were equally weak and the artillery support was still only a single battery. Acutely aware of the impotence of his forces and the even more serious inability of the Italians to defend their positions, Rommel deployed his forces so that the Germans held the sensitive areas. Italian XX Corps, with 90th Light under command, guarded the coast road while 164th Division under XXI corps, took up position on that Corps' right flank around and east of Djebel Heidoudi. The mountain positions were all held by Italian troops and to maintain contact with Panzer Army Africa's main body and von Broich's 10th Panzer Division battle group, the Sahara Group carried out wide-ranging and frequent patrolling. There were several major movements of armour as a result of which 21st Panzer Division was posted to 5th Panzer Army, leaving 15th Panzer Division in Army reserve and positioned behind Army's left wing.

The whole Axis front lay waiting throughout the long nights of the last week of March for 8th Army's new blow to fall and in anticipation of this the outpost line in position on a low ridge three miles in front of the main body was withdrawn. The first British attack came in on the night of 3/4 April and positions were lost by Trieste Division. A counter-attack by 90th Light won these back but these were only probing attacks by the British whose main assault came in at dawn on 6 April, behind a heavy artillery barrage. At

Djebel Tebaga a silent night attack by Gurkha troops and carried out before zero hour had captured the crest of the mountain before the main attack went in. By 10.00hrs on 6 April the front held by both Trieste and Spezia Divisions had been breached and Djebel Roumana and Djebel Tebaga Fatnassa had both been lost. The 164th Division, minus the battalion from 15th Panzer, was then moved to a point behind the front centre of the line to act as Army reserve and, as the division was moving, the order came for the non-motorised units to begin their withdrawal to the Enfidaville position while the German Panzer units held the line. The Schott line could not be held and the Axis armies were moving back to new defensive positions.

But even as the rearward movement was taking place a fresh British thrust carried past the right wing of 164th Division and broke through the Sahara patrol group forcing it to give up more ground under British pressure. The Panzer Army moved back to occupy another temporary line south-west of Agareb on 9 April and, when the final stages of the retreat had been concluded on 11th, 164th and 90th Light were in position to the south-west of Enfidaville.

This new line was the southern face of the Axis-held area of Tunisia and had such excellent defensive features that it was considered to be the last ditch defence. Possession of the high ground around Djebel Zaghouan dominated a network of main roads: the Kairouan–Pont du Fahs highway, the Sousse–Enfidaville–Tunis road, and the Sousse–Enfidaville–Gromballia–Tunis road. Thus the high ground and particularly Djebel Garci, a steep and bare feature with several crests, dominated any advance from Sousse into the plains around the capital city.

To hold the last ditch positions XXI Corps held the right sector and had under command Spezia and Pistoia Divisions and the Luftwaffe Infantry Brigade. The Italian XX Corps held the left flank with Trieste, Young Fascist, and 90th Light Divisions. As usual the German units held the most threatened sectors. The 164th Division was blocking the Pont du Fahs road, east of Djebel Garci the Luftwaffe Brigade dug in to control the Zaghouan road, while 90th Light covered the Enfidaville–Gromballia highway. The Italian units held the high ground with Spezia on the extreme right flank and Trieste and Young Fascist Divisions on either side of Takrouna. A secondary defence line behind the Young Fascist positions was held by non-armoured units from 15th Panzer. Parts of 10th Panzer came under command of Africa Corps and were located on the far right flank where they were joined some weeks later by elements from 21st Panzer Division.

To help hold the line there was a sudden but small spate of reinforcements and the numbers reaching 164th Division enabled second battalions to be formed for 382nd and 433rd Regiments. Battalions and artillery detachments from other units were also taken on divisional strength but the greatest number of these, and all the artillery, flak, and Nebelwerfer batteries, were taken from 164th Division when the Allied offensive opened and were then posted to 5th Panzer Army.

One of the most warmly interesting of the letters dealing with the attitudes of the German rank and file at that time is the report written by a young regimental officer after a tour of inspection to the front line. He wrote:

'On 11 April in the burning sun of mid-morning I saw eight men of 1st Battalion marching along the Kairouan–Enfidaville road in full equipment carrying arms and extra ammunition. They had had no food and had already marched for 25 miles before I met them. They were on their way to new positions at Zaghouan and refused my offer of a lift to any wounded saying that they would do the "little bit" of a march to Zaghouan. They arrived at battalion before nightfall.'

There was quiet along the sector held by 164th Division until the morning of 16 April when British artillery began to 'range in' and patrolling activity was reported. Three more days of calm passed but then Pistoia Division was hit during a night attack. The reconnaissance detachment of 164th Division, acting as reserve, was brought forward to capture the positions which the Italians had abandoned and on 21 April the Italians made their own counter-attack but this collapsed and broke in the face of British artillery fire. It was clear that Pistoia could no longer be considered an effective fighting force and it was removed from the line.

The next Italian division to come under the hammer blows of Montgomery's Army was Young Fascist but it held its ground on the Takrouna heights despite fierce attempts to drive it back, while on the Enfidaville plain the 90th Light was heavily engaged. A minor adjustment of the line to shorten this and thus to release men was carried out and these units were then sent to help the hard-pressed Hermann Goering Division north-west of Pont du Fahs. On 29 April the Spezia Division was forced off the heights which it had held.

The absence of British armour on the Enfidaville front pointed to the fact that 8th Army's tank divisions had been moved and, obviously, to Medjez el Bab from which sector would come the decisive blow. All anti-tank weapons on the southern flank were therefore rushed to the threatened western sector. Montgomery was fulfilling his plan to make the Germans 'run like wet hens' between the two Allied armies.

There were no other major British offensives against 164th Division and it remained inactive while the offensive through Medjez el Bab brought about the fall of Tunis. It is now to the battle front at that town that we return and to when, during the latter weeks of March, the American, British, and French forces having been regrouped, were preparing to make the thrust which would end the war in Africa.

12. Towards the end in Africa, May 1943

'Africa Corps must rise again'
Cramer's last message, May 1943

The air of resigned acceptance which is so evident in the OKW War Diary entry for 31 March, that 'no new Allied thrusts have been made on the front of 5th Panzer Army', indicates how completely the initiative had passed into Allied hands and the realisation that the end of the war in Africa was only a question of time.

German planners were in no doubt that the Allies were concentrating their forces for the decisive battle. As a first step there was a reshuffle of forces which brought II United States Corps to face Manteuffel's Division and in the battle line around Medjez there were several British infantry divisions, freshly arrived from the United Kingdom, as well as the advanced guards of those desert formations which were eventually to be in the van of the battle for Tunis.

Steady pressure exerted all through the last weeks of March had reduced the bridgehead area. The Medjez sector blazed into activity as British attacks came in against 334th Division on 7 April, and fighting for strategically important mountain crests continued for days. South of Medjez el Bab, there were struggles to win commanding positions around Fondouk. To the north-west of Medjez el Bab the 78th Infantry Division captured Longstop during Easter week thus regaining a feature which had been in German hands since Fischer's December offensive.

The fires of battle reached other sectors of the British front and the Hermann Goering Division came under almost continuous assault from the middle of the month although it met every British attack with a counter-attack and by such spirited defence actually lost very little ground. This German élite formation was used to spearhead an operation to determine the location of the British concentration area behind the Medjez front and by attack to delay the British preparations. This operation, code-named *Fliederblüte,* a combined panzer/grenadier attack, was launched during the night of 19/20 April. The sky behind the German line was alight with gun fire as the barrage opened the advance, with a panzer wave escorted by paratroops of the Herman Goering Division clinging to the outsides of the vehicles. The 2nd Battalion the Duke of Cornwall's Light Infantry was overrun as the armoured vehicles swept across their positions but the 25-pounder guns of 4th Division's artillery fired all night until by dawn when, with their mission accomplished, the German panzers and their Grenadiers rolled back across their start line. Through this reconnaissance in force it was clear to 5th Panzer Army that a massive build-up of Allied strength was in progress and this in a sector with few natural defences. Army Group looked for units which it could put into the threatened sector to thicken the line and moved 10th Panzer from its positions in the south, for it seemed that the Enfidaville line would be strong enough to hold.

Despite local losses this line did, in fact, hold and as the mountains absorbed the Allied strength, so more and more German troops could be transferred to the central sector. Army group intelligence appreciations located an iron ring around the Axis armies made up of 1 French and 3 American divisions on the extreme northern sector and to the west of Mateur, 5 British divisions in the Medjez el Bab area, 2 British and 2 American divisions in the Pont du Fahs region, a French Corps south of that place, and 6 British or Imperial divisions, as well as 2 brigades situated along the Enfidaville line. Of this great force no less than 7 were armoured divisions and when Montgomery moved part of his army from Enfidaville to Medjez el Bab the British had poised for battle in this sector, 2 armoured divisions and 2 armoured brigades to spearhead an attack which would be followed by 5 infantry divisions.

The panzer regiment of 21st Panzer Division was moved north and shortly thereafter followed all the anti-tank weapons which could be spared. The 15th Panzer Division moved its panzer regiment towards the central sector and located the main of division to the west of Tunis, ready to meet a deep Allied thrust.

Throughout April the Allied attacks continued, growing in frequency and intensity. From north to south small actions flared along the battle front as new units were 'blooded' in battle. But this was sometimes a 'bloody' affair for the attackers and in the battles around Peter's Corner, a bend in the Medjez–Tunis road, infantry battalions of 4th British Division lost heavily battling against the skilful, battle-hardened, and unshaken veterans of Koch's 5th Para Regiment and the Hermann Goering Division.

It is undeniable that under this Allied pressure a certain confusion existed as units moved, dug in, and received orders to move again. One officer wrote:

'Here the situation changes hourly. An order is followed by a counter-order. Since 11th (April) the fighting has entered its final stages and the task of maintaining the bridgehead is really only a question of time. With men alone we could hold the front but materially we are in an inferior position. The Luftwaffe cannot supply us and that which comes by sea is a drop in the ocean . . . we are on the defensive because we cannot fight tanks with the bodies of men and with shot guns. Yesterday Battle Group Wolff had one 7.5cm pak and a 5cm pak. The latter did not work.'

The pattern of Allied tactics was now to secure jump-off points for the final assault and the German units were switched from one threatened sector to another. One battle group commander reported that his unit had withdrawn 50 miles without loss and that the sector he was presently holding was seven miles wide. Of another battle group commander it was said that he had not slept for four days. In the north 334th Division and the Barenthin Regiment fought desperately to deny Hill 609 to the Americans but the pressure was too great and by the end of April American troops had attained the last commanding height west of Mateur. In the north Manteuffel's Division slowly gave ground as it carried out a fighting withdrawal on Bizerta and 962nd Regiment of 999th Division, moving back to new positions, turned at bay to face the Allied units which were pressing close upon it. A report written by Sergeant Scharwachter of No 5 Company 962nd Regiment, who was wounded and flown back to Germany, gives details of the fighting:

'American troops whose lines lay between one and five miles distant from our own crossed a mine-field in 'no man's land' to begin their attack on 25 April. They went to ground under our fire but under a well co-ordinated barrage they soon worked their way to within hand grenade range. My platoon covered the withdrawal of our battalion to higher ground and was heavily engaged. We had heavy losses because my men had had no recent combat experience. One 42-year-old man who had been convicted of treason and who had helped to beat back the American assaults said to me, "Sergeant, I don't care what happens now. I have redeemed my honour" and another man stood up in his slit trench firing a machine gun from the hip and driving back the advancing Americans until he was wounded.'

But even fighting such actions they could not hold back the Allied drive and Mateur was occupied by 3 May. It was now clear that, however desperately Army Group shuffled its available forces, these were neither sufficient in number, nor logistically capable of withstanding the anticipated blow. Units were being overrun by the advancing Allies. Colonel Wolff reported on one unit of his division which was overtaken by the speed of the Allied drive: 'Three hundred men were isolated behind the enemy lines but now have fought their way back to us. Some were missing for more than 10 days. One group is reported to be still free and is being fed by Arabs. They are still hoping to break through to us.'

Army group echeloned its effectives in depth along the line which they expected the British attack to follow and had brought into the final battle a miscellaneous collection. Batteries of 20th Flak Division, whose principal task it had been to defend the Tunisian cities from air raid, found themselves grouped to the south-west of the capital preparing to fight in a ground role and the last 30 vehicles of 10th Panzer were moved from the Medjerda river line and placed as a deep reserve in the Massicault area.

Contemporary diaries, letters, and reports show that in those last anxious days the morale of the front line soldier remained high. Colonel Wolff, describing the military situation in the Pont du Fahs area, finished one letter 'so we live in our little kingdom and only through the radio do we know what is happening in the outside world and in Tunisia. The flies pester us but we are happy.'

There was no breakdown in discipline even at the end and in 999th Penal

Division the only case of military justice being exercised was in the execution of five men for trying to kill an NCO. The officers' letters are full of praise for the spirit of their men; 'As is to be expected the spirit of the men in the front line is excellent but that of rear echelon units is less so. In Tunis town there are many drunken soldiers to be seen and lack of proper salutes indicates a certain slackness.' But, if contemporary accounts stress the high morale, very few of the many acts of heroism were detailed – even fewer received recognition. It is to be hoped that some staff officer at army head-quarters would have found time to accede to the request of one regimental officer who, proud of the way in which his company of military criminals had fought, made application that the men of 999th Division who had been active in the fighting should have their military honour restored to them before the campaign ended. In this he was asking for recognition which the bravery of some of the men of his unit had already gained for themselves in the award of Iron Crosses.

On 5 May an artillery and air bombardment of unparalleled ferocity crashed down upon the German positions. Breaches made in their lines were sealed by desperate attacks put in by the last remaining vehicles of 15th Panzer and by anti-tank units. One unnamed staff captain reported that one unit of his command in the Pichon area 'fired the anti-tank guns to the last round and were then rolled over by American tanks. The infantry fought their way out but on entering positions believed to be held by Italians found these to be occupied by Goums. By nightfall we had only 25 men left although stragglers have been coming in.' Through the breaches which the artillery and air bombardment had made, poured a flood of Allied armour and infantry whose long pent-up energy cast aside any counter-attacks which Army Group could still launch.

By the evening of 6 May, Massicault had fallen and the word was spread to commanders of German units that Tunis was to be evacuated by 17.00hrs on 7th. Early in the morning of that day the first evacuations began to take place although outwardly the city seemed calm and German soldiers still went about their usual business. Then in the drizzle which had set in towards 14.00hrs armoured cars of 11th Hussars or the Derbyshire Yeomanry – the point is debated still – entered Tunis as the first British troops. In the north Bizerta fell to the Americans on the same day. Army Group Africa had been split in two and 5th Panzer Army swung back to the north while 1st Panzer Army sought to establish a firm line south-west of Tunis.

When Tunis fell there were many who made long and difficult journeys from an airfield to a port and back to another airfield hoping to find a ship or aircraft which would take them from the dying front and enable them to escape to continue fighting in another theatre of operations. One subaltern officer spent the last hours before the fall of Tunis in negotiations with pilots of JU 52 transport aircraft to fly back to Sicily a divisional staff which had reached Africa only 48 hours before. His successful negotiations earned him a place in the machine but it was shot down and, slightly concussed, he had to swim from the machine and back to shore. Five hours after the first British troops had entered the city the last of the JU 52s took off and the same officer managed to squeeze himself with three others and the pilot into a single-seater fighter and to land unharmed in Sicily.

Resistance was still being offered outside the cities. In the north American and French troops crossed the Chouigui pass and cut off much of 334th Division and the flak batteries to the south-west of the city fired to such good effect that they destroyed 20 tanks of one American spearhead. Other short-lived and purely local successes were scored by German units whose vehicles no longer had fuel to move them and whose crews fought and died where they stood.

The 15th Panzer, which still had some fuel, carried out one last counter-attack north of Djebel Kechabta and during this battle fired its last ammunition. The last shots by the last German tanks were fired on 9 May to cover the removal of 5th Panzer Army's tactical headquarters and then the vehicles were blown up. With them died the 5th Panzer Army.

The line now held by the remnants of Army Group Africa was based on Hamman Lif and the Cap Bon peninsula but however much deployment and redistribution of troops might take place, the fighting was akin to the dying struggles of a Titan. When the British came in along the line from Creteville to Zaghouan the last German units, in obedience to the *Führer Befehl* to fight to the last round, defended their positions until the ammunition ran out and then destroyed their vehicles and weapons before surrendering. The 10th Panzer Division, as an example, dug in its last seven panzers which were completely without fuel to serve as pill boxes and carried on fighting around these for as long as there was ammunition. On 11 May the wireless waves were alive with sound as unit after unit, having obeyed Hitler's order to the last round went off the air and into captivity.

On the morning of 12 May von Arnim, conscious that Army Group Africa could no longer offer any organised resistance, asked for surrender terms and on the following day 164th Division – the last unit of the Axis armies in Africa – marched out and into prisoner-of-war compounds, fully aware that it, like the rest of Army Group Africa, had done its duty.

Epilogue

*'Despite recent developments the Führer and the
Duce are determined to continue the struggle in Tunisia.'*
From a letter sent by Field Marshal Keitel to
Chief of the General Staff of the Army, time-stamped
20.00hrs 8 May 1943

For several days following the 13 May 1943, I stood at the top of a street in Tunis and watched the German troops, who had surrendered in Cap Bon, coming into captivity. The British Army trusted them to drive to the prison camps with only a minimum escort, so great was the depth of their defeat. Sitting correctly in lorries, wearing equipment, but carrying no arms the convoys of vehicles streamed past all through those early summer days. The sound of German voices singing the marching songs of their army rose above the roar of the motors. The strong, young voices, the gaiety of the singers, their optimism, and the air of confidence which they showed convinced the Arabs who saw them pass that these were the conquerors and that it was they, the Germans, and not we, the British, who had won the war in Africa.

Thus it was, in an atmosphere of self-confidence, almost of arrogance, that the German force which has now passed into history as the Africa Corps, passed then into Allied prison camps.

Now only the cemeteries which run in an arc from El Alamein to Medjez el Bab remain to show that here lie the bodies of German soldiers who were sent almost by accident to a new continent and were sacrificed there by the casual negligence of their supreme commander – Adolf Hitler.

Appendixes

Appendix 1

Chronology of Panzer Army Africa

12 November 1940	OKW issues Instruction No 18 that a force be raised to support the Italians in North Africa for an autumn attack upon Egypt.
16 January 1941	According to Hitler the purpose of German intervention in Libya is to prevent the collapse of the Italians. A blocking force is to be raised and sent.
6 February 1941	Erwin Rommel named as commander of German Troops in Africa and arrives in Tripoli.
12 February 1941	The first German air raid on Benghasi.
19 February 1941	The German force in Africa is named 'German Africa Corps'.
22 March 1941	The Africa Corps advances and captures El Agheila.
2 April 1941	The Africa Corps goes on to seize Agedabia.
8 April 1941	The battle of Mechili.
12 April 1941	The first assaults upon Tobruk. The capture of Bardia and Sollum on the Egyptian frontier forms an eastern outpost for the Axis army.
15 June 1941	The tank battle at Sollum defeats Wavell's attempt to capture Halfaya.
5 August 1941	Panzer Group Africa is formed.
18 November 1941	Operation Crusader, an attempt to raise the siege of Tobruk, opens.
23 November 1941	The battle of Sidi Rezegh smashes 7th Armoured Division.
2 December 1941	Operation Crusader ends with a German tactical victory.
7 December 1941	Faced with the resumption of a new British offensive the Axis forces are withdrawn to the Gazala position.
17 January 1942	The Axis garrison at Halfaya surrenders.
21 January 1942	Rommel's counter-offensive to recapture Cyrenaica opens.
28 January 1942	Rommel recaptures Benghasi.
30 January 1942	Panzer Army Africa (the German/Italian Panzer Army) is formed
February 1942	The air offensive against Malta begins.
26 May 1942	Rommel's offensive against the Gazala position opens.
2 June 1942	The siege of Bir Hachim at the southern end of the Gazala line begins.
20 June 1942	Having destroyed 8th Army's armoured force, Rommel's force goes on to capture Tobruk.
22 June 1942	The advance begins across Egypt towards the Suez canal.
29 June 1942	Mersa Matruh falls to the Axis Troops.
1 July 1942	The first battle of El Alamein begins.

9 July 1942	The battle of Alam Halfa opens.
30 August 1942	The German armour breaks through at El Alamein but is unable to force a decision.
2 September 1942	The German offensive at El Alamein is broken off.
23 October 1942	Montgomery's offensive at El Alamein begins.
2 November 1942	The 8th Army breaks through the El Alamein front.
4 November 1942	The Axis forces retreat to the Fuka line.
8 November 1942	Operation Torch begins; the landing of the British and Americans in French North Africa.
19 November 1942	German paratroops occupy Gabes aerodrome and other detachments launch an offensive against Medjez el Bab.
20 November 1942	In the second stage of their withdrawal the Axis forces reach the Marsa el Bregha position.
6 December 1942	The offensive by 10th Panzer Division in Tunisia drives back the Allied armour in Blade Force.
8 December 1942	The 5th Panzer Army is formed in Tunisia.
24 December 1942	The British assault against the Buerat Line. In the Medjez el Bab sector the Germans capture Longstop Hill.
22 January 1943	The last German units evacuate Tripolitania and cross into Tunisia.
12 February 1943	The desert army and 5th Panzer Army link up in Tunisia. Rommel reaches the Mareth position and prepares for the forthcoming battle.
15 February 1943	The Axis offensive against Gafsa and Sidi bou Zid begins.
20 February 1943	Initial successes at Gafsa and Sidi bou Zid having been scored by the Axis forces, the advance upon Thala and Le Kef is begun.
23 February 1943	Army Group Africa is formed.
6 March 1943	The last major German attack in Africa is made at Mareth and fails on the same day.
20 April 1943	The 8th Army reaches the Enfidaville position, the last ditch defences of the Army Group Africa before Tunis.
3 May 1943	The Allies break through at Mateur and capture it.
5 May 1943	The British offensive opens at Medjez el Bab.
7 May 1943	Tunis falls to the British and Bizerta to the United States forces.
13 May 1943	The Axis armies in Africa capitulate.

Appendix 2

Order of battle of the German divisions which served in Africa

90th Light Africa Division
Organised as Africa Special Purposes
Division from units already in Africa
during August 1941. Retitled 90th Light
Division on 28 November 1941.
Composition: Infantry units only.
155th (Motorised) Infantry Regiment.
200th (Motorised) Infantry Regiment.
361st (Motorised) Infantry Regiment
Africa.
Panzer Grenadier Regiment (Motorised)
Africa.

(This division contained many unusual units.
The 361st Regiment contained many men
who had served with the French Foreign
Legion. The Panzer Grenadier Regiment
was raised out of Special Unit No 288, one
of whose battalions was composed of
Arabs from the North African
population.)

164th Light Africa Division
Sent in July 1942 from Crete to North
Africa and was the last major unit to
surrender in May 1943.
Composition
125th (Motorised) Panzer Grenadier
Regiment.
382nd (Motorised) Panzer Grenadier
Regiment.
433rd (Motorised) Panzer Grenadier
Regiment.

334th Infantry Division
Sent to Tunisia in December 1942 and
fought with distinction at Longstop Hill
in April 1943.
Composition
754th (Motorised) Infantry Regiment.
755th (Motorised) Infantry Regiment.
756th (Motorised) Mountain Infantry
Regiment.

999th Light Africa Division
This division was a penal unit made up of
specially selected officers and NCOs and
men who were to be rehabilitated through
battle. Two of its regiments were sent in
late March to Tunisia.

Composition
961st (Motorised) Africa Rifle Regiment.
962nd (Motorised) Africa Rifle Regiment.

**von Broich (later von Manteuffel)
Division**
Formed from units already in Tunisia and
taken over by von Broich in November
1942. When von Broich was sent up to
take over command of 10th Panzer
Division, Hasso von Manteuffel replaced
him and the division then took the latter's
name.
Composition
Fallschirmjäger Regiment (Motorised)
Barenthin.
T3 Infantry Battalion.
From March 1943 the divisional
composition was:
Fallschirmjäger Regiment (Motorised)
Barenthin.
160 (Motorised) Panzer Grenadier
Regiment.
Corps Para Engineer Battalion.

Hermann Goering Division
A Luftwaffe formation which was sent to
Tunis over a period of months beginning
in November and ending in March.
Composition
Grenadier Regiment Hermann Goering.
Jäger Regiment Hermann Goering.
Various Panzer Grenadier companies and
T battalions.

10th Panzer Division
Transferred from southern France to Tunisia
during November 1942.
Composition: Armour and Infantry only
7th Panzer Regiment.
69th (Motorised) Infantry Regiment.
86th (Motorised) Infantry Regiment.

15th Panzer Division
Sent to North Africa between April and June
1941.
Composition
8th Panzer Regiment.

15th (Motorised) Infantry Brigade:
115th (Motorised) Infantry Regiment.
200th (Motorised) Infantry Regiment.
8th (Motorised) Machine Gun Battalion.
15th (Motorised) Motor Cycle Battalion.
33rd (Motorised) Reconnaissance
   Battalion.

21st Panzer Division (formerly 5th Light Division)

The 5th Light Division was first sent to North Africa during February 1941 and was retitled as 21st Panzer Division on 1 October 1941.

Composition
5th Panzer Regiment.
104th (Motorised) Infantry Regiment.
3rd (Motorised) Reconnaissance
   Battalion.

Appendix 3

The major groupings of the German Army in Africa

The German Africa Corps
This unit evolved out of Reconnaissance Detachment Rommel which had been formed in February 1941. Hitler bestowed the title German Africa Corps upon the formation on 19 February 1941.
Order of Battle
5th Light (later 21st Panzer) Division.
15th Panzer Division.

Panzer Group Africa
On 15 August 1941 the German Africa Corps was raised to the status of Panzer Group Africa.
Order of Battle
GERMAN AFRICA CORPS:
15th Panzer Division.
21st Panzer Division.

90th LIGHT DIVISION

XX ITALIAN CORPS:
Ariete Panzer Division.
Trieste Infantry Division.

XXI ITALIAN CORPS:
Pavia Infantry Division.
Bologna Infantry Division.
Brescia Infantry Division.

SAVONA DIVISION (ITALIAN)

Panzer Army Africa
This evolved from Panzer Group Africa on 30 January 1942 and was known as German/Italian Panzer Army until 23 February 1943, when the title was changed again to 1st Italian Army.
Order of Battle: 15 August 1942
GERMAN AFRICA CORPS:
15th Panzer Division.
21st Panzer Division.

90th LIGHT DIVISION

164th INFANTRY DIVISION

RAMCKE PARACHUTE BRIGADE

X ITALIAN CORPS:
Brescia Infantry Division.
Pavia Infantry Division.

XX ITALIAN (MOTORISED) CORPS:
Ariete Armoured Division.
Littorio Armoured Division.
Trieste Motorised Division.
Folgore Parachute Division.

XXI ITALIAN CORPS:
Trento Infantry Division.
Bologna Infantry Division.

90th Corps
This unit began life as Nehring's Staff on 14 November 1942, shortly after the opening of the campaign in Tunisia and was upgraded to Corps status on 19 November 1942.
Order of Battle
TUNIS BRIDGEHEAD
No 3 Company, 1st Tunis Field Battalion.
5th Para Regiment.
14th Company, 104th Panzer Grenadier Regiment.
BIZERTA BRIDGEHEAD
No 1 Company, 1st Tunis Field Battalion.
No 4 Company, 190 Panzer Battalion.

5th Panzer Army
Created out of 90th Corps on 8 December 1942.
Order of Battle: 17 December 1942
10th PANZER DIVISION

DIVISION VON BROICH

20th FLAK DIVISION (LUFTWAFFE)

Order of Battle: 1 March 1943
10th PANZER DIVISION.

21st PANZER DIVISION.

334th INFANTRY DIVISION.

DIVISION VON MANTEUFFEL (FORMERLY VON BROICH).

19th FLAK DIVISION (LUFTWAFFE).

20th FLAK DIVISION (LUFTWAFFE).

SUPERGA DIVISION (ITALIAN).

BRIGADE IMPERIALI (ITALIAN).

Army Group Africa
This, the last grouping of the Axis armies in
  Africa, was formed on 23 February 1943.
Order of Battle
1st ITALIAN ARMY
  (German/Italian Panzer Army).
5th PANZER ARMY

Appendix 4

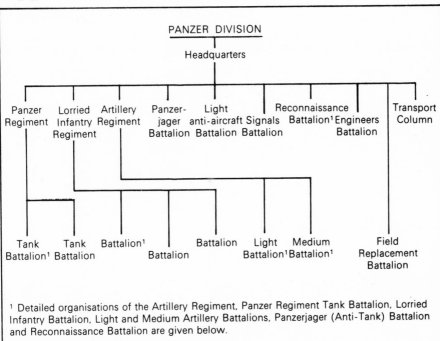

PANZER DIVISION

Headquarters

| Panzer Regiment | Lorried Infantry Regiment | Artillery Regiment | Panzer-jager Battalion | Light anti-aircraft Battalion | Signals Battalion | Reconnaissance Battalion[1] | Engineers Battalion | Transport Column |

| Tank Battalion[1] | Tank Battalion | Battalion[1] | Battalion | Battalion | Light Battalion[1] | Medium Battalion[1] | Field Replacement Battalion |

[1] Detailed organisations of the Artillery Regiment, Panzer Regiment Tank Battalion, Lorried Infantry Battalion, Light and Medium Artillery Battalions, Panzerjager (Anti-Tank) Battalion and Reconnaissance Battalion are given below.

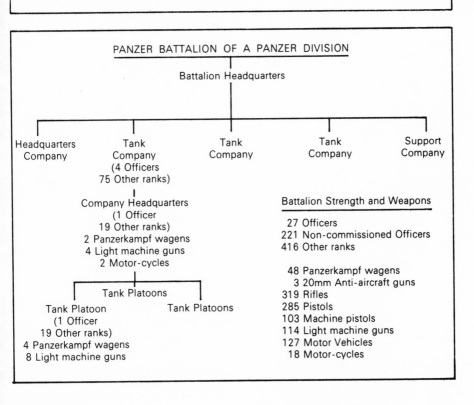

PANZER BATTALION OF A PANZER DIVISION

Battalion Headquarters

| Headquarters Company | Tank Company (4 Officers 75 Other ranks) | Tank Company | Tank Company | Support Company |

Company Headquarters
(1 Officer
19 Other ranks)
2 Panzerkampf wagens
4 Light machine guns
2 Motor-cycles

Tank Platoons

Tank Platoon
(1 Officer
19 Other ranks)
4 Panzerkampf wagens
8 Light machine guns

Tank Platoons

Battalion Strength and Weapons

27 Officers
221 Non-commissioned Officers
416 Other ranks

48 Panzerkampf wagens
3 20mm Anti-aircraft guns
319 Rifles
285 Pistols
103 Machine pistols
114 Light machine guns
127 Motor Vehicles
18 Motor-cycles

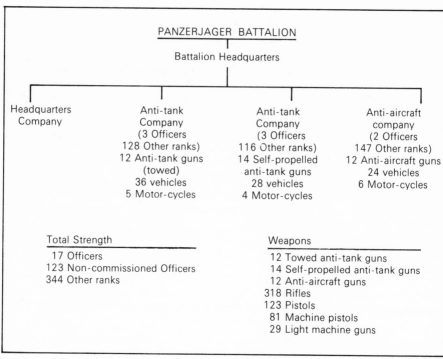

PANZERJAGER BATTALION

Battalion Headquarters

| Headquarters Company | Anti-tank Company (3 Officers 128 Other ranks) 12 Anti-tank guns (towed) 36 vehicles 5 Motor-cycles | Anti-tank Company (3 Officers 116 Other ranks) 14 Self-propelled anti-tank guns 28 vehicles 4 Motor-cycles | Anti-aircraft company (2 Officers 147 Other ranks) 12 Anti-aircraft guns 24 vehicles 6 Motor-cycles |

Total Strength

17 Officers
123 Non-commissioned Officers
344 Other ranks

Weapons

12 Towed anti-tank guns
14 Self-propelled anti-tank guns
12 Anti-aircraft guns
318 Rifles
123 Pistols
81 Machine pistols
29 Light machine guns

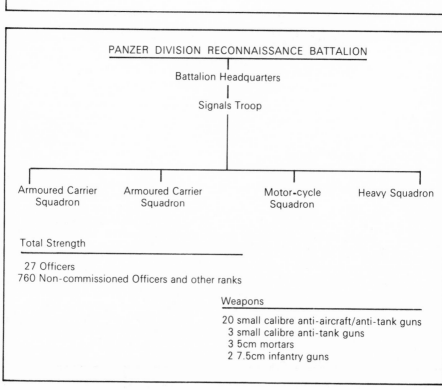

PANZER DIVISION RECONNAISSANCE BATTALION

Battalion Headquarters

Signals Troop

| Armoured Carrier Squadron | Armoured Carrier Squadron | Motor-cycle Squadron | Heavy Squadron |

Total Strength

27 Officers
760 Non-commissioned Officers and other ranks

Weapons

20 small calibre anti-aircraft/anti-tank guns
3 small calibre anti-tank guns
3 5cm mortars
2 7.5cm infantry guns

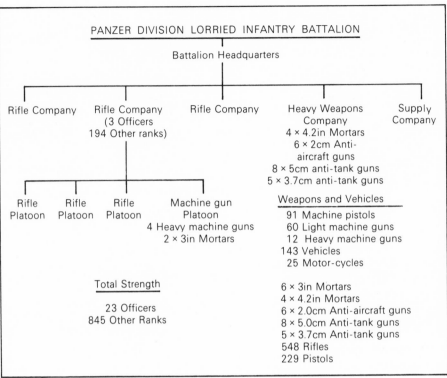

PANZER DIVISION LORRIED INFANTRY BATTALION

Battalion Headquarters

Rifle Company | Rifle Company (3 Officers 194 Other ranks) | Rifle Company | Heavy Weapons Company 4 × 4.2in Mortars 6 × 2cm Anti-aircraft guns 8 × 5cm anti-tank guns 5 × 3.7cm anti-tank guns | Supply Company

Rifle Platoon | Rifle Platoon | Rifle Platoon | Machine gun Platoon 4 Heavy machine guns 2 × 3in Mortars

Weapons and Vehicles

91 Machine pistols
60 Light machine guns
12 Heavy machine guns
143 Vehicles
25 Motor-cycles

Total Strength

23 Officers
845 Other Ranks

6 × 3in Mortars
4 × 4.2in Mortars
6 × 2.0cm Anti-aircraft guns
8 × 5.0cm Anti-tank guns
5 × 3.7cm Anti-tank guns
548 Rifles
229 Pistols

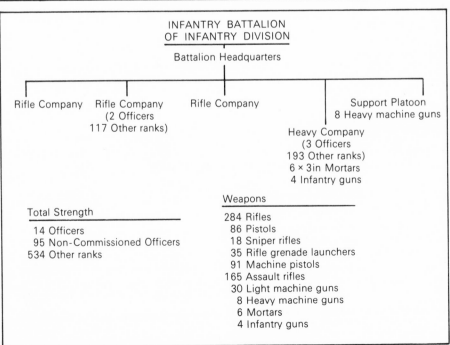

INFANTRY BATTALION
OF INFANTRY DIVISION

Battalion Headquarters

Rifle Company | Rifle Company (2 Officers 117 Other ranks) | Rifle Company | Support Platoon 8 Heavy machine guns

Heavy Company
(3 Officers
193 Other ranks)
6 × 3in Mortars
4 Infantry guns

Weapons

Total Strength

14 Officers
95 Non-Commissioned Officers
534 Other ranks

284 Rifles
86 Pistols
18 Sniper rifles
35 Rifle grenade launchers
91 Machine pistols
165 Assault rifles
30 Light machine guns
8 Heavy machine guns
6 Mortars
4 Infantry guns

Select Bibliography

Select Bibliography

AGAR-HAMILTON and TURNER, L. C. F.,	*The Sidi Rezegh Battles: 1941,*	Oxford University Press, 1957
ALMAN, K.,	*Ritterkreuzträger des Afrikakorps,*	E. Pabel Verlag, 1968
AUSTERMANN,	*Von Eben Emael bis Edewechter Damm,*	Verlag der Fsch. Pionier Gemeinschaft, Holzminden, 1971
BENDER, R. J. and LAW, R. D.,	*Afrikakorps,*	Bender Publications, 1973
BRADDOCK, D. W.,	*The Campaigns in Egypt and Libya 1940/1942,*	Gale & Polden, 1953
BUSCHLEB, H.,	*Feldherren und Panzer im Wüstenkrieg,*	Vowinckel Verlag, 1966
CHAPLIN, H.,	*The Queens Own Royal West Kent Regiment, 1920–1950,*	Michael Joseph, 1954
ESEBECK, H. VON,	*Helden der Wüste,*	Die Heim Bucherei, Berlin, 1942
ESEBECK, H. VON,	*Sand, Sonne, Sieg,*	Berlin, 1942
HOWE, G. H.,	*North-west Africa: Seizing the Initiative (The U S Army in World War II),*	Department of the Army, Washington, 1957
HOWE, G.,	*Battle History of 1st Armoured Division,*	Combat Forces Journal, Washington, 1954
KESSELRING, A.,	*Soldat bis zum letzten Tag*	Athenenäum Verlag, Bonn, 1953
KUROWSKI, F.,	*Brückenkopf Tunesien,*	Maximil. Verlag, Herford
LEWIN, R.,	*Rommel as a Military Commander,*	Batsford, 1968
MAUGHAN, B.,	*Tobruk and El Alamein,*	Australian War Memorial, Canberra, 1966
MELLENTHIN, F. W. VON,	*Panzer Battles,*	Vowinckel Verlag, 1953, 1958
MINISTERO DELLA DIFESA,	*La Ia Armata Italiana in Tunisia,*	Rome, 1950
MINISTERO DELLA DIFESA,	*Le XXX Corpo d'Armato Italiano in Tunisia,*	Rome, 1952
NEHRING, W.,	*Die Geschichte der Deutschen Panzerwaffe 1916–1945,*	Propylaen Verlag, Berlin, 1969

PLAYFAIR, I. and
MOLONY, C.,

*The Mediterranean and the
Middle East, Volumes II, III,
and IV,*

HMSO 1956, 1960, 1966

SCOULLAR, J.,

Battle for Egypt,

Department of Internal
Affairs, Wellington, New
Zealand, 1962

WALKER, R.,

Alam Halfa and Alamein,

Department of Internal
Affairs, Wellington, New
Zealand, 1962

Unpublished sources

LIEBENSTEIN,
K. VON,

*Die Kämpfe der 164ten leichte Afrika Division von der Schott
Stellung bis zum Ende der Kampf in Afrika*

TOPPE,

An Account of the Battle of Sidi bou Zid, 14–15 February 1943

———

Feldzug in Afrika: Teil 1 8 February 1941–18 June 1941
           2 19 June 1941–7 February 1942
      Band 2(1) 8 February 1942–21 June 1942
      Band 3   1 March 1943–13 May 1943
      Band 3(A) December 1942–13 May 1943

VAERST, G. VON,

Operations of 5th Panzer Army in Tunisia

WEBER, F.,

Battles of 334th Division

BUERKER, U.,

10te Panzer Division in Tunesien

NEHRING, W.,

XC Korps

Kriegstagebuch: 15ten Panzer Division, June 1942–September 1942

Kriegstagebuch: 21 Panzer Division, 30 July 1942–30 September 1942

Kriegstagebuch 90te Leichte Division

Kriegstagebuch: 999 Afrika Division

Kriegstagebuch: Afrika Korps: Panzer Armee Afrika

The German military publication *Signal* 1941–1943
Die Wehrmacht 1941 and 1942

Various British military regimental histories and magazines, war diaries, and personal
accounts.

Index

Index

Abiod, 138–40 *passim*
Acroma, 42, 48, 54
Agedabia, 38, 39; captured by Rommel, 91; Axis plan to use as depot, 94
Alam Halfa, 33, 117, 118
Alexandria, 3, 8, 114
Algeria, 129; Allied assault begins, 130
American Army, 129, 133, 146, 153–4, 159, 166–8, 174; *et passim*
Anderson, General, 155
Arco dei Fileni, 37
Armaments
  British: 3.7cm, 33; 7.5cm, 33; 2-pounder, 27, 33; 6-pounder, 27, 33; 25-pounder, 27, 32; Grant tank gun, 27
  German: 5cm, 27, 146; 7.5cm, 146; 7.6cm, 27; 8.8cm, 26
  Italian: 32
  See also Tanks
Army Group Africa. *See* German Africa Corps
Auchinleck, General, 62, 113

Badoglio, 9
Bald Hill. *See* Djebel el Ajred
Bardia, 12, 48, 49, 60, 64, 66, 71, 79, 82, 84, 85
Barenthin, Colonel, 143
Barre, General, 136
Bastico, General, 61, 65, 90, 109, 113
Beja, 138, 169
Belhamed, 70, 72, 86: captured, 84
Ben Gardane, 175
Benghasi, 37, 39, 40: airport falls to Rommel, 91
Bight of Bomba, 39
Bir el Aslagh, 104
Bir el Gerrari, 42
Bir el Gobi, 66–75; *passim*
Bir el Halad, 75
Bir el Schine, 114, 116
Bir el Tamar, 104
Bir Hachim, 67, 69, 71, 72, 103, 104–6;

Bir Harmat, 100, 104
Bir Sidi Muftah, 102
Bismark, General, 118
Bizerta, 129, 133, 135, 136, 138
Bone, 135
Bou Arada, 158
Bou Djebel Toum, 156
Bougie, 135
British Army, 3, 9, 32; *see also* Eighth Army
British Hill. *See* Djebel el Azag
Buerat, 123, 125
Buerker, Colonel, 4, 152

Cap Bon, 186
Cap Serrat, 148, 172
Capuzzo, 50, 58, 59, 60, 82, 83; as vital target, 84; German attack on, 85
Cauldron, Battles of the, 104ff
Cavallero, General, 94, 109, 116, 117
Chouigui, 147, 151, 156, 186
Churchill, Winston S., 3–4
Commando Supremo, 12, 13, 14, 122, 123, 163, 168, 174; *et passim*
Corsica, 8, 130
Cramer, General, 175
Crüwell, 79
Cunningham, General, 64, 69
Cyprus, 3
Cyrenaica, 8, 12, 37, 39, 52, 55: recaptured by Germans, 43; Rommel realises its indefensibility, 90; necessity for Germans to abandon, 123; *et passim*; *see also* under names of places and battles

Derna, 40, 42, 46, 91
Desert Warfare, 5: problems posed by, 18–21, 41; terrain, 20, 23–4; campaigning seasons and effects of climate, 24
Djebel Abiod, 140, 147, 169, 173
Djebel bou Aoukaz, 155
Djebel Bou Daboussa, 158
Djebel Bou Mouss, 145
Djebel Chirich, 157, 158
Djebel el Ahmera. *See* Longstop Hill

Djebel el Ajred, 147
Djebel el Azag, 147
Djebel el Hamra, 169
Djebel Garci, 179
Djebel Heidoudi, 178
Djebel Kechabta, 186
Djebel Kralif, 159
Djebel Ksour, 162
Djebel Lanserine, 156
Djebel Lessouda, 165, 166
Djebel Maiana, 154
Djebel Mansour, 157, 158, 173
Djebel Roumana, 179
Djebel Tebaga, 177, 179
Djebel Zaghouan, 179
Djedeida, 135, 143, 145, 147
Djerid Schott, 162

Egypt, 3; *see also* under names of places and battles
Eighth Army, 26, 32–4: at Mechili, 41–4; losses at Sollum, 60; losses during Operation Crusader, 74, 77; defensive positions at Gazala, 95–6; losses on Aslagh ridge, 105; defeated in Gazala line battles, 107; losses at Gazala and Tobruk, 110; withdrawal to Alamein, 113; losses, 115; strength October 1942, 120; advances on Tarhuna Pass, 126; *et passim*; *see also* under Armaments and Tanks
Eisenhower, General Dwight D., 129
El Adem, 42, 48, 96, 106
El Agheila, 4, 36, 37, 39, 90, 123
El Alamein, 4, 24, 30, 114, 115
El Aouina, 135
El Aroussa, 141, 143
El Auda, 109
El Bathan, 141
El Daba, 114
El Duda, 84: captured by Germans, 87
Eleut el Tamar, 100, 107
El Guessa, 155
El Hamma, 178
El Regima, 91
Enfidaville line, 162, 179, 180, 182
Esher, Lord, 3
Evelegh, General, 148, 149

Faid Pass, 159, 164, 165
Feriana, 163, 168
Fischer, General, 149, 150: at Tebourba Gap,

152; death, 159
Fondouk, 182
Fort Capruzzo, 49
Foum Tatahouine, 173, 177
French Army, 137, 141–2, 158
Fuka, 114, 122
Funck, General, 13

Gabes, 123, 136, 140, 141
Gabr Saleh, 64, 67, 68, 69, 70, 79, 82
Gafsa, 159, 162, 163, 164, 168
Gambut, 58, 68, 72, 74, 85
Gariboldi, General, 14, 37, 52, 61: his timidity, 37–8
Gasr al Abd, 83
Gasr el Arid, 69, 77, 79
Gazala, 27, 46, 58, 91: Eighth Army's defensive positions at, 95–6; battle for Gazala line, 95–107
German African Corps. *See* Panzer Army Africa
Gialo, 64, 71, 79: Oasis occupied by Axis troops, 92
Giarabub, 68, 69
Gibraltar, 3, 8, 10, 130
Got el Ualeb, 102–3
Goubellat, 142, 145, 173
Graziani, Marshal, 10, 11, 12, 13: replaced by Gariboldi, 14
Green Hill, *See* Djebel el Azag
Grenadier Hill. *See* Djebel Bou Mouss

Halfaya, 48, 49, 50, 58, 60, 64, 66, 70, 71, 81, 82: German garrison surrenders, 90
Hamman Lif, 186
Harlinghausen, Colonel, 135
Hitler, Adolf, 4, 9, 11, 12, 14, 109, 122, 123: sends forces to North Africa, 13–14; and Rommel, 29–30; obduracy, 125; misjudges importance of North Africa, 130; orders troops to Tunisia, 131; disagreement with Rommel, 176–7; *et passim.*
Homs, 126

Italian Army, 2, 4, 10, 31–2, 61, 157: establishment, 32; advances into Egypt, 10; morale improves, 43; some troops placed under Rommel's authority, 74; losses, 117· *et passim*; *see also* under Armaments

Jefna, 140

Kairouan, 141, 164
Kasserine Pass, 134, 164, 168
Kesselring, Field Marshal, 4, 30, 90, 113, 116, 117, 123-4, 127, 130, 131, 163; advises Hitler, 131; forms XC Corps, 137; differences with von Arnim, 174; *et passim*
Kippenberger, Brigadier, *Infantry Brigadier*, 87
Knightsbridge box, 96, 101-6 *passim*
Koch, Lieutenant-Colonel, 131, 135, 138, 141, 142, 151
Koenen, Captain, 172
Kasr Tyr, 141

La Marsa, 135
Lederer, Colonel, 135
Le Kef, 164
Liebenstein, 168
Longstop Gap, 155, 180
Longstop Hill, 134
Lorenzelli, General, 143
Luftwaffe, 8, 37, 62, 65, 70, 72, 84, 97, 103: attacks Bir Hachim 105; attack on Tobruk, 108; units move into Tunisia, 130; driven from the skies, 133; in Tunisia, 135; at Abiod, 139; their importance in Tunisia, 156; *et passim*
Lybia, 8, 9; *see also* under names of places and battles

Maaten Giofer, 91
Maddalena, 82
Mahares, 159
Maizila Pass, 159, 165
Malta, 10, 12, 94, 130
Marada Oasis, 37
Mareth, 162, 164, 169, 173, 174, 175: Mareth line, 177-8
Marmarica, 8, 12; given up by Germans, 123; *see also* under names of places and battles
Marsa El Brega, 37, 38, 123
Massicault, 185
Mateur, 136, 138, 139, 172, 184
Mechili, 29, 40, 41, 42-3, 44
Medenine, 173, 175
Medjerda river, 135, 138, 142, 145, 154, 156
Medjez el Bab, 133, 135, 138, 140, 141, 142, 143, 155, 159, 172: in German hands, 143; defences, 144; Koch evacuates, 145; as key to Tunisian campaign, 157; offensive through, 180; *et passim*
Mersa Matruh, 10, 11, 82, 113-114

Messe, General, 172, 174
Metameur, 175
Minorca, 3
Misurata, 126
Montgomery, General, 26, 33, 118, 122, 123, 177, 180
Msus, 40, 41, 91
Mussolini, Benito, 3, 4, 8, 9, 11, 14, 30, 31, 109, 122, 163-4: asks for German assistance, 12; places troops under Rommel's authority, 74; stubbornness, 125

Naduret el Gheseauso, 106
Neame, General, 42
Nehring, General, 118, 131, 140, 150: sent to Tunisia, 131; problems and plans in Tunisia, 136-7; divides Tunisian bridgehead, 143; leaves his command, 155; *et passim*
North Africa: strategic importance of, 2-4

Oberkommando der Wehrmacht. *see* OKW
Oberkommando des Heeres. *See* OKH
O'Connor, General, 42
OKH, 10, 12, 13, 20, 38, 53, 55: misapprehensions, 23, 24, 120; *et passim*
OKW, 9, 13, 14, 122, 123, 173, 174, 180: *Instruction No 18,* 11; *Instruction No 22,* 12; Operation *Sonnenblume,* 14; plan to drive through Egypt, 94; attention directed towards Western Mediterranean, 128; *et passim*
Operation Crusader, 62, 64-92
Operation *Eilbote,* 157-8
Operation *Fliedeblute,* 182
Operation *Fruhlingswind,* 163, 164
Operation *Morgenluft,* 163
Operation *Ochsenkopf,* 172
Operation *Olivenernte,* 157, 159, 172
Operation *Sonnenblume,* 14
Operation Torch, 128-9, 144
Oudna, 148
Oued Zarga, 143, 172, 173
Ousseltia, 158

Panzer Army Africa, 2: establishment, 9; tasks and duties, 14; unprepared for desert warfare, 18-21; food, 21; uniform, 22; tactics, 25-9; arrival in Tripoli, 36-7; losses at Sollum, 60-1; shortages, 62; Battle Group Stephan, 68; losses, 70; losses during Operation Crusader, 77, 84; Battle Group Böttcher, 81; setbacks at Tobruk, 85-6; Battle Group

Mickl, 88; losses after Operation Crusader, 89; shortages and reinforcements, 95; losses, 100; strength and losses, 115; reinforcements 116; shortages of supplies, 120, 122; strength October 1942, 120; establishment November 1942, 123; losses November 1942, 125; withdrawal towards Buerat 125; withdrawal from Buerat, 126; Battle Group Sauer, 134; von Broich Division, 139; command structure in Tunisia, 160; shortages of supplies, 162–3; weakness March 1943, 173–4; order of battle of the Divisions, 193–4; the major groupings 195–6; *et passim*; *see also under* Armaments, and Tanks

Patton, General, 177

Pétain, Marshal, 131

Pichon, 157, 158, 159; captured by Germans, 169

Pilastrino, 54, 109

Pont du Fahs, 141, 143, 156, 158, 168

Poste de Lessouda, 166

Protville, 150

Quattara Depression, 24, 113

Ramcke, 135

Ras el Mdauar, 53

Rebaou Pass, 159, 165

Regia Aeronautica, 8

Retma, 98

Ritchie, 96, 103–4, 106

Rommel, Field Marshal Erwin, 4, 14, 15, 29–31, 39, 43–4, 46, 60. 72, 73, 74, 79, 106, 113, 162: tactical doctrines, 25–9; independence, 37–8; opens offensive, 38; plan to destroy Eighth Army field force, 39–40; crosses the desert, 41–2; decision to advance on Tobruk, 46; at Tobruk, 46–55, 61–2; directs his forces to Madelina and Mersa Matruh, 82, setbacks at Tobruk, 85; realises Cyrenaica is indefensible, 90; prepares for renewal of offensive, 95; Gazala battle plan, 96–7; new plan to capture Tobruk, 107–8; promotion to field marshal, 109; battle plan after Tobruk, 113; new plans, 117; withdraws from Alam Halfa, 118, demands withdrawal to Buerat, 123; advocated withdrawal to Gabes line, 125; orders evacuation of Tripoli, 126; partnership with von Arnim, 163–4, 168; replaced by von Arnim, 172; disagreements with Hitler and Mussolini, 175–6; *et passim*

Roosevelt, President, 128

Rotondo Segnali, 97

Royal Air Force, 4, 8, 81, 83, 102, 114–15, 120

Royal Navy, 4, 8, 120

Ruwaisat ridge, 115, 116, 117, 118

Sbeitla, 163, 167, 168

Sbiba, 168, 169

Sbikha, 157

Schott line, 175, 177, 178–80

Schwarwachter, Sergeant, 184

Sciafsciuf, 73, 74

Sedjenane, 172

Sfax, 126, 141, 159

Sicily, 8, 12, 136

Sidi Aziz, 58, 69

Sidi Barani, 10, 12

Sidi Belafarid, 66, 104

Sidi Bou Zid, 160, 163, 165, 166, 167

Sidi el Moudjad, 148

Sidi Maftah, 108

Sidi Muftan, 71, 75

Sidi Nsir, 139, 140, 172, 173

Sidi Omar, 48, 58, 59, 60, 64, 67, 68, 69, 79, 81, 82, 83: as vital target, 84; *et passim*

Sidi Rezegh, 67, 69, 70, 71, 72, 73, 74, 76–82 *passim*, 86

Sidi Salah, 148

Sidi Suleiman, 59, 60

Siliana, 169

Sirte desert, 12, 13, 14, 37

Siwa Oasis, 12

Smidia, 143

Sollum, 12, 48–9, 50, 52, 60, 64, 66, 71, 74, 79: tank battle, 58–62; new front at 122; *et passim*

Souk el Arba, 135, 163, 164

Sousse, 141, 179

Stark, Colonel, 159

Stolz, Colonel, 143

Streich, General, 38, 48

Stummc General, 120, 121

Suez, 113

Suez Canal, 44, 65, 114

Tabarka, 136, 138, 172, 173

Tanks, 18–19, 25–29:
British: Crusader, 33; Grant, 27, 33, 98; Matilda, 27, 33; Valentine, 33
German: Panzer II, 28; Panzer III, 27; Panzer IV, 27; *et passim*

Tebessa, 163, 164, 168, 169: Pass captured by Germans, 169

Tebourba, 135, 141, 143, 150, 151, 153, 154: falls to British, 147; captured by Germans, 154

Thala, 169

Tmimi, 43

Tobruk, 12, 13, 47–55, 62, 105: German advance on, 46–7; defences, 47; the battles, 47–55; frontal assault on, 51–2; second assault, 53–5; Operation Crusader, 64–92; German decision to resume efforts to capture, 94–5; Rommel's new plan of attack, 107–8; attack and capture, 108–9

Toulon, 8

Touzeur, 163

Trigh Capuzzo, 66, 69, 70, 71, 72, 74, 79, 83, 100

Trigh el Abd, 41, 64, 67, 68, 69, 74, 87

Tripoli, 12, 13, 36, 37, 39, 61, 125, 126, 129: German troops arrive, 14, 36; evacuated by Germans, 125

Tripolitania, 8, 12, 14, 90, 137

Tunis, 129, 133, 136, 144, 147, 148, 180: falls to Allies, 185–6

Tunisia, 8, 9, 122, 126, German withrawal into, 126; German troops move in 131; terrain, 131–2; the Tunisian campaign, 132–86; peculiar conditions of campaign, 134; first major battle, 138; German defensive line, 146; *see also* under names of places and battles

U-boats, 130

Via Balbia, 4, 5, 23, 38, 39, 40, 42, 48, 58, 74, 81, 84, 107, *et passim*

Von Arnim, 126, 134, 155, 156, 157, 158, 171, 177: takes up post as Army Commander, 155; differences with Rommel, 163–4, 168; becomes Army Group Commander, 172; differences with Kesselring, 174; asks for surrender terms, 186

Von Brauschtisch, Field Marshal, 10

Von Broich, General, 156

Von Esebeck, 54

Von Manteuffel, 172, 173

Von Nolde, Captain, 152

Von Paulis, General, 53, 55

Von Rintelen, General, 13, 14

Von Thoma, General, 10–11

Wavell, General, 12, 31–2, 58, 59, 60, 62, 90: ordered to support Greeks, 15

Witzig, 137, 138–40, 146, 149, *et passim*

Wolff, Colonel, 184

Zaafran, 72, 86

Zarhouan, 141

Ziegler, 165, 167

Zuetina, 39